THUNDER BAY PUBLIC LIBRARY
Waverley Resource Library

UKRAINIANS IN

NORTH AMERICA

OREST SUBTELNY

UKRAINIANS IN

UNIVERSITY OF TORONTO PRESS

TORONTO
BUFFALO
LONDON

NORTH AMERICA

AN ILLUSTRATED

HISTORY

© University of Toronto Press 1991
Toronto Buffalo London
Printed in Canada

ISBN 0-8020-5920-1

Printed on acid-free paper

Canadian Cataloguing in Publication Data

Subtelny, Orest
　Ukrainians in North America

Includes index.
ISBN 0-8020-5920-1

1. Ukrainian Canadians – History.　2. Ukrainian Canadians – History – Pictorial works.　3. Ukrainian Americans – History.　4. Ukrainian Americans – History – Pictorial works.　I. Title.

FC106.U5S8 1991　　971'.00491791　　C91-095037-7
FC106.U4S8 1991

Design and page production by
Counterpunch/Linda Gustafson & David Vereschagin

This book has been published with assistance from the Canada Council and the Ontario Arts Council under their block grant programs.

To those who dared —
To those who cared

CONTENTS

Preface ix

Introduction 3

The First Wave: Before the First World War 11
    Immigration to the United States 13
    Immigration to Canada 37
    Community organization 61
    Links between the United States, Canada, and the homeland 91

The Second Wave: Between the Wars 101
    Key features of the period 104
    The interwar period in Canada 118
    Ideological currents 122
    The churches 153
    Secular organizations 160

The Third Wave: After the Second World War 189
    The German interlude 191
    The organizational upsurge 203
    From émigrés to ethnics 233

The North American Diaspora 249
    The Ukrainian Americans 251
    The Ukrainian Canadians 254
    The homeland and the diaspora 257

Abbreviations 270
Selected readings 272
Index 275
Photo Credits 282

PREFACE

Exactly one hundred years ago the first Ukrainian immigrants came to Canada. They had begun to arrive in the United States about a dozen years earlier. Over this impressive time span they have maintained in their new homelands a continuous and unusually vigorous community life, one that boasts a colourful history and that, in the age of glasnost and perestroika, has begun to exert a considerable impact on the ancestral homeland. Surprisingly, to date no comprehensive historical treatment of the multifarious activities of this tenacious community has appeared. Therefore, the centennial celebrations of Ukrainian settlement in Canada and the fast-approaching centennial of such venerable Ukrainian-American institutions as the Ukrainian National Association seem to be a most appropriate occasion to present to the general reader this historical survey of the Ukrainians in North America.

The scope of this work in unconventional in that it encompasses the Ukrainians in both Canada and the United States. Traditionally, scholars have studied Ukrainian immigrants in one country or the other, but never both. What, therefore, is the rationale for treating them together? An obvious reason is the fact that the immigrants were one and the same people, coming from exactly the same regions of their homeland, reacting to the same socioeconomic and political pressures. Not only was their point of origin identical, but their destination, with all due respect for the differences between the United States and Canada, was similar in many ways. Both countries constituted for these immigrants the New World, with its promising but demanding opportunities, its English language, and its Anglo-Saxon culture and values. True, at the outset the lives and livelihood of the settlers in Canada and the miners in the United States differed greatly. But with every passing decade these differences diminished. Meanwhile, the religious, cultural, and ideological currents and issues that swept through the communities in the two countries were essentially the same. Certainly today, one can view the Ukrainian communities in the United States and Canada as having far more similarities than differences. And even the differences that do exist can be used, for the purposes of this study, to advantage because they allow one to compare and contrast, at least cursorily, the experience of the two communities.

Another feature of this work is that it treats the full span of the history of Ukrainians in North America, from the outset to most recent times. This is a first and, admittedly, a hazardous endeavour. The problem is that research in Ukrainian immigration history has been most uneven. Certain periods, such as that of the pioneers in Canada, are relatively well researched. But much of the rest, especially the post–Second World War era, is practically untouched. Consequently, we have been unable to provide the depth of analysis and the wealth of detail that many aspects of Ukrainian immigrant life certainly deserve.

All too often, and this is particularly true in Ukrainian studies, historians have failed to appreciate the usefulness of visual images in helping the reader grasp the spirit of the moment and the times. Yet as one peruses the photographs presented in this book it is patently clear that they capture and transmit much more graphically than can most historians the confusion and anxiety of arrival in a strange land, the strain of back-breaking labour, the sense of common purpose, and the feeling of community. Thus, another function of this book is to acquaint the reader with a long-neglected source for Ukrainian immigration history, one that not only illustrates but enlightens.

This book is organized in terms of the successive waves of Ukrainian immigrants who arrived in North America. Although a traditional, even obvious, way of looking at the flow of Ukrainians to the New World, it is also, for our purposes, the most useful. Indeed, the division into waves is essential to establishing periodization and to treating the changing nature and direction of community activity. It is, moreover, an effective means of elucidating the central theme of this work, namely, the impact that Ukrainian (and generally European) conditions, events, and concepts continued to exert on Ukrainians living in the North

INTRODUCTION

During the last century, millions of Ukrainians left their homeland in search of more favourable conditions elsewhere. Most did so for socio-economic reasons. Vast numbers of East Ukrainians, that is, those who lived within the confines of the Russian empire, moved, or were moved, to Russia's and, later, the Soviet Union's, Asian territories. By contrast, West Ukrainians headed westward across the oceans to the New World, where they encountered not only unfamiliar lands but radically different political, socio-economic, and cultural systems. It is they who are generally considered to be emigrants par excellence. Other Ukrainians abandoned their homes primarily for political reasons. Unwilling to accept Soviet rule, they preferred exile. Together these emigrants and political émigrés formed the three distinct waves of Ukrainians that fate has, up to now, brought to North American shores.

The emigrants came from one of Europe's largest lands. It was also a little known and even less understood part of the continent. To the few Canadians or Americans who took an interest in the homeland of the new arrivals, it conjured up only vague images of a land on the fringe of Western civilization – 'Ukraine' means borderland – a country of vast steppes, rich black earth, and endless fields of wheat that served as the 'granary of Europe.' But if one glanced at a map of Europe in 1900, there was no country called 'Ukraine' to be found. Indeed, for many centuries there had been no Ukrainian state, no time when the Ukrainians had ruled themselves. Thus, they were practically invisible among the family of nations. And the vast territories that they inhabited were known merely as provinces of the Austro-Hungarian and Russian empires.

Under the circumstances, at the turn of the century Ukrainians had difficulty defining their national identity, to themselves

Ukrainian Hutsul highlanders in the Carpathians in the early 20th century.

as well as to others. Originally, they called themselves by their traditional name, Rusyns (Ruthenians). Early in the twentieth century, they adopted the modern 'Ukrainian.' But many of the newcomers to North America, confused by the similarity between 'Rusyn' and 'Russian,' identified themselves as 'Russians.' Others still called themselves 'Austrians' because they came from the Austro-Hungarian empire. This terminological confusion emphasized how hazy was the sense of national identity among the early immigrants. And one of the major themes in the story of their new life in the New World is, paradoxically, their growing awareness of their ethnic, Old World, origins and, along with this, of their desire to preserve this cultural heritage.

While there was confusion about the national identity of the newcomers, there was no question about their economic status: they clearly came from one of Europe's most impoverished areas. How was one to reconcile the stereotypical image of Ukraine as a granary of Europe with the distressing poverty of its inhabitants? A large part of Ukraine certainly did consist of vast, fertile plains as well as other, abundant natural resources. But they were mostly located in the central and eastern parts of the country that belonged to the Russian empire. Moreover, because of the empire's backward, exploitive policies, Ukraine's peasants derived little benefit from their land's natural riches. More to the point, however, the vast majority of Ukrainian immigrants to North America did not come from the fertile plains of the Russian-ruled east but from the western regions that were part of the Austro-Hungarian empire. Hilly, relatively poor in natural resources, and overpopulated, these western provinces – Galicia and much smaller Bukovyna and Transcarpathia – were the homeland of approximately 20 per cent of all Ukrainians.

Although nominally ruled by the Vienna-based Habsburgs, the three provinces were actually controlled by powerful, local élites. Galicia or, more specifically, Eastern Galicia was inhabited by about 3.3 million Ukrainians and dominated by Polish nobles. About 300,000 Ukrainians lived in Bukovyna where Romanian boyars were the predominant political force and, across the Carpathians, in the Hungarian part of the empire, lay Transcarpathia, home to about 400,000 Ukrainians. In all these provinces, Ukrainians were, to an overwhelming extent, peasants. Cities and

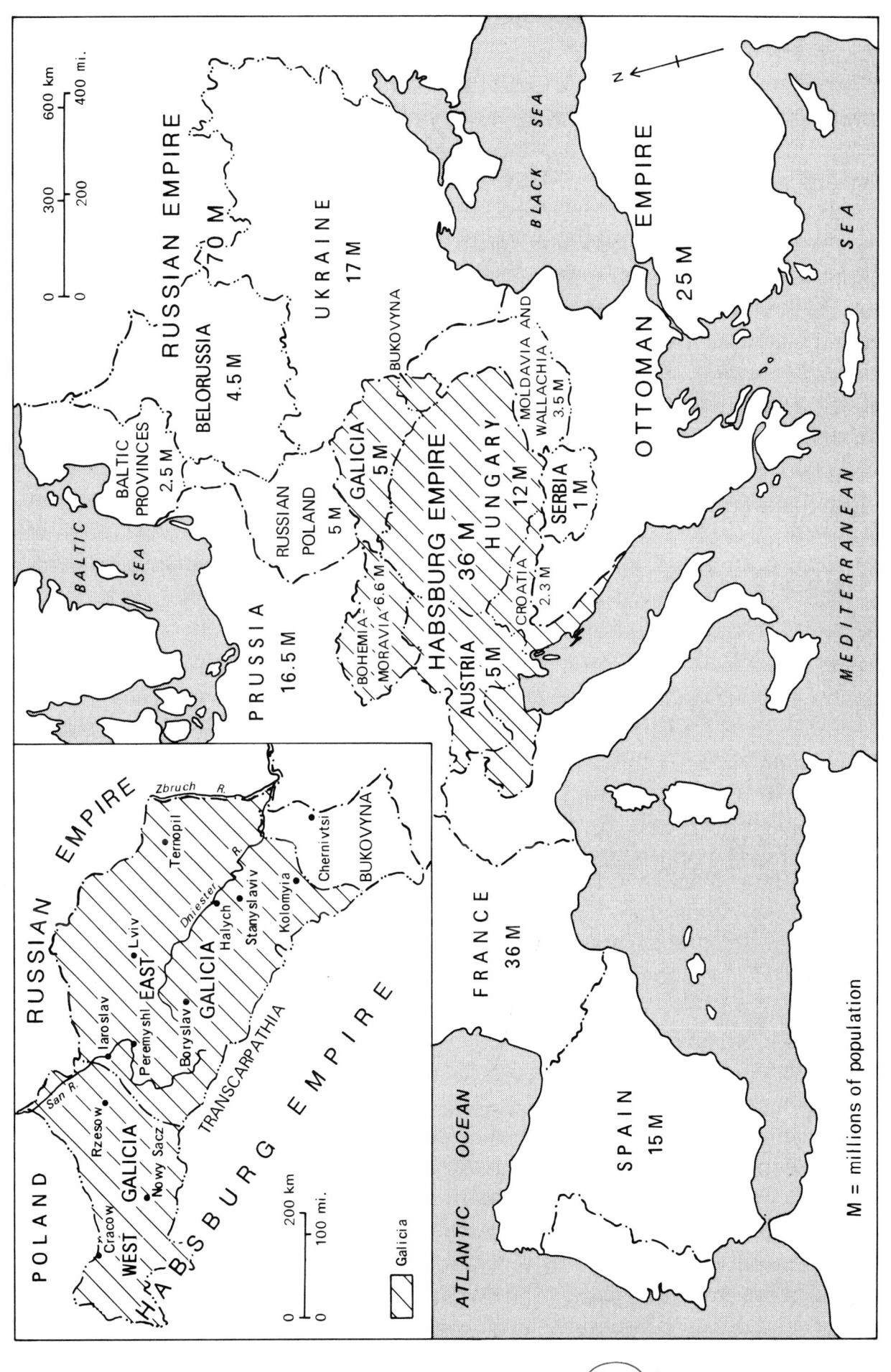

especially the towns were largely the domain of Jews, who carried on what little commerce there was.

While it is common knowledge that poverty forced people to emigrate from the region, a closer look at the socio-economic conditions that existed in Western Ukraine in the late nineteenth century might help one comprehend more fully the intense pressures that led people to leave behind their homeland. Galicia, as well as Transcarpathia and Bukovyna, was sometimes referred to as 'a storehouse of economic absurdities.' One of the major economic drawbacks of these provinces was their lack of major exports. An insurmountable barrier to the development of industry, even on a modest scale, was the competition from such heavily industrialized provinces as Bohemia, Lower Austria, and Moravia, which easily overwhelmed the few Galician attempts to industrialize. The policies of Vienna only worsened the situation. Not only did the imperial government show little interest in improving conditions in its eastern lands, but, by means of unbalanced tariffs, it clearly favoured the western provinces. Even more so than Russian Ukraine, the lands inhabited by West Ukrainians were the internal colonies of the Austro-Hungarian empire.

The landowning élite of the province, moreover, was not eager to introduce economic changes for fear that development, particularly industrial growth, might deprive it of cheap and plentiful labour. Thus, Galicia as well as Romanian-controlled Bukovyna and Hungarian-dominated Transcarpathia remained an agrarian society, with little capital accumulation, weak internal trade, low urbanization, minimal industry, and the lowest wages and highest labour surplus in the empire.

Population was one of the few growth areas in the lands inhabited by the West Ukrainians. In Galicia it jumped from 5.2 million in 1849 to almost 8 million in 1910. But this was a mixed blessing because the rising population density in the countryside – 32 people per sq. km in 1780 and 102 per sq. km in 1910 – only exacerbated socio-economic problems. And while their numbers increased rapidly, their occupational profile changed very little. Ukrainians remained an overwhelmingly agrarian people. In 1900 about 95 per cent of them were engaged in agriculture; only 1.2 per cent were in industry, what little there was of it, and 0.2 per cent in trade. The Ukrainian intelligentsia, consisting mainly of priests, teachers, and lawyers, was small, probably numbering between 12,000 and 15,000 individuals.

It was clear that Habsburg imperial reforms, while improving the legal status and political rights of the peasantry, did not improve their economic position. Indeed, they worsened it. Essentially, the problem was one of rising costs and declining incomes. A major burden on the peasantry was the debt owed on the lands they received after the emancipation of the serfs in 1848. Originally, the Vienna government promised to cover the cost of the land transfers itself, but in 1853, after order was restored, it shifted the entire expense to the peasantry. In addition, the peasants were subjected to direct and indirect taxes, including the costs of maintaining schools and roads.

But most infuriating to the peasants was the issue of the so-called servitudes. Under the conditions of the emancipation, the landlords generally retained ownership of the servitudes, that is, forests and pastures to which villagers had previously had access. This meant that the peasant now had to pay whatever price the landlord stipulated in order to obtain firewood and building materials or to feed his livestock. Usually the landowner's price was so high that it seemed to a peasant that he had simply exchanged the legal serfdom of the pre-1848 era for the economic enserfment of the post-1848 period.

As their costs mounted and their numbers grew, the plots of land owned by peasants, and therefore their income, shrank rapidly. While in 1859 the average size of a peasant holding in Eastern Galicia was 5 ha, in 1880 it slipped to 3 ha and in 1902 to 2.5 ha. Or, to put it differently, the percentage of peasants who could be classified as being poor, that is, who owned less than 5 ha of land, rose from 66 per cent in 1859 to 80 per cent in 1902. The primary reason for this shrinkage was the subdivision of a peasant's land among his children, the average number of whom was five or six per family. As peasant holdings became smaller, the large estates grew even bigger since the wealthy bought up the lands of the peasants who could no longer survive on their tiny plots as well as the estates of bankrupt nobles. Thus, Eastern Galicia was a land of about 2400 large landowners who held over 40 per cent of the arable land and hundreds of thousands of tiny peasant plots that accounted for about 60 per cent of the total territory under cultivation.

For peasants who sought to supplement their incomes, the prospects were not encouraging. If they hired themselves out as labourers to an estate-owner, they could expect to receive the lowest wages in the empire – about one-quarter of those paid in Austria proper. And if they were so desperate as to borrow from local moneylenders – mostly Jewish tavern-keepers in the villages and shop-owners in the towns, for there were no banks – they courted economic disaster. With interest rates ranging from 150 to 250 per cent annually (another reason why capital stayed in moneylending rather than being invested in industry), a small loan taken out by a peasant to tide him over to the next harvest could in a short time turn into a crushing burden. Large debts were also inadvertently incurred by the naïve, uncomprehending peasants since local moneylenders would often encourage them to drink or to buy on credit and, after allowing time for interest to accumulate, would present them with huge bills. In any case, the indebtedness of the peasantry rose rapidly and by 1910 it was eighteen times as great as it had been forty years earlier. When peasants could not pay their debts, their creditors either took over their land or auctioned it off.

Although peasants needed little encouragement to drink, their depressing economic plight certainly contributed to the alarming spread of alcoholism. Inducement also came from the estate-owners who had a monopoly on alcohol production and from the tavern-keepers who sold it. One form was the aforementioned extension of credit; another method was paying labourers in chits that could only be cashed in taverns; and then there was the great availability of taverns. In 1900 in Eastern Galicia there was one tavern for every 220 inhabitants (but only one elementary school per 1500 inhabitants).

Not surprisingly, the health of the West Ukrainians was the most neglected of all the empire's subjects. Over 50 per cent of the children died by age 5, usually as a result of epidemics or malnutrition. For example, in 1900 in Eastern Galicia, over 7000 people died of diphtheria, while in the Czech lands only 194 perished from the disease. But perhaps most shocking was the fact that about 50,000 deaths a year were attributed to malnutrition, that is, famine. In a famous book, *The Misery of Galicia*, the Polish author Stanisław Szczepanowski showed that the productive capacity of a Galician was one-quarter that of an average European while his food consumption was one-half. Little wonder that at the turn of the century the life span of a West Ukrainian male was six years less than that of a Czech and thirteen years less than that of an Englishman.

Being an agrarian, sedentary people, the Ukrainian peasants felt an extremely powerful attachment to their native soil and only the most pressing conditions would force them to leave it. By the late nineteenth century, it was clear that such conditions were at hand and many peasants were confronted with the heart-rending necessity of emigrating. They would have to go halfway around the world, to Canada and, more often, to the United States, in search of more promising opportunities.

THE FIRST WAVE

BEFORE THE FIRST WORLD WAR

Immigrants on their way to Canada, c. 1900–10.

INDIVIDUAL UKRAINIANS found their way to America long before the massive wave of immigration in the late nineteenth and early twentieth centuries. Ukrainian names appear among the founders of the Jamestown colony in Virginia as well as among the combatants in the American Revolution and Civil War. When Russia established colonies in Alaska and California in the early nineteenth century, Ukrainian cossacks and civilians were among their inhabitants. However, the man who is commonly recognized as the first nationally conscious Ukrainian in the United States is Ahapii Honcharenko, an Orthodox priest from the Kiev region, who had been personally acquainted with Taras Shevchenko, Ukraine's national poet, and had espoused revolutionary ideas. In 1867–72, this original and adventurous individual served as the editor of the *Alaska Herald,* the first U.S. publication that carried some information about Ukraine and its inhabitants. Later, Honcharenko became a prominent figure in California where he attempted to establish a Ukrainian socialist colony in the early years of the twentieth century. Another colourful individual was Nicholas Sudzilovsky-Russel, a physician and revolutionary from Kiev who settled in California in the 1880s and later moved to Hawaii where he became the president of the Hawaiian senate. He too attempted to attract Ukrainians to his new homeland.

IMMIGRATION TO THE UNITED STATES

The first large influx of Ukrainian immigrants to the United States was very different from these picturesque forerunners. Composed mostly of hard-working peasants – young single men predominated – it originated in Transcarpathia and the Lemko regions, the westernmost and least developed of Ukrainian lands. News about the semi-mythical land far across the sea where one could earn ten to twenty times as much as at home first reached the Lemkos and Transcarpathians from their Slovak, Polish, and Hungarian neighbours. In 1877, an opportunity arose to test the veracity of these tales. That year, a Pennsylvania coal company, confronted by a strike, decided to bring in cheap labour from the poorest areas of the Austro-Hungarian empire to act as strikebreakers. When its agents offered young Lemkos and Transcarpathians money for the journey – to be deducted later from their earnings – it found many eager takers. As encouraging news (often exaggerated by agents of the steamship companies) and impressive amounts of money began to arrive from the early emigrants in their home villages, the exodus to the United States grew rapidly.

The journey was long, arduous, and expensive. It began with the heart-wrenching experience of leaving one's native village, often for the first and last time. A lengthy ride on a rickety wagon brought the emigrants to a railroad station in a neighbouring town where they were packed into crowded, second-class compartments. It usually took a week or more, punctuated by frequent, intimidating checks of documents, to reach the major ports of embarkation. These were, most often, Bremen and Hamburg in northern Germany. The Dutch ports of Antwerp and Rotterdam also attracted many of the travellers. Those who emigrated from Transcarpathia often boarded ship at Trieste on the Adriatic.

Father Ahapii Honcharenko at his home in Hayward, California, c. 1905.

Predatory agents, who received $2 for convincing a single male to go to North America and $5 for a family, continued to prey on the unsophisticated travellers, extorting huge charges for helping to obtain a passport, selling steamship tickets for two or three times the actual price, and cheating on the currency exchange. A favourite ploy was to convince the peasant-traveller that it was necessary 'to wait' several weeks in port for his ship. This allowed the agent to pocket a large commission for the grossly inflated costs of food and lodging. When the harried and exhausted emigrants finally boarded ship, they were invariably packed into steerage – a large, dark, poorly ventilated common area crammed with bunk beds and with barely room to move about. For many of the steerage passengers, the lengthy two-to-three-week sea voyage was pure agony. Seasickness, exacerbated by the dank, claustrophobic, malodorous quarters, cut them down in droves. Barely able to move in their bunks and convinced that death was near, many cursed the day they left home.

An advertisement for ship tickets to Canada and the United States by a Ukrainian (Ruthenian) travel agency in Chernivtsi, Bukovyna, in 1910. It urges Ukrainians to patronize their own businesses.

A Forerunner

> I was still a young lad – not even ten years of age – when in 1878, word got out in my part of Lemkivshchyna (Lemko region) that Pavel Khyliak of the town of Luhy, of the parish Zhdynia in the province of Horlytsko had returned from the army and was preparing to leave for a distant land beyond the sea, America ... When the priest announced in church that Pavel Khyliak, the son of Semen Khyliak is preparing for America and that a divine liturgy will be celebrated on his behalf, a large group of people came to the church. On that day I didn't go to school because I wanted to see how a man prepared for America. A large group of people had gathered at the home of Semen Khyliak. A buffet was served at the home. The father rose to speak. He recited the Our Father and then blessed his son ... The people spoke about how Pavel Khyliak had learned about America from his Czech friends in the army.
>
> *From the memoir of an early immigrant*

Immigrants arriving in New York harbour in the first decade of the twentieth century.

Slavic immigrants at Ellis Island, 1906.

Yet even the most exhausted and discouraged felt a thrill when they caught sight of the Statue of Liberty in New York harbour. There was, however, one more major hurdle to surmount: Ellis Island and the immigration authorities. In the cavernous hall of a huge building on this tiny island at the mouth of the Hudson River, the immigrants went through a medical examination and other clearance procedures. Then papers were checked once more. The lengthy, nerve-wracking procedures, which raised the nightmarish possibility of being sent back, were not mere formalities. In 1905, for example, of about 14,000 newly arrived Ukrainians, over 200 were sent back. In that year, a total of 11,500 immigrants were rejected. One can, therefore, imagine the sense of relief that an immigrant felt when he finally set foot on the American mainland. Now, with rarely more than $10–15 in his pocket and a motley crowd of money changers, 'guides,' and hotel or employment agents hounding him, he was on his own.

Settlement patterns

The growing influx of Slavic immigrants coincided with, indeed was directly related to, America's industrialization. Because, in the late nineteenth century, Pennsylvania lay at the centre of this vast process, it became the primary destination of the immigrants. The Commonwealth's industrial pre-eminence was due, first and foremost, to anthracite coal. Huge deposits of this crucial source of energy – analogous in importance to oil today – were found in the Lehigh and Wyoming valleys in the central and western parts of the state. By the 1870s these areas were dotted with mines near towns such as Olyphant, Shenandoah, Shamokin, Mt Carmel, Hazelton, Wilkes-Barre, and Scranton. With coal readily available, iron foundries and mills also proliferated, particularly in the vicinity of Pittsburgh and such nearby towns as Johnstown, McKeesport, McKees Rocks, Homestead, and New Castle.

East Europeans on the crowded stairway to the processing area of Ellis Island in New York City harbour, c. 1900–10.

Bigness characterized these booming industries. The mines, foundries, and factories needed a vast army of workers, men who had strength and endurance, and who were willing to work in difficult conditions. Since specialized skills were not a necessity, Eastern Europe's millions of excess workers fit the bill perfectly. Available, mobile, and plentiful, they arrived unencumbered by families. Moreover, they were more tractable than the unionized German, Scottish, and Irish workers. Steamship companies cooperated with coal-mining concerns by directing the flow of East Europeans to Pennsylvania. Poles and Slovaks were the first Slavs to appear in the minefields in the 1870s. Ukrainians followed a few years later. As mentioned earlier, the first sizeable group, consisting of Transcarpathians, was brought in in 1877 to act as strikebreakers. Soon afterwards came the Lemkos and then the Galicians.

As industrial development spilled over into nearby states, the Slavic labourers followed. By the turn of the century, concentrations of Ukrainian labourers could be found in the factories and foundries of New York State, in towns like Elmira, Binghamton, Syracuse, Rochester, and Buffalo. The steel mills of Ohio, located in Cleveland, Youngstown, and Akron, also attracted them. Inevitably, the big cities such as New York, Philadelphia, Chicago, and Detroit also began to draw Ukrainian workers. Few went further

Agencies such as this one in New York City in 1910 often recruited immigrants for work in the coalmines.

A coalmining town in Pennsylvania at the turn of the twentieth century. The Eastern-rite church in the background indicates that there were probably many Ukrainians among the miners.

afield. Indeed, before the First World War close to 98 per cent of Ukrainians lived in the northeast and well over 70 per cent were concentrated in Pennsylvania.

Be it in a large city or a small mining town, Ukrainians, like most immigrants, invariably 'clustered,' that is, they settled en masse in what might be described as urban villages. Within these communities, which usually abutted on those of Old World neighbours such as Poles, Slovaks, or Jews, Ukrainians evolved networks of 'our people' who helped each other. Grimy, seedy, invariably on the 'wrong side of the tracks,' these neighbourhoods none the less re-created the sense of community that the transplanted villager sorely missed and badly needed. At the core of these communities was, invariably, a church, a saloon, a general-goods store, and crowded boarding-houses owned by countrymen. For the most part, American society was a world apart for the immigrant.

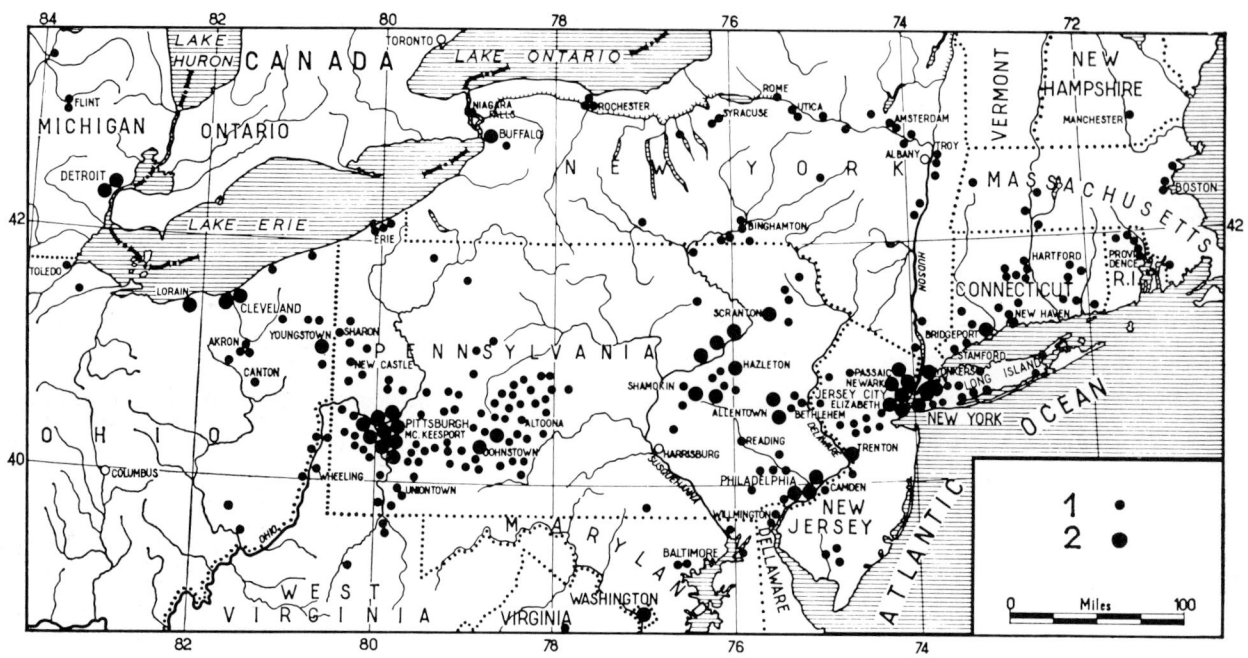

Ukrainian communities in the USA, 1958. (1) Ukrainian parish; (2) 2–5 Ukrainian parishes.

Farming

Since Ukrainians were an overwhelmingly agrarian people in their homeland, why did not a large number engage in farming in the United States? By the time they arrived almost all of the free land in the West was already distributed. And almost none had the capital to buy the necessary acreage and inventory. Moreover, initially the goal of the typical single immigrant was to earn sufficient money to establish himself in his homeland, not in the United States. Finally, mining and factory work put money in an immigrant's pocket quickly and steadily. Farming, in contrast, was a risky, long-term undertaking. None the less, there were several Ukrainian forays into agriculture.

In 1892, a group of Protestant Stundists (Evangelicals) from Eastern Ukraine, harassed by Russian imperial authorities because of their religious beliefs, arrived in Virginia and commenced farming. Reinforced by several more groups of co-religionists, some moved on in 1898 to South Dakota while others settled in North Dakota. At about the same time, Galician immigrants, who had originally planned to settle in Canada, also moved into North Dakota, acquiring land around the towns of Belfield and Wilton. By 1906 they built a church in a community that came to be called Ukraina, North Dakota. The area continued to attract

Ukrainians, especially from Canada, and by 1933 there were about 5000 in the region.

In time, individuals or small groups of immigrants also acquired farms in the East, primarily in New England, New York, and New Jersey, particularly near the town of Millville where in 1912 an enterprising Ukrainian real-estate agent convinced about two hundred families to buy land. Small groups of Galician homesteaders also moved to Montana, Georgia, Texas, and Oklahoma.

While most of those who decided to work the land eventually prospered, for some it proved to be a bitter experience. This was especially true of the approximately four hundred Ukrainians who were enticed to Hawaii in the late 1890s by the machinations of a dishonest agent. Assigned to work on the islands' plantations, they were treated as virtual slaves until they paid off the huge costs of a four-month sea voyage. When the immigrants went on strike, many were arrested. Only in 1900, when they managed to inform their countrymen in Pennsylvania about their conditions and the latter brought the matter to the attention of congressmen by means of a letter-writing campaign, were these indentured plantation workers freed from their contracts. Although some remained on the islands and eventually acquired farms, most moved to the United States or Canada.

In time, as Ukrainian communities grew and their leaders began to ponder the long-term future of their countrymen in the United States, some looked with renewed favour on farming. They argued that it was, both physically and psychologically, a healthier alternative to the dirty work in the mines, that it would allow the immigrants to work for themselves, not for the profit of others, and that Ukrainians would be better able to ward off assimilation if they lived in isolated farm communities like their brethren in Canada. In the early 1900s, several projects called for the acquisition of cheap land in Mexico and the establishment of Ukrainian farming communities there. Other projects investigated similar opportunities in Virginia. And others still argued that Ukrainians should take whatever capital they accumulated to Canada and strengthen the burgeoning farm communites there. But none of these projects ever went beyond the discussion stage. The lure of quick earnings in the mines and factories and the attractions of urban life were too strong.

Stundists (Baptist Evangelicals) from Russian-dominated Eastern Ukraine who arrived in America in the 1890s. They belonged to the small minority of those who engaged in farming in the United States. Initially they settled in Virginia and later many moved to North Dakota.

Work

The Ukrainian immigrant was accustomed to hard work. In the Old Country it was a prerequisite of survival. In the United States he was ready to work even harder because he was in a hurry to earn the money that would enable him to keep or maybe expand his plot at home. Because of his limited skills, his options were limited. Therefore, if a job paid relatively well he was willing to take it, no matter how difficult the conditions of employment.

Mining attracted most of the immigrants because the pay was relatively good, jobs were plentiful, and no special skills were required. For the most part they worked as common labourers, not as skilled miners. The work was simple but exhausting. Far below the surface some labourers shovelled coal on to carts, which others hauled out of the shafts and other still unloaded. During an average working day, which consisted of 9–10 hours of back-breaking, monotonous, unhealthy, and dangerous work, a labourer earned about $2. While the wages of Ukrainian and other East European workers were not necessarily lower than those of other unskilled labourers, the newly arrived Slavs were usually expected to put up with poorer accommodation, longer hours, and greater dangers.

Work in the foundries and steel mills also required strength and endurance, and little else. Slavic workers pushed carts of iron-ore to the furnaces, extracted and cooled red-hot iron bars, and stoked the furnaces. They earned somewhat less than their compatriots in the mines. The glass factories, textile mills, shipyards, and docks that employed numerous Ukrainains also utilized them primarily as unskilled labour. Tradesmen such as tailors, bricklayers, and carpenters were relatively well paid but they were few and far between among the Ukrainians.

In time, a few small businessmen began to appear among the immigrants. The earliest, most primitive, and widespread form of business consisted of taking in boarders. An enterprising individual who managed to save $20–30 would rent large quarters of three or four rooms, furnish them with beds, and, in addition to housing his family, take in 10–12 countrymen as boarders. Thus, he not only covered his rent but often made a very considerable

Ruthenian steelworkers at a boarding-house in Homestead, Pennsylvania, 1907.

This early example of subterranean photography shows miners shoring up support beams in a Shenandoah City, Pennsylvania, coalmine in the mid-1880s.

The First Wave

Homestead, a typical Pennsylvania industrial town in the pre-1914 period. The Carnegie Steel Company dominated the town.

$10–15 profit a month. An essential element in such an undertaking was an industrious and strong wife who was capable of feeding not only the family but the numerous boarders in the overcrowded quarters. Other early enterprises were groceries, meat markets, and, most profitable, taverns. Indeed, saloon owners were usually some of the most influential men in a community.

Average Budget of a Slavic Immigrant Family in Pre-1914 Pennsylvania Earning under $12 per Week

Food	$4.64	Tobacco	$0.07
Rent	1.62	Liquor	0.55
Fuel	0.27	Medicine	0.00
Clothing	1.57	Furniture	0.00
Housekeeping expenses	0.13	Insurance	0.77
		Other	0.41

Byington, Homestead, 140

Pushing large chunks of coal down a chute to be broken up. Ukrainians and other East Europeans were often used for unskilled labour such as this.

The First Wave

25

A Pennsylvania steel foundry at the turn of the twentieth century. After coalmining, work in the foundries was the most widespread form of employment among the early Ukrainian immigrants to the United States.

The faces of child labour. Breaker boys in a Pennsylvania coalmine in the 1890s.

Early Ukrainian immigrants interested in business often started out with a combination grocery store and meat market. This store, owned by Joseph Dragan, was photographed in 1915.

The Surma Book and Music Store in lower Manhattan. Founded in 1918, this oldest Ukrainian bookstore in the USA has been continuously owned by the Surmach family.

The First Wave

The women

As some of the men decided to remain permanently, they had their wives or fiancées join them. Later, women ventured overseas on their own. But even as late as 1905, only one of three Ukrainian immigrants was a female. However, while many of the men returned to their homeland, women rarely did so. This helped to raise the ratio of women to men to somewhat less than one to two.

Female immigrants were certainly living proof of the adage that a woman's work is never done. While men sought work in the mines and foundries of central Pennsylvania, Ukrainian women, who began to arrive in appreciable numbers in the decade prior to the First World War, gravitated to the large coastal cities where they usually found employment as domestics. Their working days were generally thirteen hours long and, except for Sunday evenings off, they worked all week. And they frequently impressed Americans with their endurance and dependability. The pay varied. If their employers were Ukrainians, it was $3–5 per month plus room and board; Jews, who frequently employed the women because they spoke their language, usually paid twice as much, and Americans almost triple. Others worked as cleaning ladies in hotels or kitchen help in restaurants. In time, women were frequently employed in light industry, especially factories manufacturing cigarettes, cigars, textiles, and clothing. But even for the same work, their wages were much lower than those of the men. Especially great were the demands on women who had to hold down a full-time job while raising large families. And worst off were wives of boarding-house owners whose life was usually one of endless drudgery.

A group of First Wave Ukrainian immigrants to the United States. Usually men arrived first and later brought over their wives and children.

Immigrant quarters in Pittsburgh, 1908.

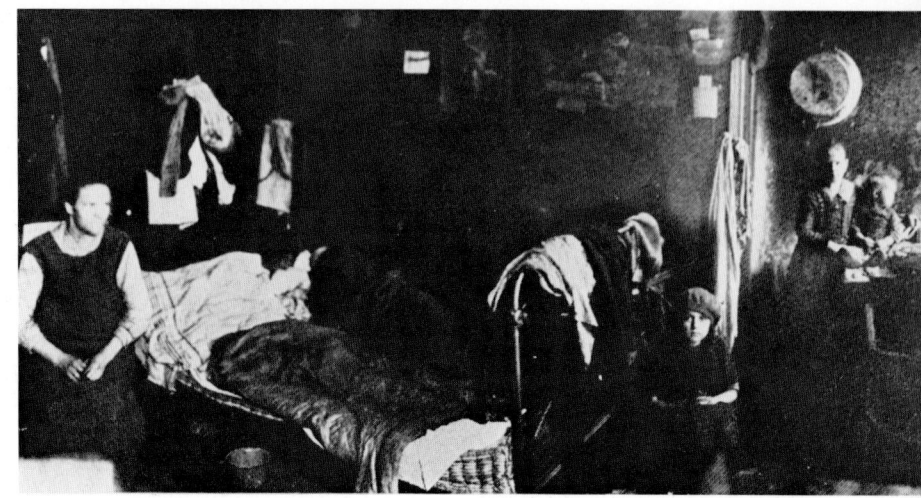

The living quarters of recently arrived Slavic immigrants in a large east-coast city before the First World War.

A Woman's Perspective

From early morning until late in the evening, she is always on her feet, always working in miserable, perpetual, and monotonous boredom. She awakens in the morning and prepares breakfast for her boarders; then she washes the dishes and cleans the house; later, she cooks supper and again she washes the dishes and cleans the house; in her spare moments, she washes the boarders' clothes and in the anthracite region she heats wash water and washes the boarders' neck and back. And so it goes, day after day. All that and children too!

But in all that boring and depressing life, so fraught with health-killing forces, the wife-slave did look, often desperately, for some respite. And she found it – in whiskey. Opportunities for indulgence were all around – so many boarders. 'How about it, landlady, let's have a short one' – today she drinks with one boarder, tomorrow another. Everyone offers. Slowly she becomes so accustomed to whiskey that soon she can't live without it. And with whiskey, all kinds of things happen – so many boarders – and all so young, so healthy ... And it happens. The husband returns from work one day and his wife is gone – left with a boarder.

Bachynsky, Ukrainska emigratsiia, 227

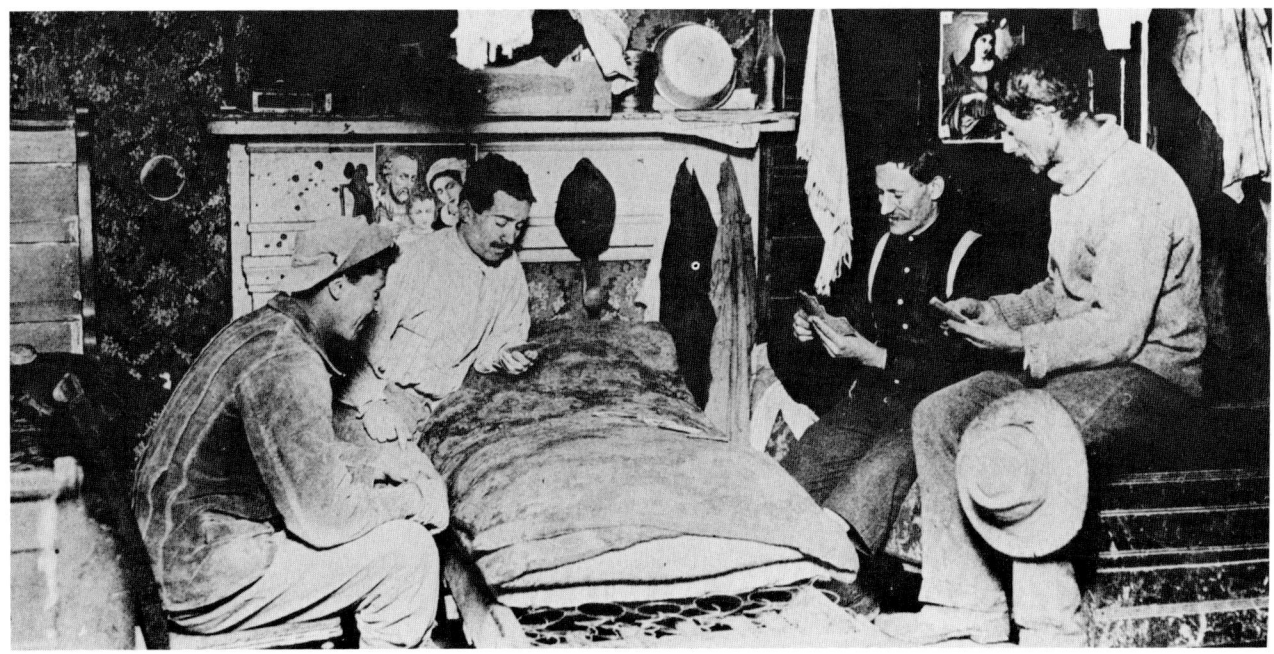

Daily life

As might be expected, the immigrants' lifestyle changed drastically from what they were accustomed to in their homeland. The earliest and easiest transformation involved clothes, especially Sunday suits, ties, and hats that the newcomer eagerly purchased as soon as he had some spare money. Since only 'gentlemen' wore such garments in the Old Country, the immigrant took special pleasure in donning them on a Sunday. It signalled, to him at least, a major rise in his social status. Despite their meagre earnings, newly arrived females showed even greater alacrity in 'dressing like ladies.' In general, they were much faster than men in mastering English and acquiring American customs and dress.

The immigrants' diet also improved. But, accustomed to more modest fare and eager to save every cent, they spent much less on food than did native Americans. And, by all accounts, they had little liking for American cooking. Housing, however, was often worse than at home. Like all immigrants, they could only afford the worst of what was available. To make matters worse, however, their quarters were invariably badly overcrowded. The desire to economize led to the widespread practice of having eight to ten single men live in rooms that normally accommo-

Workers relaxing in their cramped quarters, 1909.

dated only three or four. Dirty and exhausted after a day in the mines, they often ignored the basic rules of cleanliness and hygiene. Consequently, the squalor of immigrant workers' quarters was notorious and contrasted sharply with the tidiness of their village homes.

What did the immigrants do with their free time? There was, first of all, very little of it. Men usually worked until Saturday afternoon. Women, if they were domestics, were free only on Sunday afternoons and evenings. Thus, the first consideration was to get a rest. After work on weekdays, the men usually lay about in their crowded rooms, talking about their jobs or reminiscing about the Old Country. Often such conversations turned to 'politics,' that is, church affairs that usually focused on the virtues and vices of their parish priests. Heated debates, sometimes involving fisticuffs, over the relative merits of Greek Catholicism and Orthodoxy were also frequent. For those who preferred reading, this usually took the form of a literate worker reading a newspaper or book aloud to the illiterate majority. Those with less serious inclinations relaxed with beer, whisky, and song. On Sundays, the men, dressed in their new-bought finery, congregated at church services and, later, in a tavern.

Given the scarcity of women, finding a wife was difficult. The men invariably preferred women of their own ethnic back-

---

The Pitfalls of Emigration

> A trial was held involving Vanko Koralia, accused of polygamy. Vanko left his wife in Galicia, came to America and got married in Jersey City a second time and later, in ... Michigan, a third time. He was arrested because Wife #2 accidentally discovered the existence of Wife #3 ...
>
> Later, after serving his sentence, Vanko returned to his fatherland, found his house, his fields, his trees, his Mary, and his children, which, unfortunately, instead of two, now numbered four.
>
> Svoboda, 1896

The traditional and modern. While the mother is, and probably always will be, part of the Old World, her daughter is well on the way to successfully adapting to the American way of life.

ground, if only because of easier communication. But the women were usually employed in and around the large coastal cities, far from the mines and foundries of central Pennsylvania. Passaic, New Jersey, was particularly well known for its high concentration of Ukrainian girls. Because excursions to such centres were expensive, courtships tended to be brief, especially since the girls, bereft of family and relatives, were also very eager to marry.

Weddings were major social affairs in the immigrant community, often costing $200–300, which was a huge amount in relationship to a couples' earnings. Little wonder that Ukrainian weddings gained renown as lively, lengthy affairs where alcohol flowed freely and brawls were frequent. For those still seeking mates, dances were a favourite haunt. Before they organized their own 'balls,' Ukrainians frequented Slovak and Polish dances. Here, too, heavy drinking and brawls were de rigueur.

Yet, despite the liberal use of alcohol, the crime rate among Ukrainians was low. Between 1904 and 1908, only 0.02 per cent were accused of breaking the law, in contrast to 4 per cent of the Irish, 1.8 per cent of the German, and 1 per cent of the Polish immigrants who were charged with criminal offences. Ukrainians also had one of the lowest representations among those seeking charity.

While the immigrants were notably slow in adjusting to American ways, their children mastered them easily and quickly. With both parents at work and no grandparents about, immigrant children spent much of their time in the street. There they learned English so quickly that they were soon indistinguishable from the children of the native-born. Outpaced by their children, Ukrainian parents fought a losing battle in trying to inculcate in their quick, street-wise, self-confident offspring the obedience and respect that elders were accorded in the Old Country. But it was not only the relations between parents and children that were often strained. On the pages of Ukrainian newspapers one often read complaints of men who claimed that America spoiled women and, specifically, that it was a land of *babske pravo*, that is, where the law favoured women. As proof, the scandalized letter-writers cited cases of women demanding equal rights with men, refusing to tolerate beatings, and abandoning their husbands for more attractive mates. Consequently, one frequently heard of marriage-minded males going back to the Old Country to find spouses.

Discrimination

Like most immigrants, the Ukrainians, and Slavs in general, encountered prejudice and discrimination. There was, first of all, a strong economic motivation for the native Americans' antagonistic attitudes towards the newcomers. Originally brought over as strikebreakers and invariably willing to work under more difficult conditions than the original English, Welsh, and Irish miners in the region, the Slavs were an ominous threat to the native Americans' economic well-being. Moreover, the Slavs possessed another prerequisite for prejudice: they were markedly different from the native population.

Constituting the first major wave of non-English-speaking immigrants to the region, they had little contact with the general populace and congregated only with their own kind. As they observed the largely illiterate, bedraggled immigrants living in crowded, abysmal quarters, many Americans were only too ready to consider them as members of a primitive culture, even a lower race. Soon ethnic slurs were cast their way with increasing frequency and derision. They were called, as a matter of course, 'Bohunks,' a derivative from Bohemians that was applied to all Slavs, or the more pejorative 'Hunkies,' a term originally used for those from the Hungarian part of the Austrian empire and later for all East Europeans.

Dire warnings and bitter complaints about the newcomers began to appear in the press. For example, in 1892 an article in Forum magazine fulminated against the 'scum of Europe' that 'diseased' the once prosperous, safe, and civilized towns of Pennsylvania, forcing out the English, Scottish, Welsh, Irish, and American miners that 'once gave stability to the coal regions.' Alarmed by the increasing waves of Slavs, the author of the Slav Invasion proclaimed that a 'struggle for industrial race supremacy' was taking place and the Slavs were winning. Among the Slav's advantages were, according to the author, 'his fewer wants, his lower cost of living, his lower price of labor ... and his characteristic indifference to difficult conditions.' Moreover, because contacts between them were very limited, the Slav 'assimilated very few, if any, of the ideals of the the English-speaking worker.' Even government bodies reflected the anti-immigrant attitudes. In 1897, Pennsylvania passed a discriminatory tax against miners and other workers who were not naturalized Americans.

Because initially most of the Slavic immigrants planned to return to their homeland after several years, these attitudes, while irritating, did not appear to be overly threatening. But as more and more decided to stay in America and brought their families to join them, prejudice and discrimination became a major burden in their already difficult lives.

An example of immigrant humour and a comment on the institution of marriage. This 1921 postcard depicts a Ukrainian upset by the sight of his neighbour flying off with his wife and his home-brew. He is willing to let the neighbour keep the wife as long as he returns the brew.

The First Wave

A Bukovynian family in Quebec on their way to Edna-Star, Alberta, 1897. Most of them wear the sheepskin coats by means of which Canadians identified Ukrainian newcomers.

IMMIGRATION TO CANADA

One of the great agricultural regions of the world, the Canadian prairies – currently the provinces of Manitoba, Saskatchewan, and Alberta – encompass a huge area. With 1,200,000 sq. km they are larger than Western Europe and over two times as large as Ukraine. In 1870, when much of these territories were purchased from the Hudson's Bay Company and incorporated in the dominion, they were largely empty. Even in the 1890s, after decades of sporadic colonization, their population was only 200,000. Thus, at the turn of the century, for a variety of economic and political reasons – the United States, with its open land almost gone, was uncomfortably close – Canadian authorities felt intensely the need to populate the prairies.

Consisting mostly of British Canadians, and reinforced by English, Scots, Irish, and Americans, the initial wave of colonists arrived soon after 1870. It and subsequent reinforcements established, and retained, an overwhelming majority, thereby assuring that English-speakers and their culture maintained a position of pre-eminence in the new lands. About a decade later, Germans, Jews, Icelanders, and religious sects from the Russian empire, such as the Mennonites, began to arrive. Soon afterwards, the first Ukrainians found their way to the prairies.

The adventurous Ivan Pylypiw and Vasyl Eleniak are commonly considered to be the first Ukrainian immigrants to Canada. After learning about its vast, open spaces from a German friend, the two set out for Western Canada in 1891. They liked what they saw and upon his return to Galicia, Pylypiw convinced six families from his home village of Nebyliw to move to Canada. Consequently, in 1892, the so-called Nebyliw Group established the first permanent Ukrainian settlement in Canada in the locality of Edna-Star, near Edmonton in present-day Alberta.

But the individual who was most responsible for transforming the early trickle of immigrants to Canada into a massive migration was Josef Oleskiw. A professor of agriculture in Lviv (Eastern Galicia) and a populist committed to aiding the peasantry, he vis-

Dr Josef Oleskiw, 1860–1903.

Sir Clifford Sifton, Minister of the Interior, 1896–1905.

A Canadian government advertisement proclaiming the availability of 200 million acres of land in Western Canada. It offers 160 acres of free land to every settler.

ited Canada in 1895 to examine conditions firsthand. Impressed by the opportunities that the Canadian West offered for agricultural settlement, Oleskiw published a number of widely circulated pamphlets in Western Ukraine that discouraged the growing emigration to Brazil and advised peasants to go to Canada instead. In his successful efforts to popularize emigration to Canada, Oleskiw received encouragement from Canadian authorities. The minister of the interior, Clifford Sifton, was particularly impressed by the suitability of the hardy Ukrainians for taming the wild prairies. He expressed his views as follows: 'I think a stalwart peasant in a sheepskin coat, born on the soil, whose forefathers have been farmers for ten generations, with a stout wife and half a dozen children, is good quality.'

Because of Oleskiw's efforts, on the one hand, and the Canadian government's direct involvement, on the other, the flow of Ukrainians to Canada was much more directed than that to the United States. The immigrants usually landed in Halifax, Saint John, or Quebec City from where, unlike their compatriots who went to the United States, they still had a tremendous distance to travel to reach their destinations. But the Canadian government was more helpful than the American, usually providing interpreters and guides who helped the immigrants on the long trek westward. Boarding the Canadian Pacific Railway, they commenced the journey of over 4000 kilometres, much of it over endless plains and bush to Winnipeg (East Selkirk). There, in the Immigration Hall, they went through clearance procedures, and decided on where to acquire land. Here, as in the course of the journey, they were often besieged by swindlers. 'Poles, Jews and even Canadians,' a government official wrote in 1898, 'try to take all the money they have from them.' Many a newcomer was sold useless or substandard equipment and even non-existent land in the vicinity of Winnipeg. The final stage of the long journey that took them halfway around the world usually ended the way it began: on foot or by wagon, following trails for want of roads, the newcomers followed their guides to an isolated place in the unpopulated bush that was to be their new home.

New arrivals at a railway station in Quebec preparing for the long train ride to the Prairies, pre-1914.

Newcomers shortly after their arrival in Winnipeg, c. 1908. At this point many Ukrainians made the decision about where to establish their homesteads.

The First Wave

A Galician in Calgary, c. 1903–5. Clearly confused by the urban surroundings, he still wears the clothes in which he left his native village.

Indians on the corner of Jasper Avenue and Grierson Street in Edmonton, 1902. Ukrainian settlers frequently encountered Indians when they established their homesteads in the prairies. Relations between them were generally friendly.

Immigrant women and children outside the Canadian Pacific Railway station in Winnipeg, c. 1890–1914. Exhausted by weeks of travel, they rest on the pavement amidst all their earthly possessions.

Part of The Ukrainian Pioneer mural by William Kurelek.

The First Wave

A Government Survey of Ukrainian Homesteaders, 1897

I have the honour to forward the following report re settlers that came in this Spring, who I visited with the Interpreter:–

Wasel Mariajan (Wasyl Marian, S. 22, Tp. 56, Rge. 17, W4). Has no horses, 1 cow. Said he had about $150.00 stolen from him on board the ship. This man is very good to work, having built a house and fixed it for the winter. Has 3 small children.

Danytra Balan (Dmytro Balan, S. 16, Tp. 56, Rge. 17, W4). Has nothing. This man has also built a house and is working out when he can get any work. Has 4 small children.

Giorgi Klapacyuk (George Klapatiuk, NE 1/4 16, Tp. 56, Rge. 17, W4.) Has nothing. Three children. He owed Iwan Scraba $200.00 for passage money to this country ...

Giorgi Melnyk (SW 1/4-20-56-17-W4). Has one horse, 1 cow, and 4 children. His wife had twins about two months ago and caught cold from laying on the ground. He started to take her to Edmonton once, but had not gone any more than a quarter of a mile before she started to groan and say she could not stand being taken that distance. She has not been any better since ...

Nycola Tapylnitzki (Nykola Topolnitsky, NW 1/4 28-56-17-W4). Has nothing at all. This man has been sick for about 5 weeks and is just getting round again. Symptoms like grippe. (Three in the family.)

There are 5 families who had had the misfortune to lose their boxes with all their clothes. The only clothes they have now is what they stand in. The last they saw of the boxes was in Galicia ...

Most of these people when asked how they are going to get through the winter, and what they are going to live on, say they do not know, they will have to get through somehow. They all want to know if they cannot get work somewhere from the Government, the Government to give them flour and meat in exchange.

There are only 3 of the whole lot who came in last Spring who have any money at all, I have not mentioned them in the report at all, and there are quite a few more who will need looking up, but I have not time before sending in this report.

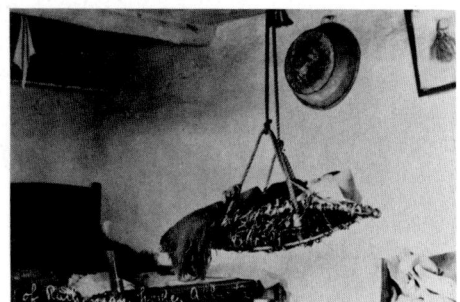

The interior of a Ukrainian (Ruthenian) home in Alberta pre-1910. Despite the poverty, the owner hung a portrait of Taras Shevchenko, Ukraine's national poet, on the wall beside the makeshift cradle.

A primitive shelter that the family of Stefan Waskewicz inhabited while they built their permanent home (below) near La Corey, Alberta, in 1930.

The First Wave

Sawa Szalapaj working his land near Athabasca, Alberta, in the late 1920s. The cleared land and broken soil is the result of years of back-breaking work.

A typical bloc settlement. Township 19-22W: Settlement northeast of Oakburn.

The conditions under which they obtained land were as follows: a settler received 160 acres for $10 (the market rate was $10–15 per acre). However, within 3 years he had to clear and farm at least 30 acres of prairie or bush and build a house valued at a minimum of $300, and he had to live on the land for at least six months a year before he received final title.

Selecting the area in which to settle was a crucial decision. And in making it Ukrainians differed significantly from the Anglo-Saxon settlers. For a variety of reasons they often chose or received poorer-quality land. One reason was that much of the prime land was already distributed. Another reflected Old World thinking: because wood was scarce and expensive in Galicia and Bukovyna, Ukrainians tended to choose wooded terrain that others avoided because it was difficult to clear. Sometimes prejudiced government officials knowingly assigned them to inferior lands. And frequently the desire of the immigrants, who often arrived in groups from a single village, to be near friends and relatives led them to choose poorer-quality land.

The first Ukrainian house in Manitoba was built in 1896 near Emerson.

The First Wave

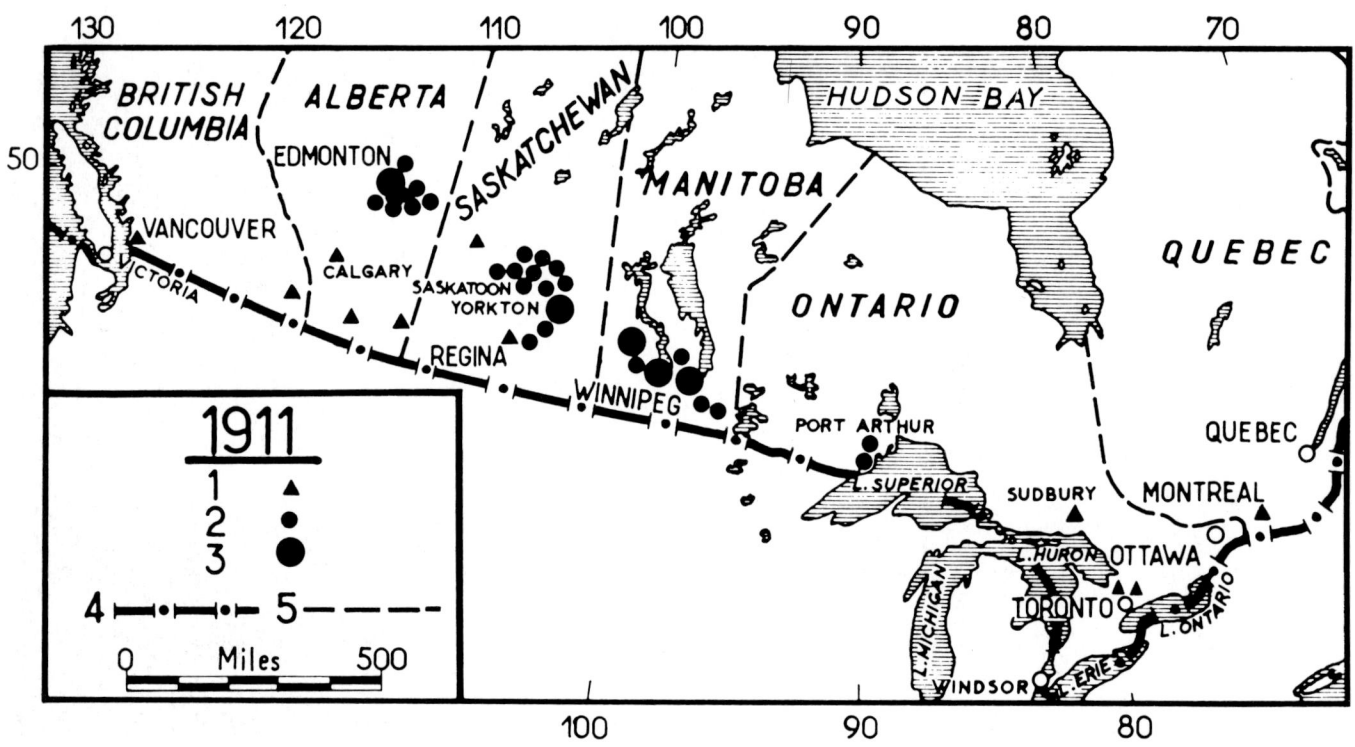

Distribution of Ukrainians in Canada, 1911. (1) 500, (2) 1000, (3) 10,000.

Ukrainian women plastering the walls of their primitive, one-room dwelling.

This exceedingly pronounced tendency to 'cluster' had crucial ramifications. As one group after another settled near each other, it became clear that a large, contiguous, and expanding Ukrainian enclave might be in the making. However, this was what the government, intent on 'Canadianizing' newcomers as soon as possible, wished to avoid. Consequently, a compromise of sorts emerged. The Ukrainians, who stubbornly insisted on seeking out their own kind, were allowed to settle in groups. But instead of forming a single, contiguous bloc, their areas of settlement were broken up into smaller, disconnected blocs that stretched out across the prairies from Edmonton to Winnipeg. Such were the origins of the famous bloc settlements that became a key feature of Ukrainian life in Western Canada.

A Galician farm near Stuartburn, Manitoba. It probably took over a decade for the proprietor and his family to clear the land and raise the buildings.

Part of The Ukrainian Pioneer mural by William Kurelek.

The First Wave

A pioneer family wedding, 1911. These important social events, which usually lasted three days, were celebrated in rural Canada much like in Ukraine.

Immigrants who chose to stay in the urban centres of Canada, and specifically in Winnipeg, could expect to live in quarters such as those pictured here.

Only 9 per cent of the Ukrainians settled in urban areas before the First World War. Almost all of them congregated in Winnipeg, the gateway to the prairies. For the most part, they were single men who worked as unskilled labourers on construction sites or in railway yards, factories, and foundries. The few women who found their way to urban areas were usually employed as domestics or as help in restaurants and hotels. Because the cities of Canada expanded more slowly than those in the United States, work was rarely steady and even those who were based in cities spent a large part of the year laying railway track, cutting lumber, or working in mines.

An Orthodox priest visiting an immigrant family, most probably in Winnipeg during the pre-1914 period.

Jasper Avenue in Edmonton, c. 1903.

The First Wave

Ageing pioneers with what was clearly a life of hard work behind them. Seated are Wasyl and Wasylyna Zahara and standing are Sanda and Maria Sandul. Stuartburn, Manitoba, 1920.

Making a living

Even under the best of conditions, farming is a demanding undertaking. It is immeasurably more daunting when one begins literally from scratch, on uncultivated land, amidst vast and desolate prairies. Little wonder that even well-prepared English-speaking homesteaders, with capital of $1000, generous credit, and the best lands, often gave up after several frustrating years. The statistics are sobering: in the early decades of the century, 20 per cent of the homesteaders in Manitoba, 45 per cent in Alberta, and 57 per cent in Saskatchewan failed. What, then, were the chances of a penniless, illiterate, confused Galician or Bukovynian peasant, whose only assets were his and his wife's bare hands and who was dumped amidst the bush, often on poor-quality land, with a brood of shivering children and with the fearsome Canadian winter fast approaching?

Yet, for the most part, these severely disadvantaged newcomers not only survived but in the process managed to transform millions of acres of prairie and bush into bountiful wheat fields. And their success is generally included among the major achievements in the history of Western Canada. Performed, as it were, on an empty stage, the accomplishments of the Ukrainian settlers stood out much more than those of their compatriots to the south who were submerged among the faceless millions that fuelled America's industrial boom. Literally and figuratively, the early Ukrainian settlers in Canada broke new ground. And in time, a pioneer mystique enveloped, quite deservedly, their impressive efforts.

Initially, almost none of the Ukrainian settlers was able to devote himself to farming full time. If he arrived with a family, an immigrant and his wife, armed with axe and spade, first had to move into the bush to put up a primitive shack and clear a tiny garden plot. But as soon as possible the settler left his makeshift home, usually in the fall, to seek work as a hired hand or a railway worker so as to earn enough money for the purchase of winter supplies, farm implements, or livestock. For years, the settler depended on seasonal labour, primarily on the railways, to acquire cash. Meanwhile, his wife, left on her own for months,

Galicians threshing grain with their own machinery near Stuartburn, Manitoba, c. 1900. Such undertakings were usually communal efforts and they did much for maintaining a sense of community among the early settlers.

Digging the foundation of the Prosvita (Enlightenment) Society reading hall in Winnipeg in the pre-1914 era. The workers probably provided labour free of charge.

The First Wave

Because their homesteads could not support their families in the early years, many Ukrainian males worked on the railways during the summer months and late fall.

Ukrainians working for the Canadian Pacific Railway relax by making music with an improvised orchestra, 1912.

tried to improve the hut, enlarge the garden, and somehow feed her children. Only in summer was there time to clear laboriously one acre after another. It would take five to ten years before the entire farm was self-supporting.

The many men who arrived alone usually approached farming somewhat differently. By and large, they first sought employment on railway gangs, in mines, in lumber, or as unskilled labour in Winnipeg and other cities. If and when, after several years of poor wages and frequent layoffs, they managed to save enough, they brought over their families and, with at least a minimum of capital, launched into homesteading. But either alone or with a family, starting out in farming under these conditions was extremely difficult.

For the newcomers, the thought of profiting from farming was alien since in Galicia and Bukovyna peasants viewed their land as a means of feeding themselves and their families, not as a business. When they first began to homestead in Canada, this Old World view of farming prevailed. But in time, as the amount of cleared acreage grew, as farm machinery gradually replaced oxen, and as the North American business ethos became more familiar, increasing numbers began to market their growing surplus. A breakthough in this reorientation came during the First World War when the price of grain rose dramatically. Because many

Clad in sheepskins and travelling by sleigh, Ukrainian settlers gather at the hay-market in Edmonton, 1903.

Ukrainians were not yet Canadian citizens, they did not render military service. This allowed them to take advantage of the profits to be made in grain production. Thus, by end of the war, in some sectors of the Ukrainian community, signs of prosperity finally began to appear.

Daily life

Hard work and endurance. These words are used most often in explaining Ukrainian achievements in agriculture. If the work load of the average farmer was huge, that of the Ukrainian homesteader was more so, especially in the early years. Not only did he have to transform, literally with his bare hands, 160 acres of bush land into a productive farm but, because he lacked sufficient capital, it was necessary to leave home for months every year in order to earn desperately needed money. On the homestead, endless, back-breaking tasks, made all the more difficult because they were performed under primitive conditions, awaited him: he had to break the land, pull out roots, stumps, and rock, plough and seed, and take in the harvest. Given the short Canadian farming season, all this had to be done hurriedly and punctually or else the harvest was lost. In addition, there were granaries to be built, wells to be dug, bins, roofs, and fences to be repaired. Upon returning from the field, the farmer fed the livestock and looked after other chores in the barn. Normally, the working day began at five in the morning and lasted until ten at night.

In the summers as well as winters the homesteader turned to cash-producing jobs. Finding them was no easy matter. It often involved travelling, practically penniless, for hundreds of miles.

A Galician woman delivering milk in Manitoba in the pre–First World War period.

The First Wave

A Ukrainian family harvesting in 1918.

Women digging potatoes in East Kildonen, Manitoba, c. 1915. Gardening, which was one of a woman's many tasks, was a crucial source of cash in the early days of homesteading.

Moreover, since landless immigrants from Winnipeg and other cities were also looking for work, their competition not only made jobs even more difficult to find but drove down wages. If the farmer was fortunate enough to find work, it was usually on the railways, in the mines, or as an unskilled labourer. For laying track in the winter, the pay was $10–20 a month plus food and board; in mining, 40 cents for a ton of shovelled coal; a labourer received about 45 cents per hour for digging out a basement with a pick and shovel. Some of the work was dangerous. On the railways, there were, over a 25-year period, about 4200 labourers killed and more than 13,000 injured. None the less, the Ukrainian worker had few options and his employers knew it. As one contemporary noted, 'The common labourers were for the most part Ukrainians. These naive, trustful, bearded giants worked like elephants, laughed like children, and asked no questions. They were shamelessly exploited' (Kostash, 205).

The ability of the disadvantaged Ukrainians to survive on the land surprised many Canadians. Some argued that, in addition to being industrious, they were exceptionally frugal. Others noted their inherent love of the land. But all agreed that the Ukrainian woman's prodigious capacity for work was a crucial factor. With her husband away for months, an immigrant woman had to, with barely a dollar in her pocket, feed, clothe, and maintain the

health of her numerous children. Myrna Kostash provides a vivid description of their many labours:

> While waiting for the garden to produce and for the husband to show up again with wages, they picked wild mushrooms and berries, snared rabbits and shot game birds, trapped muskrats, skinned them and sold the pelts. Leaving the older children alone and carrying the baby on their backs, they got jobs in the neighbourhood hoeing gardens, pulling roots and digging potatoes ... They walked to town to sweep out the boxcars on the sidings for whatever grain was left on the floor. They spun and wove their own wool, ground grain for flour, pressed their own oil, wove rope from hemp and made their own soup. If a cow died, they skinned it

Settler women selling their produce at the Dufferin Street market in Winnipeg, c. 1915, much as they did in the towns near their native villages in Galicia or Bukovyna.

A well-earned pause for refreshment in the wheatfields of Alberta.

and tanned the hide. If a child got sick, they concocted herbal medicines. Not to mention pasturing and milking the cow, weeding the garden, cooking meals, doing laundry, knitting, sewing and mending, making bread, cheese and sauerkraut, washing dishes and ironing clothes. In addition, of course, to rearing the children. (Kostash, 206)

For their efforts these women received little in the way of recognition. Indeed, among the many Old Country attitudes that survived on the isolated homesteads was the view that it was a woman's duty to be subservient. All too often, men were ill-mannered, uncouth, and even brutal in their treatment of wives and children. Despite their tremendous contributions, women had little or no control over the family budget. Because children had to work from an early age, their education often ended with the first few grades of elementary school. Although Ukrainian families were known for being exceptionally close-knit, some collapsed under the strain of pioneer life. One result of the pressure was that the crime rate among the Ukrainians in Canada, in contrast to their generally single countrymen in the United States, was higher than average.

There was, of course, practically no leisure time. Holidays like Christmas and Easter were celebrated much like in Ukraine, that is, with considerable ceremony. But for women this meant even more work. Perhaps only during a wedding could the women who were not involved in preparing the event enjoy themselves. The weddings, which were always big affairs and lasted three days, were also held in traditional fashion. Usually, they involved the entire community and provided one of the few occasions when both men and women could break away from the demanding routine of farm life.

Pioneer settlers from Bukovyna in front of St Michael's Greek Orthodox Church in Gardenton, Manitoba, in 1915. While married women indicate their marital status by wearing wraps around their scarves, the unmarried girls don floral cylindrical hats.

A Canadian Expert's View of the Ukrainian Woman

The average Ukrainian woman often contributes more to the work of the farm than does the average hired man, whether in the interest, strength and ability she brings to the task, or in the variety of work she performs. A Ukrainian woman in the Canora district, Saskatchewan, gave us an outline of her day's work in the summer. She gets up between four and five in the morning and goes to bed at eleven at night. When she gets up she does the chores outside, feeds the cattle and milks the cows. She then prepares breakfast and washes the dishes, after which she follows the family to the field where she may hoe or drive a gang-plow, stook, etc. She comes in shortly before dinner, prepares it and cleans up, a matter of one and a half or two hours, then returns to the field until eight o'clock when she milks, after which she gets supper. This is a man's share in any other community. Along with the contribution of all the other members of the family – and they are usually several – the woman's labour goes far to explain the undeniable progress of the Ukrainian farmer.

                    Young, The Ukrainian Canadians, 88

Main street in 1898 of Fort Saskatchewan, Alberta, a typical prairie town. For many Ukrainian settlers, towns such as this were the closest they came to an urban centre.

Lunch-time on market-day in Sheho, Saskatchewan, c. 1907. A Canadian woman tries to communicate with the Ukrainian women who have come into town.

Prejudice

That anti-Ukrainian prejudice emerged was not surprising. The newcomers were the largest non-Anglo-Saxon group to arrive in the West. They came in an unexpected and threatening wave. And, wearing their exotic dress and clinging closely to their traditions, they were very conspicuously different from the dominant Anglo-Saxons. While Sifton and a few government officials recognized their usefulness, many Canadians did not. The English-speaking residents of the prairies were angered and appalled by the 'hordes' of outlandish 'men in sheep-skin coats,' together with their large families, which the trains disgorged in Winnipeg. Soon an outcry against the newcomers, led by some newspapers, arose.

While the need for immigration was obvious, editorials argued that newcomers should be 'stalwart, enterprising' North Europeans who were closely related to Anglo-Saxons and therefore easily capable of attaining their levels of civilization. However, the strange-looking Ukrainians, with their unpronounceable names, were, according to some newpapers, a 'mass of human ignorance, filth and immorality,' 'ignorant and vicious foreign scum,' and 'the dregs of Europe.' The *Winnipeg Telegram*, for example, characterized the Ukrainians as follows: stupid, dishonest, uncooperative, immoral, and lawless. A fear often expressed was that the immigrants would lower the moral and intellectual standards of Canadian society, dilute British racial stock, and threaten the British character of the new territories. Moreover, the sight of thousands of acres being given away to suspect foreigners badly jarred the Anglo-Saxon sense of proprietorship in the prairies.

Because they were viewed as a major obstacle to the assimilation of Ukrainians, their bloc settlements were frequently

singled out for criticism: they were a 'positive misfortune to a [neighbouring] enlightened community,' they would repel 'desirable' immigrants, they could be bribed en masse by irresponsible politicians, they perpetuated Ukrainian language and customs, and they kept their inhabitants out of touch with British institutions and ideals. Yet, the fierce criticism notwithstanding, the colonization process had proceeded too far and the Ukrainian bloc settlements remained, to the great irritation of the militant assimilationists.

There were, of course, more temperate reactions to the 'Ukrainian threat,' voices of the 'positive' racists, as Myrna Kostash calls them, who sought to reassure the English-speaking public. They pointed out that the vast majority of newcomers to the prairies continued to be Anglo-Saxons. For instance, the *Toronto Globe* in 1909 wrote: 'The West is today definitely Anglo-

During a huge war-veterans parade in Winnipeg in June 1919 anti-foreigner sentiment was much in evidence. The growing socialist influence among the immigrants led many Canadians to identify Ukrainians with Bolshevism. Consequently, several Ukrainian buildings were attacked and ransacked by the veterans.

Saxon ... The legislators, the teachers, lawyers, ministers and newspapermen are almost invariably from the (Anglo-Saxon) East and, at this formative period, the West is to them as clay in the hands of a potter.' Some newspapers, such as the pro-Liberal *Winnipeg Free Press*, anxious to win votes for its party, consistently presented Ukrainians in a positive light. Other opinion moulders, such as Reverend J.S. Woodsworth, generously commented that the Ukrainian immigrant 'is a patient and industrious workman ... The girls as a rule make good domestics.'

The Ukrainians often reacted to prejudice by turning inward. They avoided government officials whenever possible, tried to establish their own schools, and patronized their own or, more likely, the Jewish merchants, who were such a familiar feature in the Old Country and who knew their language. Social interaction between Ukrainians and non-Ukrainians, especially Anglo-Saxons, was rare and intermarriage was rarer still. In short, they seemed ready to live in a world apart, hoping not so much for acceptance as to be left alone.

Ukrainian (Ruthenian) settlers in Alberta before the First World War. While their parents clung to traditional ways and dress, the younger generation adapted quickly to their Canadian surroundings.

Reverse Stereotyping

People in this area generally frowned upon a mixed marriage. 'He's taken an English girl. What's the matter with him?' I think I would have disappointed my parents had I not married a Ukrainian girl. The Anglo-Saxon people here in town were the bank manager, the station agent, the teachers. They held important positions. Almost without exception these people's wives were lazy. They'd hire people to weed their radishes! They'd devote too much of their time to leisure. They became stereotyped by our people. But you could count on a Ukrainian girl to work hard, keep a clean house, cook for you. That's why so many of the Anglo-Saxons liked to have Ukrainian cleaning ladies. They'd earn every penny. There was an inkling of the feeling among us that Ukrainians who married non-Ukrainians were a bit like social climbers.

Second-generation Ukrainian Canadian from Alberta

COMMUNITY ORGANIZATION

Churches in the United States

Accustomed to living in tight-knit villages, the Ukrainian immigrants found it exceedingly difficult to live on their own in the New World. Their difficulty in communicating in English and unfamiliarity with North American ways exacerbated their sense of isolation. Therefore, the urge to re-create in the new, alien environment a sense of community, the comforting feeling of being among 'our people,' quickly came to the fore. Its effect was somewhat surprising. In Europe peasants were known for

St Josaphat's Ukrainian Catholic Church in Gorham, North Dakota. Erected in the 1890s, it burnt down in 1915.

The First Wave

their notorious inablity to organize, to band together for a common goal. Yet in the New World, these same peasants exhibited unexpected energy, skill, and commitment in forming organizations and institutions that could serve as the core of the new ethnic communities.

The church was the focus of spiritual and social life in the Ukrainian village. All the major events in a peasant's life – christenings, weddings, and funerals – and most communal festivities were associated with religion. When they arrived in the United States, Ukrainian immigrants sorely missed their churches, without which their lives seemed monotonous and grey. Consequently, the earliest forms of communal organization they set up among themselves were churches and parishes.

In 1884, the approximately seventy immigrant families living in Shenandoah, a small mining town in Pennsylvania, petitioned Archbishop Sylvester Sembratovych of Lviv for a priest. By the end of the year, Ivan Voliansky, an energetic young priest, arrived, together with his wife – a fact of major significance – to minister to the spiritual needs of the immigrants. By 1886, he built in Shenandoah the church of St Michael, the first Byzantine-rite edifice in the United States. This was only the first of Voliansky's numerous, ground-breaking achievements. During his five-year stay, the dynamic priest initiated the construction of about a half-dozen other churches. In his Shenandoah parish he formed, in 1885, a mutual-aid society called the Brotherhood of St Nicholas. The next year Voliansky established *Ameryka*, the first, albeit short-lived, Ukrainian newspaper in the New World. Other firsts included a choir, an evening school, a reading-room, and cooperative general store that would benefit the immigrants. Moreover, he sought out and visited most of the workers' colonies between the east coast and Colorado. Also noteworthy was the fact that in the famous coal strike of 1887–8, he was the only Catholic priest who openly sympathized with the striking miners. The efforts of this outstanding pioneer of Ukrainian organizational life caught the attention of the local press. An article in a Shenandoah paper read: 'Although young, barely more than 30 years of age, tall and slim, though compactly built, and fairly good looking, Father Voliansky has no superior as a worker. He scarcely permits himself any rest, so thoroughly is his soul in his work. If life and

Father Ivan Voliansky, 1857–1926, the first Ukrainian Catholic priest in America.

health stands the test, his religious standing and that of his church will in a decade or two rank high and firm in America, and he will then be able to enjoy with ease the honors he will have richly earned' (Procko, 5).

By 1889, five more Greek Catholic priests arrived, four from Galicia and one from Transcarpathia. But that year the budding Greek Catholic church suffered a major setback: pressure from the Roman Catholic hierarchy, incensed by Voliansky's married status, succeeded in having him recalled to Galicia. Growing difficulties with the Roman Catholic hierarchy notwithstanding, the influx of Greek Catholic priests continued. However, it now consisted mostly of priests from Transcarpathia. Thus, in 1897, when Father Nestor Dmytriw published an almanac, the first Ukrainian book to appear in America, it contained a list of 29 priests, 25 of whom were from Transcarpathia. By 1916 the number was 258, almost evenly divided between Galicians and Transcarpathians.

The influence of the clergy on the masses of uneducated immigrants was overwhelming. In the Old Country it was also extensive but there, at least in Galicia, the growing secular intelligentsia tended to balance it off. Only in 1887 did the first Ukrainian with a higher education, Volodymyr Simenovych, come to the United States. And for years he was the only one of his kind in the New World. Consequently, in the early decades it was the clergy, almost by default, that occupied positions of leadership, moulded opinions, and initiated projects among the immigrants. And priests could take credit for most of the constructive initiatives and endeavours of this early period. But, by the same token, they were largely responsible for the numerous, divisive conflicts that wracked the community.

The clergy was far from homogeneous. An essential distinction was whether a priest came from Galicia or Transcarpathia. Because the latter stemmed from a politically, culturally, and economically underdeveloped province, they tended, for the most part, to be commited conservatives. Many of them aped the élitist manners of the Hungarian nobles who ruled their homeland, adopted their language, distanced themselves from the 'simple people,' and often used their positions for their own self-enrichment. The fact that they were married and had to care

The original St Michael's Church in Shenandoah. Founded in 1884 by Reverend Ivan Voliansky, it was the first Ukrainian Catholic church in the United States.

The so-called American Circle. Clockwise from the top: the Reverends Ivan Konstankevych, Nestor Dmytriw, Mykola Stefanovych, Ivan Ardan, Antin Bonchevsky, Stefan Makar, Pavlo Tymkevych, and Mykola Pidhoretsky.

for their families increased this tendency to concentrate on material advantages. In popular parlance, they were known as Magyarones. Yet, even among the Transcarpathians there were distinctions. Those who belonged to the eparchy of Mukachiv viewed themselves as being more 'aristocratic' than their 'plebeian' colleagues from the Prešov eparchy. The latter, meanwhile, were more likely to identify with interests of their parishioners than the former.

Although Galicia was also a badly underdeveloped region, its Ukrainian inhabitants were politically and ideologically far ahead of their Transcarpathian brethren. This was readily evident in the attitudes, views, and actions of the Galician priests. Many of the younger ones were populists, often members or sympathizers of the socialist Galician Radical party, who actively sought to improve the lot of their community. Furthermore, they were much more influenced by modern concepts of nationhood, and specifically Ukrainian nationhood, than were their Transcarpathian colleagues. Such were the characteristics that defined the so-called American Circle, a group of young seminarians who, while still in Lviv, resolved to emigrate to the United States in order to improve the religious, civic, and cultural status of the Ukrainian immigrants. To avoid complications with the Roman Catholic hierarchy, they remained celibate. Members of this extremely influential cohort were Ivan Konstankevych, Nestor Dmytriw, Ivan Ardan, Antin Bonchevsky, Stefan Makar, Mykyta Pidhoretsky, Mykola Stefanovych, and Pavlo Tymkevych.

This, of course, is not to say that Transcarpathian priests were retrograde conservatives while their Galician counterparts were irreproachable altruists. Both factions obviously had a mixture of the praiseworthy and the reprehensible. Moreover, they had much in common, notably language, culture, and, first and foremost, their Byzantine rite, which they would have to defend jointly against the assimilationist policies of the Roman Catholic hierarchy. None the less, the differences between the Magyarone 'aristocratics' of Mukachiv and the 'radical-boy-priests' (*radykalypopyky*) of Galicia were too great for either side to ignore. Sooner or later, they would emerge to set the tone in relations between the immgrants from the two regions.

The Galician-Transcarpathian schism. Competition for well-established parishes first divided the two factions. Later, the appointment in 1907 of Soter Ortynsky, a Galician, as bishop infuriated the Transcarpathian clergy and they launched a vicious campaign against him and all Galicians. In order to alienate their parishioners from Ortynsky, they exaggerated the regional differences between Transcarpathians and Galicians. Because their rivals were nationally conscious Ukrainians, the Ukrainian national movement became a major focus of their attacks. Ortynsky and all Galicians were accused of caring more about nationalism than religion. They were denounced as traitors to Rusyn (Ruthenian) traditions for adopting the modern ethnonational name, Ukrainian. For good measure, the socially conservative and élitist Transcarpathian priests warned their parishioners that the Galician clergy were godless, socialist radicals.

A Magyarone Diatribe

> Ukrainian priests are pushing the lying *Svoboda* into the hands of peasants instead of the lives of the saints which they themselves haven't read. Ukrainian priests are leading the way to Ukrainian slavery, one in which our national ideals will be lost. 'Ukrainchiks' are confusing our meetings. We have reached a time when our 'Ukrainchiks' offer division, robbery and thievery ... A priest is supposed to spread the Kingdom of God and not the Kingdom of Ukraine ... Ukrainians are ripping our Christian faith from our hearts. The Pole is stealing our rite. The Ukrainian is stealing our very faith ... Ukraine is separating children from parents, brothers, sisters, priests from parishes ... evil and diabolical hatred burns in the hearts of Ukrainians ... Our tattered, hungry sons of Ruthenian soil run to America but even here they are caught by the Ukrainians.
>
> Vestnik, *Greek Catholic Union newspaper*, 1908

For their part, the Galician priests denounced their Transcarpathian rivals as Magyarones who were more loyal to Hungarian interests than to those of their own people. In fact, the Transcarpathian clergy generally did speak Hungarian at home and, quite often, even in church. Some continued to receive money from the Budapest government even after they reached North America. Many openly cooperated with the Hungarian government's so-called American Plan, which provided the Mukachiv clergy with large sums of money that was used in sowing dissension between Transcarpathians and Galicians as well as in blocking the spread of Ukrainian national consciousness among the former. In the United States, as in the Old Country, this was usually done by arguing that the Transcarpathian Rusyns constituted a nationality distinct from that of their Galician compatriots.

Unable to have one of their own appointed bishop, the Transcarpathian clergy demanded that the Vatican create a separate Greek Catholic diocese. In their words, they could not 'acquiesce

The second St Michael's Ukrainian Catholic Church in Shenandoah, Pennsylvania. Built in 1908, it was destroyed by fire in 1980 and rebuilt.

in being ecclesiastically united with the Galician Ukrainians,' because 'under the guise of the Catholic Church they might be thrown into the slavery of Ukrainianism.' Anxious to eliminate the constant feuding, the Vatican gave in. In 1916 it created a separate diocese, based in Pittsburgh, for what came to be called the Byzantine Ruthenian Catholic church. In 1924 it consisted of 155 churches, 129 priests, and about 290,000 parishioners.

Meanwhile, the original Philadelphia diocese became the base of the Ukrainian Catholic church, which numbered 144 churches, 129 priests, and about 240,000 parishioners. Thus, the Transcarpathian-Galician split became institutionalized, dividing the American Ukrainian community into two increasingly estranged parts.

In the decades after the split, the Transcarpathian church vacillated over which national orientation it should adopt. Unable to decide, it opted to avoid the issue altogether. Consequently, today it de-emphasizes ethnicity and urges its faithful to identify themselves primarily in terms of their Greek Catholic rite. But the legacy of this bitter Transcarpathian-Galician feud of the late nineteenth and early twentieth centuries remains: although the people of Transcarpathia today call themselves Ukrainians, their distant relatives in the United States still subscribe to the view that they are 'anything but Ukrainians.'

Other aspects of church life. Another effect that the arrival of new priests had was the so-called church-building fever that swept through the immigrant communities in the 1890s. Besides the desire to re-create a familiar spiritual haven, a variety of other factors provided fuel: the urging of the clergy, the vested interests of local businessmen, the desire to outdo neighbouring communities, and the internal conflicts that caused breakaway groups to form their own churches. In any case, building a church was the

Transcarpathians about the 'Ukrainian Threat'

> Dear Brothers! It is about time to know more about ourselves ... Why are you so afraid of the Ukrainians? People say there are twice as many of us as there are of them so what is there to be frightened of? ... Ukrainians ... have a national ideal and they work on its behalf. That is why they seem so frightening to us. It's about time that we too, brothers, began to do this kind of national work.
>
> Vestnik, 1908

immigrants' first communal project and it inevitably brought out their best, as well as worst, qualities.

Obviously the cost of building a church varied greatly. At the turn of the century, small communities generally constructed wooden structures that cost between $4000 and $8000. Stone churches usually required $30,000 to $40,000, although in several of the larger communites, like Chicago or New York, churches were built that cost well over $100,000. In terms of architectural style, the churches were unremarkable. Unable to duplicate Byzantine styles, American architects generally created an architectural mishmash, usually topped off by a onion-dome cupola. To pay for the costs of construction the immigrants relied on self-imposed quotas: families were assessed $15–20, while those who were single paid half the amount. In addition, parishioners were expected to contribute $0.50 a month in dues. Much of this went towards the maintenance of a priest, at the considerable salary of $60–90 a month, and a cantor who doubled as a teacher.

The churches not only served as a focus of communal life; they also became an arena for bitter conflicts engendered by the new American environment. Indeed, for the early immigrants, 'church politics' were usually the only politics that mattered. A major problem, which became acute before the appointment of Soter Ortynsky, was the strained relations that developed between the Greek Catholic immigrants and the largely Irish hierarchy of the Roman Catholic church. Ignorant of the particularities of the Greek Catholic rite and contemptuous of all East Europeans, Roman Catholic bishops often made matters difficult for them. For their part, Greek Catholic parishes frequently refused to surrender the deeds to their newly built churches to the 'foreign' bishops as was the practice in the Roman Catholic church. Often the results were bitter lawsuits, forced evictions of parishioners by the police, minor riots, and a deepening of ill-feeling on both sides.

Greek Catholic priests who came to North America with their families had additional reasons for being dissatisfied with the Roman Catholic hierarchy. Because Roman Catholic priests, unlike their Greek Catholic colleagues, were not allowed to marry, Roman Catholic bishops often refused to recognize married clergymen from Transcarpathia and Galicia as legitimate priests.

Soter Ortynsky, OSBM, was consecrated in 1907 as the first Ukrainian Catholic bishop in the United States.

The funeral of Bishop Soter Ortynsky, who died in Philadelphia on 24 March 1916. Priests carry the portrait of the deceased bishop through a crowd of about 15,000 mourners.

As the case of Alexis Toth illustrates, the controversial issue of celibacy soon had major repercussions for both Greek and Roman Catholicism in America.

A respected professor of theology in Transcarpathia, a consecrated priest, and a widower, Alexis Toth arrived in Minneapolis in 1889 to serve as the pastor of the local Greek Catholic parish. But because he had been married, the Roman Catholic archbishop refused to accept him. Unable to gain redress and convinced that the ancient Byzantine traditions of his rite, which Rome had recognized, were being trampled upon, Toth and his 365 parishioners made a dramatic decision in 1891 – they went over to Orthodoxy. In the following decades tens of thousands of Lemko, Transcarpathian, and Galician immigrants, urged on by the well-financed Russian Orthodox Mission in the United States, opted for membership in the Russian Orthodox church. By 1914, they constituted the overwhelming majority of the Orthodox in the United States and Alexis Toth was hailed as the 'father of Orthodoxy' in that country.

The rush to Orthodoxy had important national-ethnic implications for the Ukrainian-Rusyn immigrants. Since most of them came from isolated Ukrainian regions such as Transcarpathia, they were generally untouched by the developing sense of Ukrainian national consciousness. Moreover, as it had been in the Old Country, Russophilism was widespread among their clergy. Consequently, when the uneducated Rusyns (Ruthenians) entered the Russian Orthodox church in the United States, its hierarchy often succeeded in convincing them that they were ethnic Russians. Today, at a time of heightened consciousness of ethnic orgins, the Americanized descendants of these pseudo-Russians are often at a loss to explain why their 'Russian roots' lead back to patently Ukrainian lands.

To summarize, as a result of these religious and regional controversies, about 20 per cent of the early immigrants from West Ukrainian lands became Orthodox 'Russians,' another 40 per cent identified themselves as Greek or Byzantine Catholic Ruthenians/Rusyns, and the remaining 40 per cent called themselves Ukrainian Catholics.

The Path of Least Resistance

> I usually say I'm Russian. If you say you're Ukrainian, the guy tells you, 'Jesus Christ, what's that?' and you have to go into a whole history of Ukraine and explain to the guy what you mean. It is easier to say you are Russian. Everybody has heard of that — especially now, during the war. You could say 'Ruthenian,' they seem to know that one, too. So few people have ever heard of the Ukrainians that it's embarrassing to say you are one.
>
> *A Chicago Ukrainian in the 1940s*

The First Wave

Members of the Saints Cyril and Methodius Society arrayed before their church in Shamokin, Pennsylvania, 1908.

Chaos reigned among the Greek Catholics in America in the early years of the twentieth century. Conflicts with the Roman Catholic bishops, countless lawsuits over church property, growing factionalism among the clergy, and, most important, the fact that there was no Greek Catholic hierarchy to maintain ecclesiastical law and order among the faithful all had their effect. As noted above, in 1907, the Vatican, in consultation with Metropolitan Andrei Sheptytsky of Lviv, took a decisive step: it appointed the Galician priest Soter Ortynsky bishop for Greek Catholics in America. Initially the new bishop was subordinated to a Roman Catholic superior and his rights were limited. However, despite the many daunting difficulties that confronted him, Ortynsky resolutely pushed ahead. He established himself in Philadelphia, founded an orphanage there that became the source of numerous vocations, regulated the training of new priests, and founded a Catholic fraternal organization and a newspaper. In the process, he had constant conflicts with both the clergy and the laity. None the less, by 1913 Ortynsky's accomplishments were impressive enough to convince the Vatican to raise his status to that of full bishop and to create an independent diocese for the Greek Catholics. It consisted, before the Galician-Transcarpathian schism, of 152 churches, 154 priests, 43 missions, and approximately 500,000 faithful.

From a UNA Sketch of a Pennsylvania Community

In 1907 [in Ambridge, Pennsylvania – os] all the Ukrainians from Galicia and Transcarpathia together founded one Greek Catholic parish, that of Sts Peter and Paul, and immediately bought a church ... It consists now of 235 families and 50 unmarried members. The parish has Galicians, 20 families of Transcarpathian Ruthenians and one family from Bukovyna.

The value of the church, parish hall and cemetery is over $50,000. The church choir has 50 members. The parochial school has ... 146 children.

The first to break away from this parish, almost at the outset, were the Muscophiles (Galicians and Transcarpathians) and they founded the Russian Orthodox church of the Holy Spirit ... It has about 150 families.

The second to break away, in 1922, were the Transcarpathian Ruthenians and they established the second Greek Catholic church of St John the Baptist ... they have about 150 families. Now they do not have a permanent parish priest nor a cantor-teacher (*diak-uchytel*).

In 1925 the third group broke away from the original Greek Catholic parish and established a new Ukrainian Orthodox Church of St Volodymyr ... About 100 families belong there.

As long as the Ukrainians were united they had their own National Home on Eighth Street, but they lost it after they broke up.

From a UNA jubilee publication, 1936

The Brotherhood of St Nicholas, organized in Shenandoah, Pennsylvania, by Father Ivan Voliansky in 1885, was the first Ukrainian fraternal benefit society in the United States.

A certificate of membership of Basil Kuzmych in the Ruthenian National Union of America of Scranton, Pennsylvania. In 1918 it changed its name to the Ukrainian Workingmen's Association.

Secular organizations in the United States

Having established their churches, the Ukrainian immigrants next attempted to find communal ways of dealing with their pressing practical needs. Foremost among them was the desire for at least a minimal sense of economic security. Work in the mines and factories was exhausting and dangerous. The hours were long and, by American standards, the pay was poor. As might be expected, cases of serious illness, loss of limbs, and fatal accidents were all too frequent. Furthermore, there were no company or government plans to aid those who were incapacitated or their families. In response to the problem, fraternal benefit societies or brotherhoods (bratstva) emerged among the various immigrant groups to aid their members.

For a modest monthly payment, these fraternal associations provided insurance in case of illness, incapacitation, or death. Moreover, as their membership and capital grew, they usually sought to address the cultural and educational needs of their members. For the immigrant, the appeal of the fraternal associations was not only their economic benefits, but also the fact that they brought together people of his 'own kind' and used his native language. Unlike the churches, the fraternal associations had no roots in the Old Country; they were an organic response to the environment the immigrant encountered in America.

In 1885, Reverend Voliansky organized the first Ukrainian fraternal benefit society in the United States. Consisting of several dozen members, its primary goal was to provide burial costs for deceased colleagues. When Voliansky returned to Galicia, the society disbanded. But others cropped up throughout Pennsyl-

The funeral procession of a prominent Ukrainian on the way to church.

vania. The Greek Catholic Union of the USA was established in 1891 and grew to considerable size. However, it soon fell under the domination of the pro-Hungarian Transcarpathian clergy and adopted an increasingly hostile attitude towards nationally conscious Ukrainians.

The impetus to found an avowedly Ukrainian fraternal benefit society came from young, dynamic, and committed priests of the American Circle. Imbued with the activist spirit of the Galician intelligentsia, the group formed the backbone of the Greek Catholic church's drive for ecclesiastical autonomy. One of its members, Ivan Konstankevych, and a fellow priest, Hryhorii Hrushka, became the founders, in 1894, of a fraternal benefit society called the Russky narodny soiuz (Ruthenian National Association) based in Jersey City. In 1914, this organization changed its name to the Ukrainian National Association (UNA).

A branch of the Ukrainian National Association, the Zaporozhian Sich of Syracuse, New York, 1909.

Although its beginnings were exceedingly modest — a mere 439 members and $220.35 in the treasury — the Ukrainian National Association adopted an ambitious agenda. It sought to become the representative body of all Ukrainians in the United States and its annual conventions were to function as a kind of parliament that discussed all matters of concern to the community. To publicize its position and attract new members, the UNA acquired *Svoboda*, a newspaper founded by Hryhorii Hrushka in 1892. Fervently committed to Ukrainianism, as early as 1900 the UNA came out in support of a separate, democratic Ukrainian state, long before many Ukrainians in the homeland were ready to accept the idea.

Another of the UNA's goals was to raise the cultural level of the Ukrainian immigrants. Therefore, it supported the spread of reading-rooms (*chytalni*), enlightenment societies (*Prosvita*), sport

The Ten 'National Commandments'

I am *Svoboda* that wishes to lead Ruthenian Americans out of the darkness of ignorance and spiritual slavery.

1. You will not read any newspapers printed in Ruthenian but devoid of the Ruthenian spirit.
2. Do not call yourself Ruthenian if you are indifferent to the Ruthenian cause in America.
3. Do not forget to become a member of the Ruskyi narodnyi soiuz and belong to a reading club and make sure that you subscribe to *Svoboda*.
4. Honor, respect, and support sincere Ruthenians and you will lead a long and happy life in America.
5. Do not kill your body and spirit by leading a life of drunkenness and debauchery.
6. Do not engage in friendly relations with the Magyarophile clique, hostile to the Ruthenian cause.
7. Do not seek to obtain *Svoboda* free of charge. First pay for it, then read it.
8. Do not testify falsely against the Ruskyi narodnyi soiuz or Svoboda but make sure you know where the truth lies.
9. Do not seek to become a traveling agent of *Viestnik* or you will suffer for it.
10. Do not seek the purse of the haughty Magyarophiles because it is empty; the people are wise and do not throw away 'quarters'; neither seek their bigotry nor their fox-like shrewdness – they belong to them.

Svoboda, 1894

The first issue of Svoboda, the oldest Ukrainian newspaper in the diaspora (and in the world). Founded in Jersey City, NJ, in 1893 by the Reverend Hryhorii Hrushka who was also its first editor. The paper played a crucial role in raising the Ukrainian national consciousness of the immigrants to the United States.

organizations (Sich and Sokol), choirs, drama societies, and ethnic heritage schools in the immigrant communities. Much attention was devoted to the socio-economic plight of the immigrants. Reflecting the socialist proclivities of the American Circle, *Svoboda* advised Ukrainian workers to join unions, even to form Ukrainian ones. Unlike other ethnic fraternal associations, the UNA did not limit its field of activity to the United States alone. For example, the association dispatched Father Nestor Dmytriw to aid their recently arrived countrymen in Canada and *Svoboda* regularly reported on the condition of Ukrainian immigrants in Brazil, Canada, and Hawaii.

But there were also major setbacks. Despite the leading role of the clergy in the UNA, it remained a secular organization open to Ukrainians of all religions. In 1910 Bishop Ortynsky attempted to take control of the UNA and transform it into an exclusively Greek Catholic organization. Angered by the 'priestly meddling,' a significant portion of the membership led by, ironically, Ivan Ardan, a former priest, broke away from the UNA and formed another fraternal society, strongly socialist and anticlerical, which was eventually called the Ukrainian Workingmen's Association (UWA). The new association chose Scranton as its base.

Meanwhile, Ortynsky's machinations failed. Consequently, in 1911 the frustrated bishop ordered his supporters to leave the UNA and join an exclusively Greek Catholic fraternal society that eventually adopted the name 'Providence' Association of Ukrainian Catholics and established its headquarters in Philadelphia. As a result of these internal struggles – quite typical for most ethnic communities – the UNA hopes of becoming the sole secular representative body for all Ukrainian immigrants were dashed.

These developments also had a brighter side because the new organizations helped to expand the organizational infrastructure of Ukrainian immigrant society. For example, both of the new associations established newspapers to present their point of view. The UWA's newspaper was called *Narodna Volya* while that of the Providence association adopted the name *Ameryka*. The fraternal associations also competed in organizing reading-rooms, enlightenment societies, sports groups, choirs, and the like. Thus, while Ukrainian organizational activity became more factionalized, it also gained in diversity.

A Ukrainian elementary school in McAdoo, Pennsylvania, in 1902.

The Besida Choir in 1916.

Reverend Petro Poniatyshyn on a visit to the pupils of the School of Ukrainian Studies in Bronx, NY, 1926.

The First Wave

The celebration of the feast of Jordan by Bishop (Metropolitan) Seraphim in Winnipeg, c. 1904.

Churches in Canada

In Canada, as elsewhere, churches were the earliest and strongest institutions established by the immigrants. As in the United States, their growth was also accompanied by bitter controversies. But there were also crucial differences. One of the most significant was the total absence at the outset of Greek Catholic priests in Canada, a condition related to the relative isolation of the prairie communities. Initially, the settlers turned to their brethren to the south for help. In 1897, responding to their appeal, Reverend Nestor Dmytriw travelled from Pennsylvania to visit the pioneers on the prairies and to celebrate the first Greek Catholic mass on Canadian soil. In subsequent years, several other Ukrainian priests from Pennsylvania made similar visitations. But these stopgap measures were clearly incapable of providing stable ecclesiastical leadership and organization for the immigrants.

For its part, the local Roman Catholic hierarchy, which was French-Canadian, attempted to impose its jurisdiction over the newcomers. However, in the face of opposition, it retreated and, later, showed a greater tolerance of Greek Catholics than did the Irish bishops in the United States. None the less, problems remained. Most pressing was the lack of priests. Because a papal edict in 1894 forbade married Greek Catholic priests from serving in North America and because the few celibate priests who emigrated from Galicia usually went to the United States or Brazil, Canada could not depend on the Old Country for clergymen. In 1902, three Basilian monks and four Sisters Servant of Mary Immaculate arrived to minister to the immigrants. But they were clearly too few for their needs.

Under the circumstances, other denominations began to make inroads among the settlers. One of the most successful at the outset was the Russian Orthodox church, which had among its missionaries many Galician Russophiles and Ukrainians from the Russian empire who could communicate with the immigrants in their native language. Moreover, the Orthodox church did not demand deeds to parish property, the salaries of its priests were not a burden on the congregation because they were paid by the Holy Synod in Russia, and Orthodox rites were very similar to those of the Greek Catholics. And since the Bukovynians were Orthodox already, they provided the church with a promising base of support.

Between 1905 and 1911, with the archpriest Arsenii Chekhovtsev of Winnipeg at the helm, the Canadian mission of the Russian Orthodox church scored some of its greatest successes. And by 1916, it had 65 churches and 26 priests in Western Canada. Russian Orthodox/Russophile newspapers also appeared. Without exception they refused to recognize the existence of a distinct Ukrainian nation, supported Russification, and proclaimed slogans such as 'Russia, one and indivisible – One Orthodox Nation.' Yet even before the downfall of the Russian empire in 1917 undermined the Russian Orthodox church in Canada,

competition appeared from an unexpected quarter.

In 1903, Bishop Seraphim, a Russian Orthodox cleric of dubious background, came to Winnipeg from the United States. A group of radical Ukrainian intelligentsia, led by Cyril Genik, Ivan Bodrug, and Ivan Negrych, allied themselves with the Russian cleric in order to create a church that would be independent both of Roman Catholicism and of Russian Orthodoxy. Thus arose the Independent Greek church, which soon attracted as many as 60,000 adherents.

However, Seraphim's intelligentsia allies had a hidden agenda: rejecting the mysticism of Eastern Christianity and enamoured of the 'rationality of Protestantism,' they hoped to use the Independent Church to draw Ukrainians over to Protestantism. Their efforts received the discreet backing, financial and otherwise, of the Presbyterian church, which was avidly interested in proselytizing (and Canadianizing) the Ukrainian settlers. Inevitably, conflicts between Seraphim and his erstwhile intelligentsia allies erupted. Meanwhile, the clandestine links with the Presbyterians became known and led to numerous defections. Thus, within a few years of its meteoric rise, the new church experienced an equally rapid collapse.

Confronted with a very real threat of losing its faithful – in 1912 there were only seven Ukrainian priests in Canada – Rome

A mid-week church celebration in Mundare, Alberta, c. 1920.

granted Canada's first Greek Catholic bishop, Nykyta Budka, far-ranging authority. The new bishop quickly demanded and obtained title to the property of all Greek Catholic parishes. And in 1914 he assembled his clergy at a *sobor* (council) that produced detailed guidelines for the behaviour of priests. With the situation finally stablized, the Greek Catholic church was ready to make up for lost ground. Soon, Greek Catholic churches, parishes, and schools multiplied in the prairies. By 1931, the Greek Catholic church encompassed about 58 per cent of the Ukrainians in Canada and had 100 priests and 350 parishes. But since about 80 per cent of the immigrants had originally been Greek Catholic, it was evident that Budka's church had suffered serious losses.

Convention of the Petro Mohyla Ukrainian Institute, Saskatoon, Saskatchewan, 1918.

Many of those who rejected Greek Catholicism entered the Ukrainian Greek Orthodox church, formed in 1918. In his ardour to restore Catholic pre-eminence, Budka and his clergy, many of whom were non-Ukrainians who accepted the Eastern rite, strove to extend control not only over parishes but also over secular institutions such as community halls, reading-rooms, and enlightenment societies. The church even perceived a threat in the rising sense of Ukrainian national consciousness, believing that it undermined commitment to Catholicism. 'Rome before Kiev' was one priest's succinct summary of this attitude.

The simmering dissatisfaction that this approach engendered

The First Wave

Parishioners awaiting the visitation of Bishop Nykyta Budka in Borshchiw, Alberta, 1916.

among many Ukrainians, especially the more educated, came to the fore when Bishop Budka attempted to transform the Mohyla Institute in Saskatoon, a student residence that strove to provide a patriotic Ukrainian environment for Ukrainians of all denominations, into a strictly Catholic institution. When the bishop was rebuffed, he attacked the institute as 'an agency of godlessness' and threatened to excommunicate its leadership. This led to open revolt. A group of prominent community leaders, led by Wasyl Swystun, called a conference that formed a Ukrainian Greek Orthodox Brotherhood which was mandated to establish the new church. Soon about one in four Ukrainians in Canada belonged to the Ukrainian Greek Orthodox church. The Presbyterian church, which continued to proselytize among the Ukrainians, also attracted a considerable number of immigrants.

Julia Fedorky, Annie (Svarich) Gregory, Nancy (Melnyk) Ruryk, and Stella (Melnyk) Porayko Svarich in front of the Ukrainian cultural centre in Vegreville, Alberta, in 1914.

Secular organizations in Canada

Like the churches, the first secular organizations among the immigrants in Canada were transplants from the Old Country. The *Prosvita* (enlightenment) societies, reading-rooms, and community centres, which at the turn of the century were multiplying in the villages of Galicia and Bukovyna, soon began to appear in the Ukrainian communities throughout the Canadian prairies: by 1925 there were about 250 of them. A major reason for this organizational dynamism was the presence in Canada of a relatively numerous, in comparison with the United States, Ukrainian intelligentsia. Concentrated in Winnipeg, it consisted initially of a small cohort of so-called village intelligentsia – former teachers, cantors, educated peasants, and young gymnasium (secondary school) students. Moreover, the Ukrainian Canadians acquired, for a brief but crucial period, a Canada-based source of educated Ukrainians. Because their rural communities were totally or largely Ukrainian, they were allowed to establish publicly funded bilingual school systems. Attempts by Canadian political parties, especially the Liberals, to win votes also encouraged this development. To provide qualified teachers for these schools, the government established the Ruthenian Training School in Winnipeg in

An instructor teaching Ukrainians reading and writing at a railway construction site prior to the First World War.

The first school for Ukrainians in Manitoba, the Plum Ridge School, was built in Pleasant Home, 1898, and originally named 'Galicia.' The photograph was taken in 1908.

Resistance to English Teachers in All-Ukrainian Schools

> 'The last move of the agitation,' reports the Edmonton Bulletin of early January 1914, 'was against the English teacher, and women seem to have been employed as the instruments in this case. On January 4, when Mr Armstrong returned to his shack alongside of the school after the vacation, two women came into his shack, and when his back was turned struck him on the head with a pot, and proceeded to beat him up generally, using teeth upon him fiercely. He succeeded in ejecting them from the house. He was then set upon by a couple of men with clubs who beat him up unmercifully. Of course, the offenders will be prosecuted.

1905. Similar institutions were founded in Saskatchewan and Alberta. Well-versed in both English and Ukrainian, their graduates, who numbered over two hundred, soon formed the core of a secular, educated community leadership.

As the Canadian authorities understood it, the primary function of the bilingual schools was to ease the pupils' transition from Ukrainian to English. But the settlers had different ideas. As taxpayers they demanded that their schools hire more Ukrainian teachers and that they teach more subjects in their native language. Bitter confrontations between provincial authorities and Ukrainian communiites ensued. In 1913, when the Alberta government forced a number of Ukrainian teachers from their schools, the latter responded by running in a local election. Although their bid to resist the powers that be failed, it indicated that the Ukrainians in Canada, unlike their brethren in the United States, had a secular leadership that was independent of the church and not intimidated by the Anglo-Saxon establishment.

It was in this small but growing milieu of the educated and semi-educated that the first signs of ideological evolution appeared. Since many of the more sophisticated immigrants had been associated with the Galician Radical party, it is not surprising that interest in socialism grew. A small reading circle in

The students and principal of the Ruthenian Training School, Winnipeg, 1906.

This theatre group was based in Edmonton. The photograph was taken in 1914 in Fernie, British Columbia, during the group's tour of the region.

Participants of the Ivan Franko Readings in Edmonton, 1910.

which Mykhailo Drahomanov, Ivan Franko, and Karl Marx were discussed appeared in Winnipeg. And in 1902, some of its members made an abortive attempt to set up a utopian commune, called the Ukrainian Brotherhood, in Hayward, California. Undaunted, a group led by Pavlo Krat and Myroslav Stechishin founded a Ukrainian branch of the Socialist Party of Canada in 1907. Some, however, rejected socialist tenets. They argued that their Ukrainian nationality, not class, should be the primary basis for communal organization. Consisting mostly of Ruthenian Training School graduates and led by Taras Ferley, they also attracted independent farmers and small businessmen. Others still, men like Genik, Bodrug, and Negrych, argued that Protestantism, with its rationalism, its well-developed moral and ethical codes, and its rejection of the mystifying ritualism of traditional Ukrainian religions, was the best hope of salvation and progress for their people.

To popularize their views, adherents of these evolving ideological orientations established newspapers. The various churches did likewise. Even the Liberal party of Canada funded a Ukrainian-language paper, *Kanadiisky farmer*, so as to exert an influence in the community. Thus, by 1912 sixteen weeklies had already made their appearance. Some quickly collapsed. None the less, nine, including two from the United States, circulated on a regular basis.

A Ukrainian bookstore in Smoky Lake, Alberta, in 1925.

The First Wave

A Social-Democratic group in Hamilton, Ontario, in 1916. Members display the Ukrainian socialist newspapers that they support.

Given their compact settlements and their tendency to vote in blocs, it was only a matter of time before Ukrainians realized that they could exert an impact on Canadian politics. The earliest major indications that they were ready to test the political waters came in 1903 when over one thousand of them gathered at a rally in Winnipeg to discuss the merits of the various Canadian parties. Because it was the Liberals who first opened the country's doors to the Ukrainians, they often got their votes. Before long, Ukrainians themselves stood for election. Initially, this occurred on the municipal level and in townships where the newcomers lived in considerable numbers. In 1908, Ivan Storozuk became the first Ukrainian to win elected office when he became the reeve of Stuartburn, Manitoba. Five years later Andrew Shandro, a Russophile, was elected to the Alberta legislature and in 1915 Taras Ferley, a leading community activist and graduate of the Ruthenian Training School, became a Liberal member of the Manitoba legislature. Thus, in contrast to their compatriots in the United States, the Ukrainians of Canada soon became a force in the local and provincial politics of the prairies.

LINKS BETWEEN THE UNITED STATES, CANADA, AND THE HOMELAND

As hundreds of thousands of Ukrainians came to the United States and Canada and began to establish their organizations and institutions, one might wonder about the contacts that evolved between the two neighbouring immigrant communities. Because the UNA in the United States believed it had a mandate to search out and organize Ukrainian immigrants wherever they may be, it took the initiative in forging links with the newcomers to Canada. Thus, it was with the support of the association that Father Nestor Dmytriw set out from Pennsylvania in 1896 to minister to the settlers on the Canadian prairies. His colleague, Father Ivan Zaklynsky, came soon after. Dmytriw's reports about 'Canadian Rus' were sent back to Pennsylvania, where they appeared regularly in *Svoboda*. Indeed, for the early immigrants to Canada, the American *Svoboda* was the only Ukrainian newspaper available and they valued it highly.

There are indications that a number of Ukrainians who managed to accumulate cash from their work in the mines or factories of Pennsylvania later moved to Canada and commenced farming. Conversely, some of those settlers who abandoned farming moved south to look for jobs in the United States. By and large, however, contacts between the two communites did not evolve beyond those mentioned above (although the topic is, admittedly, little

Ukrainian newspapers in Canada in the pre–First World War period.

studied), probably because, in the early days of settlement, the immigrants were too involved in making a living – and, at best, setting up local institutions and organizations – to look further afield.

Despite the fact that Ukrainian immigrants to the United States and Canada came from the same regions, had the same reasons for leaving, and lived in similar, Anglo-Saxon dominated societies, there were crucial differences between the two immigrant communities. Those who went to the United States were largely single persons or those who had left their families behind. They intended, at least initially, to remain only temporarily, usually worked in mines, foundries, and factories, and lived in a crowded urban environment. In sharp contrast, immigrants to Canada came in families, planned to stay permanently, and struggled to make a living as independent farmers in isolated and difficult rural surroundings. While the flow of migrant workers to the United States was largely an uncontrolled, spontaneous movement of people looking for ways to earn money and then return home, Ukrainian immigration to Canada was a more controlled and directed process of colonization.

While in both societies the function of Ukrainians was to fulfil basic labour needs, in the United States they were largely lost in the mass of 25 million immigrants who arrived before the First World War and crowded into well-established industrial centres where a place was reserved for them at the bottom of the social scale. In sharp contrast, the Ukrainians in Canada, despite the stronger prejudice they encountered, were able, in time, to claim a unique, pioneering role.

The internal dynamics of the two communites also varied greatly. While internecine conflicts and fissures are a typical immigrant phenomenon, they had a lasting impact on the early immigrants to the United States. Unhappy with the attitude of the Roman Catholic hierarchy towards the Eastern rite, many joined the Russian Orthodox church and came to view themselves as Russians. Even more catastrophic was the schism between the immigrants from Galicia and Transcarpathia that split their community into two, increasingly alienated parts. While in Canada the immigrants certainly had their share of internal conflicts, especially on the religious level, these were not as severe as those of their neighbours to the south.

Delegates to the Fifteenth Convention of the Ukrainian National Association in Philadelphia, 1920.

Each of the communities had assets that the other lacked. In the case of the Ukrainians in the United States it was primarily the fraternal societies like the UNA that attained a recognized, albeit not unchallenged, position of leadership. In Canada such organizations did not take root because farmers, unlike miners, were more self-sufficient and therefore had less need of mutual support associations. The Canadian community, for its part, had a relatively large and activist secular intelligentsia. Finally, the compactness of its bloc settlements allowed Ukrainians to become a significant factor in the politics of the Canadian West.

How did Ukrainian immigrants assess the relative merits of the United States and Canada? Judging from numerous letters and articles in *Svoboda* and other publications, the general opinion was almost unanimous that, in the long term, Canada had more to offer Ukrainians than did the United States. Among the arguments used to support this view were the following: the farmer, unlike the miner, was in greater control of his own fate; on the prairies Ukrainians could live en masse and therefore there was less pressure to assimilate; their lifestyle was healthier; and they could become citizens faster (in three years instead of five), elect their own representatives, and, if need be, form an alliance with the Germans and French in order to counteract English predominance.

The First Wave

The immigrants maintained an intense interest in their homeland. In the United States, where many believed that they would be returning home, this was to be expected; but it was also true among the permanent settlers in Canada. Like immigrants everywhere, Ukrainian newcomers were soon sending what little spare money they had back to their loved ones in the Old Country. This was especially so among the miners and workers in America since the wives and children many left behind depended on their financial aid. But the fact that Ukrainians were a stateless people added another dimension to the flow of money back to the homeland. Because the Austrian imperial and the Polish-dominated Galician provincial governments showed little interest in Ukrainian community and national needs, the immigrants felt obligated to respond to them.

Support for education was an especially popular cause. Soon after their arrival, the immigrants in both Canada and the United States organized fund drives to support elementary and secondary schools and university students. Besides these community-wide drives, immigrants from a particular locality frequently funded reading-rooms, churches, and schools in their native villages. Support for political causes also grew. Thus, funds were collected to support the campaign for electoral reform in Galicia and the student strike in Lviv. Perhaps most popular in the pre-1914 period was the fund in defence of Myroslav Sichinsky, a young student who assassinated Andrżej Potocki, the Polish governor of Galicia who, Ukrainians claimed, was responsible for a bloody crack-down on their countrymen.

While immigrants sent money to the homeland, it dispatched distinguished visitors to them. After an earlier stay in the United States in 1906, Iuliian Bachynsky, a noted political figure and the first historian of Ukrainian immigration to the United States, came to Canada to study Ukrainians in that country. In his numerous speeches he constantly and eloquently reiterated the need for immigrants to organize themselves. Moreover, he played a crucial role in convincing the immigrants to abandon 'Ruthenian,' their traditional name, and to adopt the modern 'Ukrainian.' In 1910, Metropolitan Andrei Sheptytsky toured both the United States and Canada. His presence, prestige, and tact greatly aided

The highly respected Metropolitan Andrei Sheptytsky of Lviv visiting members of his church in Philadelphia in 1910.

the struggling Greek Catholic church on the continent. And in 1912, Semen Demydchuk came to seek funds for education, specifically for the Ridna Shkola system in Western Ukraine. In terms of fund-raising among Ukrainians, his tour was by far the most successful in the pre-1914 era. It is striking that the major fund drives addressed the needs of the Old Country while none sought to meet the community needs in the New World.

The program of the first Ukrainian assembly in the United States. It was held on 30 October 1915 in New York City with the participation of 295 delegates and led to the formation of the Federation of Ukrainians in the United States.

War, revolution, and the immigrants

The outbreak of the First World War greatly heightened the interest of the immigrants in politics, especially as related to their homeland. It seemed that with the defeat of either Austria or Russia the recently born dream of Ukrainian statehood might become a reality. Community activists lost little time in urging Ukrainians to prepare to help bring this about. One Canadian community leader formulated the rationale for involvement in Old Country politics in the following terms: 'Here in a free country we became free, we fraternize with freedom, and now this freedom takes us by the hand and tells us: Let us go and liberate the land of our forefathers' (Marunchak, 329).

In the United States the UNA took the initiative in organizing in 1914 a political-action committee. It created a Fund for Liberation and established an information bureau that, by means of books, pamphlets, and articles, would inform the American public about Ukrainian aspirations. To broaden support for these efforts, all three fraternal associations called a 'Ukrainian Diet' in New York in 1915 and formed the Federation of Ukrainians in America. However, internal conflicts led both socialists and Ukrainian Catholic leaders to bolt, thus bringing about the creation of a new coordinating body, the Ukrainian Alliance of America. One of its major achievements was to persuade President Woodrow Wilson to proclaim 21 April 1917 'Ukrainian Day.'

Euphoria swept through the Ukrainian communities in North America when, as a result of the revolution of 1917, a Ukrainian state – the Ukrainian Peoples Republic (UNR) – was established. Another new American coordinating body, the Ukrainian National Council, which soon had 150 local councils, was formed to support the attempts of the various Ukrainian governments to win diplomatic recognition. The Council cooperated with the mission of the UNR in Washington, sent its representatives to help Ukrainian diplomats at Versailles, and supported the West Ukrainian People's Republic (ZUNR) mission in the American capital. But all was for naught. Wilson's government stood by its decision to respect the integrity of the Russian empire; Bolshevik propaganda argued that there was already a Ukrainian state, albeit

On 1 November 1918 West Ukrainians in Galicia initiated a bid to establish an independent state. After a protracted struggle with the Poles, the attempt failed. However, the date became a Ukrainian national holiday. A commemoration of the 1 November holiday in Fox Chase, on the outskirts of Philadelphia, in 1925.

a Soviet one, and Jewish claims that the Petliura-led UNR was unworthy of recognition because of its alleged involvement in pogroms frustrated the efforts of the Ukrainian Americans.

The Transcarpathian immigrants, meanwhile, were much more successful in influencing political developments in their homeland. In November 1918, their leaders met in Philadelphia with Tomaš Masaryk, the future president of Czechoslovakia. On behalf of their countrymen in Transcarpathia, the immigrants agreed to become a part of the new Czechoslovak state on the understanding that their region receive autonomy. On the basis of the agreement reached in Pennsylvania, and a subsequent plebiscite among the Transcarpathian immigrants that supported the arrangement, their region became part of the Czechoslovak state. It should be noted, however, that despite the opposition of the Magyarone clergy, the idea of joining a Ukrainian state enjoyed strong support among the Transcarpathian immigrants and its appeal probably would have been even greater had an independent Ukrainian state managed to survive.

In Canada, there was likewise a great desire to help the homeland, and there were attempts to form a central organization for this purpose and, as usual, internal conflicts. But there were also uniquely Canadian complications. Canada went to war in 1914, three years earlier than the United States. Moreover, its ally was

Christmas celebration at an internment camp in Canada in which Ukrainian 'enemy aliens' were to be found, 1916.

Russia. Therefore, Ukrainian organizations, which were implicitly anti-Russian, only took off in 1917 with the collapse of the Russian empire. In December of that year, a Ukrainian Canadian Citizens Committee was formed in Winnipeg. It too sent delegates to help UNR diplomats in Paris. Furthermore, it had some success in convincing the Canadian government to raise the Ukrainian issue in international negotiations. Meanwhile, an affiliate of the committee, the Ukrainian Red Cross, collected funds for humanitarian aid to the homeland.

But the war also exposed the Ukrainians in Canada to several traumatic setbacks. Since many of them were still subjects of the Austro-Hungarian empire, the outbreak of a war in which Canada and Austro-Hungary were on opposing sides placed the immigrants in a very awkward position. It was complicated even more when, just days before the outbreak, Bishop Budka, under pressure from the Austrian consulate, issued a pastoral letter reminding those who did not have Canadian citizenship that their first duty was to Austria. Once fighting broke out, the bishop hastened to retract his statement. But the damage was done. Despite the mass rallies that Ukrainians held in support of Canada and the fact that thousands volunteered for the army, doubts about their trustworthiness abounded. As a consequence, when the government established internment centres for 'enemy aliens,' about 5000 Ukrainians were incarcerated for varying periods during the war. In many cases, their property was confiscated and never returned. Thousands of others were forced to carry ID cards and were subjected to a variety of discriminatory measures. For the many Ukrainians who believed that their pioneering efforts had earned them a secure place in Canadian society, the treatment of their countrymen during the First World War was a rude awakening.

THE SECOND WAVE

BETWEEN THE WARS

Immigrants of the interwar period arriving in Winnipeg.

DURING THE INTERWAR period Ukrainian immigration to North America continued, but it differed considerably from the pre-1914 era. There was, most obviously, a drastic decline in the number of immigrants, owing largely to America's restrictive immigration policies and the Great Depression. Canada remained a favourite goal. But poor economic conditions in the farming regions and more restrictive immigration policies limited the number of new Ukrainian arrivals to 70,000. A more dramatic change occurred in the United States, where only about 15,000 Ukrainians entered the country between the wars, in contrast to the hundreds of thousands who crowded to its shores before 1914.

Immigrants of the Second Wave arriving at the CNR Colonization Depot, Winnipeg, 1926.

KEY FEATURES OF THE PERIOD

The most crucial feature of these recent arrivals was that among them there was a new type of immigrant – the political émigré. After the defeat of the various Ukrainian governments in the 1917–20 period, tens of thousands of their supporters – soldiers, officers, government functionaries, and many members of the nationally conscious intelligentsia, together with their families – followed them into exile. In order to be close to their homeland, most settled in Poland and Czechoslovakia. But many, especially rank-and-file soldiers, opted for a fresh start in North America.

The desire to help Ukraine achieve independence remained for these veterans an overriding concern. But, like all émigrés, they were prone to fractious infighting. Supporters of the various governments-in-exile often laid more blame on each other for their defeats than on the Bolsheviks. And they expended much time and effort in attempts to secure for their respective factions the mantle of national leadership. Yet, because there were many educated, talented, and committed individuals in their ranks, they had much to contribute to the Ukrainian communities in the New World.

This is not to say that the interwar immigration lacked those who left for purely socio-economic reasons. Tens of thousands of West Ukrainians continued to leave their homeland in search of better conditions elsewhere. Most gravitated to Canada. But in the 1920s and 1930s, other countries, such as France and Argentina, also attracted workers. Therefore, the outflow of Ukrainians was more limited because of immigration restrictions in North America and more dispersed because other countries opened their doors to Eastern Europe's excess labourers. Yet, even those whose motivations for leaving were primarily economic had been exposed, to a greater or lesser extent, to the fierce conflicts that wracked their homeland in the 1917–20 period and were, therefore, more sensitive to political issues than the earlier wave of immigrants had been.

About 20,000 Ukrainians marched through the centre of Philadelphia in 1930 to protest a Polish crack-down on their countrymen in Western Ukraine.

With the arrival of the interwar immigrants, new distinctions appeared in the Ukrainian communities of North America. There were now 'old,' that is, pre-war, and 'new' immigrants. The former, especially their children, were already members of a Ukrainian Canadian (or Ukrainian American) society that was, as one Canadian observer put it, 'neither Ukrainian nor Canadian, but with features of both – a marginal society with institutions peculiar to itself' (Yuzyk, 81). If they showed an interest in politics, it was in those of their new homelands, and the development of their communities in Canada or the United States was what primarily concerned them. Thus, the exclusive, even obsessive, orientation towards Ukraine of the 'new' immigrants grated on their hyphenated compatriots. However, one cannot be categorical in making these distinctions for there were many 'old' immigrants who retained an interest in and commitment to the Old Country, while among the new arrivals there were those who quickly cut their ties with their home country.

As citizens of the British Commonwealth, these Ukrainian Canadians hoped to influence the British to protest at the international conference in Genoa against the Polish occupation of their homeland. Winnipeg, 1923.

The Winnipeg General Strike and riot of 1919 in which many Ukrainian socialists participated.

Attitudes of Leftists and Nationalists

You know those Ukrainians on Western Avenue – those right-wingers, those fascists – they want the good old days back again. They want the rich land-owning class to come back into power in Ukraine. Everybody knows that they want a reactionary government back in power ...

I went to the Ukrainian Civic Center to a 'shindig' they had there once. I felt as if I was invading the camp of the enemy – no kidding. I hate 'em. After the dance, I took one of those fascist dames home from there, and as we were passing this building, I asked her, as if I didn't know,

'By the way, what is this place?'

And she said, 'Oh, that's the People's Auditorium; that's where the Bolsheviks hang out.'

Boy, I'm telling you, if she had known who she was being walked home by, I'm sure she would have died.

Young Chicago Ukrainian in the 1930s

I wouldn't be caught dead in that Bolshevik house. Those pro-Russian people – I don't know if you can call them people; hudoba (cattle) is a better word.

Young Chicago Ukrainian in the 1930s

Ukrainian women picketing in front of the White House in protest against the Polish occupation of Eastern Galicia, 1922.

Politicization

Two central and contradictory processes emerged among the Ukrainians during the interwar period. One was a marked politicization of their communities. Events in the homeland and the increased political awareness of the new arrivals encouraged the rise of Ukraine-oriented political organizations wherever Ukrainians congregated. Soon ideological confrontations began to overshadow religious rivalries as the major bone of contention. Indeed, in the Ukrainian immigrant communities, as in the world as a whole, the 1920s and 1930s might be called the Age of Ideological Commitment.

The first to organize were the socialists. As early as 1907, a Ukrainian Marxist group was founded in Canada. That same year a socialist club, called Haidamaky, emerged in New York. The appeal of these groups was that their members addressed, in

Children as well as adults were mobilized to demonstrate against Polish rule in Western Ukraine. New York, 1923.

Ukrainian, concrete issues such as better wages and working conditions for labourers and fairer pricing for farmers. The groups also provided an organizational base for those who resented the powerful influence that priests wielded in their communities. After the First World War, impressed by the Ukrainianization and modernization that was taking place in Soviet Ukraine and disillusioned by the Depression, a significant minority of the immigrants developed pro-Communist sympathies. This did not mean, however, that they were oblivious to national issues. On the contrary, many of the pro-Communists, especially in Canada, were patriots who believed that Communism offered Ukraine the best chance of progress.

On the other end of the ideological spectrum, a Ukrainian form of conservatism appeared in the early 1920s. Linked with the brief, quasi-monarchical rule of Hetman Pavlo Skoropadsky in 1918, it urged a firm adherence to traditional forms of community life and respect for established authority. Its ideologue, Viacheslav Lypynsky, added certain ideas that addressed specifically Ukrainian needs. He argued that the concept of Ukrainian nationhood should be expanded so as to appeal not only, as was traditionally the case, to the peasants and the numerically small intelligentsia but to all classes who lived on the territory of Ukraine. Only if those people who actually produced material wealth, that is, the industrialists, large landowners, businessmen, and successful peasants, could be attracted to the struggle for independent statehood would it succeed. For those who were disillusioned with the utopian populism that predominated in 1917–20, these élitist, monarchist 'Hetmanite' views seemed realistic, refreshing, and appealing.

Although it was the latest ideological movement to evolve in Ukraine, Ukrainian nationalism scored the greatest successes. Compared to the amorphous national consciousness, patriotism, and humanist values of the pre–First World War period, this was a new, extreme variety of nationalism that was rooted primarily in the setbacks of 1917–20. Convinced that socialism and democracy only encouraged the party strife, mediocre leadership, and loss of purpose that had led to their defeat, the young veterans of the war for independence called for the creation of a new type of Ukrainian, one who was unconditionally committed to his nation and to independent statehood. To dramatize and inculcate these views, the nationalists mythologized Ukrainian history, emphasizing the cult of struggle, of sacrifice, and of national heroes.

A striking feature in the rapid growth of political organizations in the Ukrainian communities was that they all had Old Country roots and orientations. Their adherents made almost no attempts to adjust these ideologies to their own, North American, environment. To a great extent the failure to do so may be explained by the fact that Ukrainians in North America simply did not have intellectuals capable of making ideological innovations. But the popularity among the immigrants of ideologies that were exclusively oriented on Ukraine was also an indication of how strong and tenacious were their emotional bonds with their homeland. Moreover, as their concrete links with and memories of the Old Country faded, the commitment of many Ukrainians focused increasingly on an abstract, ideologized notion of their homeland. Thus, Ukrainianism became increasingly intermeshed with ideology. As Myrna Kostash put it, 'Being Ukrainian was a very political thing.'

Professor Ivan Bobersky in Winnipeg, c. 1930. Bobersky represented the West Ukrainian People's Republic in Canada in the 1920s and collected data about the life of the Ukrainian pioneers.

Metro and Wasylyna Zukiwsky in 1920. They have obviously reached a level of prosperity that few could dream of in their native village.

The 'Eleven National Commandments' Aimed at Instilling a Modern National Consciousness

1. The Ukrainian child should associate exclusively with Ukrainian children and speak only in Ukrainian when in their company.
2. Parents or older members of the family should teach children to read and write Ukrainian during the child's preschool years.
3. Homes should be beautified with Ukrainian religious and historical paintings and pictures.
4. The Ukrainian child should learn Ukrainian sayings, as well as Ukrainian verses, songs, and games.
5. Let Ukrainian tradition live in the Ukrainian family. The father or older members of the family should always remember the important national dates from our history.
6. The family should read Ukrainian books in unison during the long winter evenings.
7. Every Ukrainian home should have *Svoboda*, the truly Ukrainian national newspaper.
8. The treasure of each family should be its library containing the best Ukrainian books.
9. The Ukrainian family should take advantage of every opportunity to attend a Ukrainian play, concert, or a commemoration of a national holiday.
10. Every father, mother, and older member of the family should belong to the Ukrainian National Association and they should enroll their children in the juvenile division. They should never refuse to contribute to worthwhile public and national causes.
11. Every family should try to bring back those members who have fallen away from Ukrainian traditions.

Svoboda, 1914

Assimilation

The second key process that gathered momentum in the interwar period was assimilation. While some maintained a strong commitment to things Ukrainian, others were rapidly losing it. To a great extent, this was a generational phenomenon. The older, European-born immigrants could be little else but Ukrainians until they died. Their contacts with English-speakers were limited and many lived almost totally within their ethnic communities. Matters were very different with the new, North American–born generation that began to come into its own. Through their schooling, social contacts, and employment they were exposed and attracted to the English-speaking world. In the United States of the 1920s and 1930s, when 'melting pot' views reached a

The wedding photograph of Wasyl Hryniuk and Helen Harbuz in rural Saskatchewan in 1914.

Ukrainian labourers in Fort William, Ontario, 1922. In the interwar period, the industries of Ontario began to attract an increasing number of Ukrainian immigrants.

high point, the pressures for ethnics to conform were intense. Because of its large French-speaking minority, Canada was more restrained in applying assimilatory policies. Moreover, the compact Ukrainian settlements slowed the process. None the less, the 'Canadianization' of immigrant children moved forward inexorably.

Acceptance of American or Canadian ways usually meant rejection of things Ukrainian. Proficiency in English was accompanied by a growing disinclination to use Ukrainian. As Ukrainian language use declined among the young, so too did their access to the cultural traditions of their parents. Contemptuous of the constant squabbles among the community organizations, many of the young avoided them altogether. Because they found church services too long, confessions in Ukrainian too difficult, or some practices too questionable (for example, the hygiene they learned in high school led them to doubt the wisdom of taking Communion from a common spoon), some limited their attendance at Ukrainian services or joined American or Canadian denominations.

Alarmed by these developments, the older generation unwittingly encouraged them. On the one hand, they urged their children to become an integral part of the American or Canadian socio-economic system; on the other hand, they unrealistically believed (or hoped) that the children would remain culturally apart from it. As usual, socio-economic progress meant the breakdown of ethnic neighbourhoods. As young Ukrainians moved 'up' they also moved 'out' of their enclaves, literally and figuratively. Of course, not all made a clean break. A large number took a middle road, viewing themselves as Ukrainian Americans, or Ukrainian Canadians, or Americans or Canadians of Ukrainian descent. And they attempted to straddle the two cultures, reading both Shevchenko and Shakespeare, celebrating Christmas on 25 December and 7 January, listening to jazz and folk songs, denouncing their elected officials and Stalin. Some managed to draw on the best from both worlds, but most found biculturalism confusing and demanding. Consequently, among those born in North America, the so-called second-generation blues became a common phenomenon.

Socio-economic change

These processes occurred against a backdrop of significant, if not dramatic, socio-economic transformations. By and large, the first generation of Ukrainians in North America experienced relatively little change in terms of occupations. Those who started out as farmers usually remained farmers. And those whose first jobs were in the mines rarely left them. As might be expected, their children, especially those who attained a secondary or higher education, had a much broader range of occupational choices, although many still encountered prejudice against 'Bohunks.' That Ukrainians began to take advantage of these opportunities was evident in the fact that whereas among the pre-1914 immigrants there had been one or two doctors or lawyers, there were dozens in the interwar generation. In a field like engineering, where there were no Ukrainians before the First World War, there were over a hundred after. Teaching was an especially popular profession, attracting close to one thousand in Canada alone. Many established small businesses, and they became numerous enough to organize several Ukrainian professional and businessmen's clubs. Among those who stayed in farming, a significant portion joined the ranks of the well-to-do; those who remained workers

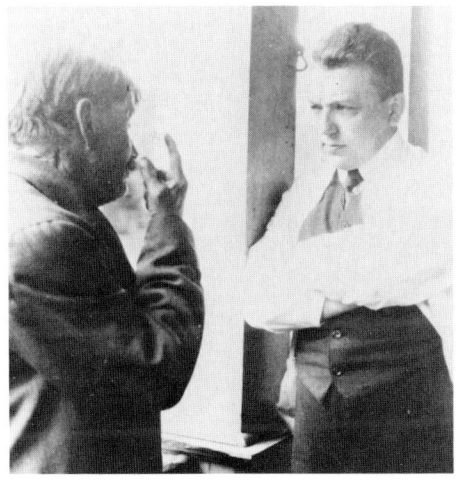

A Ukrainian physician and patient, Winnipeg, 1922.

The Providence Church Goods Ltd., owned by Jakiv Maydanyk, in 1924. The religiousness of the Ukrainians and their large number of churches provided such stores with a steady business.

rose to the more skilled categories. This is not to say, however, that Ukrainians made a quantum leap in socio-economic status. Having started so far down the socio-economic ladder, they still had a long way to go to reach the middle class.

There were also notable shifts in geographical distribution of Ukrainian communities. In the United States, Pennsylvania still had the largest number of Ukrainians, but the percentage slipped from about 75 per cent in the pre-1914 period to about 45 per cent in 1930. The states of New York and New Jersey gained much of what Pennsylvania lost. Growing communities also appeared in Ohio and Illinois. As Ukrainians spread out, they gravitated to large cities like New York, which had the largest Ukrainian community in the United States, and Philadelphia, Chicago, and Detroit. Meanwhile, the small mining towns of Pennsylvania faded as focal points of Ukrainian activity. In Canada the isolated homesteads of the pioneer era became increasingly rarer as settlements developed into small towns or farmers abandoned outlying farms to move closer to town. Many new immigrants settled in cities, especially eastern centres like Montreal, Oshawa, Hamilton, and especially Toronto. Although Winnipeg continued to be the pre-eminent centre of Canada's Ukrainians and three out of four still lived in the prairie provinces, the East was clearly gaining in importance.

M. Yonkovig, a budding Ukrainian businessman, in Pennsylvania in 1912.

By 1930, M. Yonkovig had clearly made progress.

The Ruthenian Farmers Elevator Co., a Ukrainian cooperative business venture, was established in Winnipeg in 1917. At its high point it operated 11 grain elevators in Manitoba and 4 in Saskatchewan. Lack of capital, stiff competition, poor management, and the Depression forced it into bankruptcy in 1930.

Descriptions of Assorted Ukrainian-American Communities in the Mid-1930s

Bristol, Conn. – 75 Ukrainian families. 158 children among them. The first Ukrainian, Oleksa Kalamin, arrived in 1894 from Galicia. The people are employed in various factories. There is one association, a UNA branch. Once there was a Prosvita reading hall, but it ceased to exist due to the 'Reds.'

New Britain, Conn. – About 2000 souls. Began to arrive in 1889 from Transcarpathia and in 1895 from Galicia (Sniatyn). They work in steel mills and on farms. There are 9 organizations [including]: 3 churches, a Ukrainian Orthodox, a 'Uhro-Rusyn' Greek Catholic, and a Muscophile Orthodox one. Each church has a school. There is a Ukrainian cooperative and 7 Ukrainian-owned grocery stores. There is a Ukrainian youth club, 2 youth choirs and a Sewers Club.

St Clair, Pa. – 200 Ukrainian families. Arrived 40 years ago from Galicia. Most work in the anthracite mines. They have 6 organizations, 2 Ukrainian Catholic churches, 2 parochial schools and 15 Ukrainian-owned businesses (hotels, groceries and meat stores). Of professionals, there are 3 teachers.

Milwaukee, Wis. – 2000 Ukrainians. Arrived in 1914–1917, mostly from Pennsylvania's anthracite region. Most work in steel mills. There are 2 organizations: a UNA and a UNP branch. There is a church and a library. Among businessmen there are 2 grocery stores, 2 hotels, 1 construction firm, 1 tailor. The community is largely divided because most of those from Eastern Ukraine joined the Russian Bolsheviks and the Galicians quarrel among each other over church matters.

Lorain, Ohio – 100 Ukrainian families. They came from the counties of Sanik and Sambor in Galicia. Most work in the steel mills. There are 4 organizations and 2 churches (Catholic and Orthodox). Our countrymen from Transcarpathia keep to themselves and have their own churches. There are 3 meat and grocery stores. Many of the youth are obtaining a higher education.

From a UNA jubilee publication, 1936

THE INTERWAR PERIOD IN CANADA

Ukrainians in Ternopil preparing to leave for Canada in 1923.

The second wave of immigrants to Canada had most of the old reasons for leaving as well as many new ones. With the downfall of the Habsburg empire, Galicia came under Polish control. Much of Volhynia, formerly in the Russian empire, was also incorporated in the Polish state. Bukovyna, however, became a part of Romania. Relations between the Ukrainians and the new states in which they found themselves were tense, even openly antagonistic. Moreover, much of the land was devasted by war, the economic outlook was bleak, and anti-Ukrainian discrimination was rampant. Clearly the impetus for emigrating was strong,

Mike Satychitz and his family exemplified the settlers that arrived in the Canadian West in the late 1920s. St Walburg, Saskatchewan, 1935.

but the new governments were hardly accommodating.

In 1924, when the Polish government began granting exit visas, the St Raphael's Ukrainian Immigrants Welfare Association was formed in Winnipeg. Its goal was to assist and supervise the newcomers from the point of departure to the time they settled in Canada. Later that year, the Ukrainian Emigrants' Aid Society, backed by Metropolitan Andrei Sheptytsky and led by the very experienced Iuliian Bachynsky, was established in Lviv. The work of this association was well received by the Canadian government, which made it clear that it welcomed the immigration of more Ukrainian settlers. Under Bachynsky's guidance, a reorganized St Raphael's Association undertook to process the emigrants, provide financial backing, and locate sponsors and work for them in Canada. As earlier, most of the emigrants were from Galicia. However, now Volhynia and Polissia also contributed to the outflow. Confronted with uncooperative Romanian authorities, Bukovynians had a more difficult time leaving. Many of the war veterans were brought over from exile in Czechoslovakia.

The immigration process was now much more orderly than it had been in the pre-1914 era. The Canadian government stipulated that it was exclusively interested in agriculturalists, and most immigrants fit this category. But many now had a modicum of education and at least some financial backing. Most came with

A well-established settler and his children near Warren, Manitoba, in 1912.

families, which made for greater social stability. However, a large portion of the newcomers who arrived under the guise of agriculturalists had a variety of different occupational backgrounds. This was especially so among the war veterans. These were no longer the docile, confused 'men in sheepskin coats' of the earlier era. Much more worldly, goal-oriented, and nationally conscious, they experienced fewer hardships in the new land. Moreover, they had an established Ukrainian community to turn to for support.

After serving (or feigning to serve) the obligatory year on the farms, many of the newcomers gravitated to urban centres. There some found work in industry; others, especially the younger ones, resumed their education. A considerable number of the latter went on to become professionals and small businessmen. Less adaptable older immigrants, especially those who had been politically active at home and who were slow in mastering English, often became community activists, serving as teachers in heritage schools, editors of Ukrainian newspapers, or leaders of choirs and drama clubs. Often deeply committed to the 'Ukrainian cause,' they maintained close and lively contacts with the homeland.

The time span in which the new immigrants came to Canada was very brief. Of the 70,000 newcomers, the vast majority came between 1927 and 1929. Afterwards, the Depression drastically cut the influx. Thus, as of 1931, there were about 225,000 Ukrainians in Canada, that is, 2.1 per cent of its total population. About 85 per cent continued to live in the prairie provinces, where they constituted 8.2 per cent of the population. But even in the prairies, a considerable portion of Ukrainians had settled in the cities, and overall one in five lived in an urban environment.

Matvi Probizansky, a 100-year-old pioneer, in Stuartburn, Manitoba, in 1921.

IDEOLOGICAL CURRENTS

The members of the Ukrainian Labour Farmer Temple Association of Timmins, Ontario, celebrating the 1 May holiday.

The Left

During the interwar period, Canadian public opinion developed a surprising stereotype of the Ukrainians – that of Communists or pro-Communists. Given the fact that the overwhelming majority of Ukrainians were churchgoing traditionalists and many were militantly anti-Communist nationalists, why did this fallacious perception arise? To a large extent, it was due to the dynamism of a small minority, about 5 per cent of the entire community, which did, in fact, have strong, leftist leanings. Exceptionally well

The Ukrainian Social-Democratic Party, Branch 41, of Lethbridge, Alberta, in 1917.

organized, the Ukrainian Communists and pro-Communists created a network of associations that became a major pillar of the small but active Communist Party of Canada. Indeed, one can argue that these pro-Communist organizations of the 1920s and 1930s were among the most effective that Ukrainians ever established in North America.

Many Ukrainians, especially those influenced by the Radical party of Galicia, were no strangers to socialism. In 1917, the Ukrainian Social-Democrats in Canada adopted a pro-Bolshevik stance. Within a year, as their membership rose to about 1500, they began construction of an impressive Labour Temple in Winnipeg. When the 'Red scare' of 1918 led the government to ban the Social-Democrats, they formed the ostensibly non-political Ukrainian Labour Temple Association to continue disseminating Marxist ideas among their countrymen. Bolshevik victories added to the association's appeal. By 1924 it had enough affiliates to form a nationwide cultural-educational labour organization called Ukrainian Labour Farmer Temple Association (ULFTA). Meanwhile, in 1921 delegates from the association helped to found the Workers (later Communist) Party of Canada. In the following decades, the links between ULFTA and the party remained strong since about one-third of the party's 2500–3000 members were Ukrainians and the ULFTA consistently provided the party

Delegates to the second congress of the Ukrainian Social-Democratic Party, Winnipeg, 1917.

with important financial support. Some of the outstanding activists of the association were Matthew Popowich, John Navis, Matthew Shatulsky, and John Boychuk.

The ULFTA was a 'front' organization, that is, while seemingly emphasizing cultural-educational activity, it sought to encourage the spread of Communism among Ukrainians. Although its members were pro-Communist, they were not necessarily members of the party. From its base in Winnipeg it quickly spread out to the industrial, lumbering, and railway centres. Because of their innate traditionalism and strong links to their churches, farmers were slow to join. None the less, by 1939 the organization had 113 Labour Temples, 201 branches, and approximately 10,000 members.

To extend their influence beyond the Labour Temples, Ukrainian leftists applied a variety of means. One was the creation of satellite organizations. Thus, in 1922 they formed the Workers Benevolent Association (WBA), a fraternal society that, among other activities, operated an orphanage and retirement home. The Association to Aid the Liberation Movement in Western Ukraine was founded in 1931 to attract the Ukrainian veterans. By focusing attention on Polish oppression, the leftists hoped to dissuade this vocal group from taking anti-Soviet positions. Another way of 'burrowing' into the community was the establishment of cooperative enterprises such as grocery stores, bakeries, and dairies. They also produced a great variety of Ukrainian-language publications, each designed to reach a specific segment of the community. There were papers for workers, farmers, women, and youth. By 1929 their combined circulation reached about 25,000. In addition, they published numerous school texts, books on Marxism, history, and economics, and propaganda pamphlets.

A Letter from a Leftist Farm Woman

In our locality of Simcoe, Ontario, there are quite a number of Ukrainian farmers, but only a small number of them are interested in the liberation movement. They are under the influence of two sisters: religion and ignorance. In that very spirit they bring up their children. They forbid their children to belong to the Youth Section of the ULFTA and go to the Ukrainian Labour Temple.

The consequences of that upbringing are very sad. Limited by religion and ignorance, the children grow up as though wild. They do not understand the meaning of the working class; they harm other workers and also their own parents. They leave their parents, run away from them, and not with empty hands. And these, because of the lack of understanding, say that it is God's will and make donations to the priests for prayers for their children's reform.

I advise these farmers not to rely on the priest's prayers, which will only fill the pockets and stomachs of the priests, but to undertake the necessary upbringing of the children. Send them to the Youth Section to teach them to look at the world through the eyes of science and not poison them with religious dope, and everything will be fine. They will grow up fine sons of the working class.

Robitnytsia, *a leftist newspaper*, 1931

The ULTFA sponsored many mandolin orchestras. Pictured above is the Saskatoon orchestra during its concert tour of Saskatchewan, 1929.

A Ukrainian pro-Communist youth and sports organization exhorting onlookers to support the Soviet Union. Toronto, 1930.

A Leftist Rally

Long Live the Firm Unity of Our Organized Militant Ranks. Away With Right and Left Opportunism.

Under these slogans which indicate a decisive turn in the work of our mass organizations, the Twelfth Convention of the Ukrainian Labour-Farmer Temple Association is taking place in Winnipeg with the participation of about 200 delegates who represent organized Ukrainian workers and poor farmers across the whole wide expanse of Canada. These slogans, written in large letters on red fabric, appear on the stage and on the walls on each side of the stage in the hall of the Ukrainian Labour Temple where the convention is being held ...

Immediately after the opening of the convention ... 150 Young Pioneers marched in rows into the hall ... with slogans of greetings and red kerchiefs around their necks. They mounted the stage, formed rows, sang the International and other revolutionary songs and delivered slogans of greeting ...

The appearance of the children moved the delegates and those present in the hall. In reply to the children's greetings, comrade M. Shatulsky declared that we, the elders, have laid the foundation for the ULFTA and these children will lay the foundation for and will conduct the proletarian government of this country.

Ukrainski robitnychi visti, a leftist newspaper, 1931

A music society formed by immigrants from the village of Vasylkivtsi, Ternopil region, in Winnipeg in 1919.

Major factors that fuelled this impressive dynamism were excellent leadership, patriotic appeal, and community service. No other Ukrainian organization worked as assiduously at training new cadres. 'Higher Education' courses for aspiring young activists were held periodically in Winnipeg. A number of the most promising spent one to three years training in Moscow or Kharkiv. Their graduates were not only well trained but committed. As Ukrainians, they were often at the bottom of the socio-economic ladder, constantly facing exploitation and discrimination. It is, therefore, not surprising that they were attracted to an ideology that seemed to offer salvation not only for their own people but for humanity as a whole.

Clearly, the economic crisis brought on by the Depression added greatly to the appeal of the leftists. But Ukrainian patriotism was also an important consideration. By establishing the

The Sixth Convention of the Ukrainian Labour Farmer Temple Association in 1925. Delegates stand before their impressive headquarters in Winnipeg.

Soviet Ukrainian republic and instituting a policy of Ukrainianization in the 1920s, the Soviets seemed to be well on the way to satisfying Ukrainian national aspirations. Meanwhile, the cultural-educational programs of the ULFTA also reflected a strong commitment to things Ukrainian. Consequently, their adherents were in a position to argue that the support of Communism was the most promising form of Ukrainian patriotism.

Especially enticing were the benefits that the Labour Temples provided to the community. In industrial centres, they were the only alternative to saloons, brothels, and gaming parlours. In urban and rural communities, they were often the focus of social and cultural life. Frequently, their heritage schools for children, literacy classes for adults, lectures, choirs, dance troupes, drama clubs, and orchestras were superior to those of the non-Communists. A major reason was that almost all the larger temples had a full-time teacher, their only salaried functionary, who organized much of the activity. He also expounded on Marxist ideas and saw to it that no heretical views emerged. An example of the ULFTA's organizational strength and prowess was the National Festival it held in 1939 in Toronto in which 38 string orchestras and 32 choirs totalling 1500 participants performed before an audience of 10,000.

But the ULFTA also had its share of difficulties and setbacks. In 1925, it opposed, unsuccessfully, the dissolution of nationality sections in the Canadian Communist party. When in 1928 the Communist International called for 'intensifying class struggle' and openly confronting the government, the Ukrainians, many of whom were liable to deportation as non-citizens, balked. A sign of their importance was that, in a rare move, the Moscow-based officials pardoned this breach of discipline. Many left the pro-Communist camp in the early 1930s when the Canadian government cracked down on supporters of 'class struggle.' Most demoralizing was the impact of Stalinism, the purges, and especially the famine of 1933 in Ukraine. It resulted in the defection of Danylo Lobay, editor of the association's main publication, *Ukrainski robitnychi visti*, about a dozen leading activists, and a number of major branches. But the pro-Communists weathered the crisis, in the process strengthening their adherence to the Moscow line even more. Clearly their commitment to Communism was only matched by their blindness to its faults.

Ukrainian-Canadian leftists inaugurating their first national festival of song, music, and dance in Toronto, 1939.

Reaction to the Left

We, the loyal citizens of Canada, of Ukrainian race, assembled to the number of about 700 people at a mass meeting at the Ukrainian Catholic Hall, at Mundare, Alberta, this 8th day of February 1931, for the purpose of protesting against the propaganda of Bolshevism and Communism among our people in Canada, hereby register our most vigorous protest against the agitation of paid Communist agents and their efforts to undermine our confidence in Canadian democratic institutions, and call to our brethren in Canada to demonstrate their loyalty to this our adopted land, by similar protests and active support of all our Canadian institutions.

Furthermore, we petition the government of our province of Alberta and the government of the Dominion of Canada, to prohibit the publication in Canada of all the Bolshevistic revolutionary literature and cause the deportation of all those foreigners and to suspend the naturalization of all those citizens of foreign birth who propagate and who follow the radical teachings intended for the destruction of our democratic system of government.

A Leftist View of the Nationalists

In the struggle against the Ukrainian fascist organizations in Canada it is necessary to pose clearly the question: What is the struggle about and with whom must it be conducted? To the first question it is necessary to reply that the class struggle with the Ukrainian fascist organizations is waged for the winning into the ranks of the working class of the Ukrainian working and farming masses, for the drawing away of the rank-and-file members of the Ukrainian fascist organizations from the influence of agents of the capitalist class, which is what the leaders of these organizations are.

The second question: With whom in the Ukrainian fascist organizations must we conduct the struggle?

The struggle must be against the leaders of the Ukrainian fascist organizations. It is necessary to differentiate between the upper and lower strata in the Ukrainian fascist organization. The members of the upper strata, that is, the leaders of these organizations, are the recruiting agents of the capitalist class and its mobilizers of forces from the worker-farmer strata. They consciously perform their service to further maintain the system of force and exploitation of the toilers. They are paid agents of the master class; they serve it; they invent all sorts of vague slogans and methods to attract the necessary forces for the capitalist class.

Ukrainski robitnychi visti, 1932

Winnipeg's Ukrainian Labour Temple's exhortative stage curtain

The Hartford, Connecticut, branch of the Ukrainian Federation of Communist Parties of America, 1922.

Communism also made significant inroads among Ukrainians in the United States. Indeed, at first glance it appeared to have even greater potential for growth among them than among their compatriots to the north. First, there were more than twice as many Ukrainians in the United States as in Canada and, second, almost all of them were workers, that is, the class most susceptible to pro-Communist agitation. Moreover, America's unbridled capitalism victimized many an immigrant. Finally, many of the early community leaders, most notably the young priests of the American Circle, had socialist inclinations. None the less, the impact of Communism on Ukrainians in the United States, while considerable, was never as great as it was on their Canadian brethren.

Prior to the First World War, several socialist groups appeared in the United States, most notably the Haidamaky (1907) in New York. In 1910, even the UNA advised its readers to vote for socialists since neither Democrats nor Republicans seemed inclined to help the workers. And in 1911 a group broke away from the UNA to form what eventually, in 1918, was called the Ukrainian Workers Association (UWA), a fraternal society with decidedly leftist leanings. During the Russian revolution, a Ukrainian Federation of Socialist Parties in America (UFSPA) emerged that had about 1000 members and 46 branches.

The Second Wave

But the UFSPA soon became embroiled in factional strife. One wing, the Internationalists, favoured the Bolsheviks and, in 1924, became a charter member of the American Communist party. Meanwhile, their opponents, the anti-Bolshevik Socialists, led by such luminaries as Myroslav Sichinsky, Ivan Ardan, Mykola Tsehlynsky, and Yaroslav Chyz, eventually merged with the UWA. This allowed the socialists to obtain a power base in a large fraternal organization of over 20,000 members. Thus, in the United States, unlike in Canada, the Ukrainian socialists not only avoided a take-over by the Communists but remained in a position to challenge them. Moreover, as the Americans who took over the leadership of the Communist party showed little interest in the national aspirations of East Europeans, Ukrainian issues did not have the prominence in the American party that they did in its Canadian counterpart.

But when it came to forming pro-Communist front organizations in ethnic communities, there were major similarities. The Ukrainian members of the American Communist party engineered, in 1925, the formation of Souiz Ukrainskykh Robitnychykh Orhanizatsii (Association of Ukrainian Toilers – henceforth SURO). Like the ULFTA, it too combined educational opportunities with ethnic pride to attract recruits to the pro-Communist camp. The organization set up reading-rooms, heritage schools, classes for illiterates, choirs, drama clubs, and orchestras in its labour temples. It also adopted a demonstratively critical view of Poland's treatment of its Ukrainian minority. By 1932 SURO had made significant if not dramatic progess. At that time it had 112 branches with over 2700 members and about 3400 affiliated members. However, there were only 23 temples (compared to 113 in Canada), which meant that its key institutional mechanism for reaching into communities was poorly developed. The leadership, which included George Tkach, Andrew Dmytryshyn, H. Tkachuk, and S. Soroka, was also relatively weak.

Since fraternal organizations such as the UNA, UWA, and Providence were centres of influence in the Ukrainian American community, the Communists and their allies resolved to challenge them on their own ground. In 1932, they founded Orden, a Ukrainian branch of the International Workers Organization (IWO). Apparently the combination of benefits a fraternal association provided with the utopian ideology that Orden offered hit a responsive note among many Ukrainians. Within six years of its founding, its membership reached a reported 15,000. The two pro-Communist organizations then created a common front that concentrated on accusing the clergy of rapacious avarice, equating Ukrainian nationalism with fascism, and mouthing the Soviet line, which included vehemently denying the famine of 1933.

Orden's success, however, was short-lived. Shifts in the U.S. political climate worked to its disadvantage and the opposition of the other Ukrainian fraternal organizations limited its growth. Moreover, like SURO, it had a weak infrastructure. Besides paying their dues or attending the odd demonstration, its members were barely involved in the pro-Communist cause. This was reflected in the fact that while over one hundred Ukrainian Canadian leftists lost their lives fighting against Franco in Spain, only two Ukrainian Americans did so.

The Leftist Perspective

> The Ukrainian bourgeoisie with their various 'doctors,' 'professors,' 'lawyers,' 'editors,' of various yellow rags, former Austrian corporals ... accuse the class conscious Ukrainian worker and his newspaper of being Moscowphiles of the Red variety ... The Ukrainian panky from *Narodna Volya*, *Svoboda*, *America*, and *Ukrainian Voice* accuse us of not having enough of a national emphasis ... We say too much national emphasis is wrong for the worker ... In a capitalist country, the worker really has no nation ... when the proletariat wins over the bourgeoisie, there will only be one fatherland, the world.
>
> Visti, *a Ukrainian American leftist newspaper*, 1921

Members of the Sich Society, an organization founded in 1902 that stressed gymnastics and physical fitness, gather in New York City in 1917.

The Monarchists

Throughout the 1920s the only ideological alternative to the leftists was the conservative-monarchist organization associated with Hetman Pavlo Skoropadsky, who briefly ruled Ukraine in 1918. It emerged out of the Sich movement, the Ukrainian name for gymnastics societies that were widespread among Germans and East European immigrants. Concentrating on physical fitness, Sich members believed that healthy bodies made for healthy minds. The appeal of the Sich also rested on the fact that it was the only Ukrainian organization that catered primarily to the youth. In 1920, it boasted about 3000 members in 60 branches throughout the United States. By 1935, its membership reached close to 5000 members.

During the First World War, militaristic tendencies appeared among the Sich members. The view that the Sich should train soldiers who, when the opportunity arose, would be ready to fight for Ukraine gained in popularity. And soon members were encouraged to wear military uniforms. But while the organization became more vociferous in its support of Ukrainian independence and its anti-Communism, it remained, as yet, ideologically neutral.

A Ukrainian festival in Mundare, Alberta, 1930. The local clergy and the uniformed monarchist members of the United Hetman Organization are clearly on good terms.

The Call to Activism

> The Sich organization considers only those people enlightened who are regular members of one or more Ukrainian organizations and who regularly carry some burden for the sake of their Ukrainian nation ... All others are merely ethnographic material – Little Russians or Little Poles – who, through their inactivity are undependable when the chips are down ... Therefore, the convention calls upon all Ukrainians to join the Ukrainian national organizations, to fulfill their obligations to these organizations, and to train their children to do the same.
>
> Sich, a UHO periodical, 1924

The turning point came in 1923–4, when Osyp Nazaruk, a talented journalist and a supporter of Skoropadsky, came to North America. Under his influence, Stepan Hrynevetsky, the energetic Chicago-based leader of the Sich, became a convert to Hetmanite ideas. After repeatedly haranguing the rank-and-file that only discipline, order, and respect for legitimate authority would help Ukraine gain independence, the two men convinced most members to accept the monarchist position. The Sich now became an avowedly ideological organization.

Support came from an unexpected quarter. The Ukrainian Catholic church, pressed by socialists, Communists, and the Orthodox, was in sore need of allies. Attracted by the Hetmanites' emphasis on discipline and respect for authority, it gave its imprimatur to the new organization. The Hetmanites' alliance with the church was especially close in Canada, where Bishop Nykyta Budka and then his successor, Archbishop Basil Ladyka, urged priests and their parishioners to join the Sich.

The moving spirit of the Canadian Hetmanites was Volodymyr Bossy, a post-1920 immigrant, who in 1924 convinced the Sich branch in Montreal to accept monarchist principles. Within months, branches in Oshawa, Hamilton, and Toronto did likewise. Only after it established itself in the major eastern urban

Sich members stand at attention in Toronto in 1928 during an inspection tour by Volodymyr Bossy, their leader in Canada.

centres did the organization expand into the prairies. In 1926, the Hetmanites made an unusual move: they combined the Canadian and American wings under a single executive based in Chicago.

After concluding that sooner or later Ukrainians would need a strong army, Hetmanite leaders decided that they should start building it in the United States and Canada. Therefore, in the late 1920s, even more emphasis was placed on militarism. Local branches were reorganized into army companies, a system of ranks was introduced, and members were ordered to wear military uniforms whenever possible. Emphasis on male machismo notwithstanding, women were also urged to join the Sich and to form auxiliary Red Cross units.

Military field manoeuvres became a key component of the organization's activity. Held most often in the Midwest, these involved several companies from neighbouring cities staging weekend war games on rented farms or forest preserves. A typical day consisted of a lengthy liturgy in the morning, war games – replete with nurses administering 'first aid' to 'casualties' – in the afternoon, and a gala dance in the evening. Because these events were entertaining, they added much to the Sich's popularity among the young.

The Social Aspects of Patriotism

> Our maneuvers were great fun. The day would begin with an outdoor divine liturgy and at about 11:00 A.M. or so the maneuvers would begin. The girls participated as medical support personnel and if you saw one that was particularly attractive you'd kind of make sure you were 'wounded' near her station. When the whole thing was over, the losers would buy a barrel of beer, the band would arrive, and we'd all dance until the early hours of the morning.
>
> Recollections of a former Sich member

A leaflet urging participation in Ukrainian Aviation Day in Philadelphia, 1934. The high point of festivities is to be the arrival of two Ukrainian-owned planes, the Ukraina from Detroit and the Lviv from Chicago. The event was sponsored by the local United Hetman Organization.

By 1930, however, militarization took on a more serious note. Suffering from sagging enrolments, the American militia (National Guard) allowed Sich companies to join en masse. A similar arrangement was reached with the Canadian armed forces. As a result, Sich companies, under nominal command of American or Canadian officers, received regular uniforms, equipment, and specialized training. Even a Ukrainian 'air corps' was established when the American Sich purchased three surplus military aircraft and introduced instruction in flying. Branches in Canada did likewise.

Undoubtedly, the high point of the Sich movement, renamed the United Hetman Organization (UHO) in 1934, came in 1937 when Danylo Skoropadsky, the son of the hetman, visited Canada and the United States. Handsome, well-bred, and charming, the aristocratic 'heir apparent' was well received by American and Canadian governors, church dignitaries, generals, and university officials. For the many plebeian members of the UHO, their association with this aristocratic figure provided a welcome psychological boost.

Ironically, it was the approaching war with Germany that inflicted fatal damage on this militaristic movement. Since Hetman Skoropadsky had been allied with the Germans in 1918 and currently resided in Berlin, he was accused of maintaining links with the leaders of the Third Reich. In the United States, the

Members of the United Hetman Organization who formed a machine-gun company in the Illinois National Guard in the 1930s.

Ukrainian Communists and socialists as well as the Jewish Anti-Defamation League brought this to the attention of government officials and the media. As a result, in 1938–40, a congressional committee, led by Martin Dies, investigated a number of Ukrainian nationalist organizations, including the UHO. The FBI also launched a probe of its own. Although no direct links with the Nazis were found, UHO members, fearing deportation, left the organization in droves. In 1942, after the United States entered the war, the UHO dissolved itself. It continued to exist in Canada but in a vastly weakened state.

The Hetmanite Creed

In Everyday Life and Behavior
A sincere citizen and conscientious worker on the job upon which his future depends.

He is forbidden to lie or to spread other lies like a flying crow.

He doesn't take part in intrigues nor does he stand for the intrigues and all manner of plotting by others.

In the community in which he lives and actively participates, he talks less and does more good work and with this action offers the best example to other members of the community as to how one should work for the common good ...

He behaves in a mild manner with other people and does not look down his nose at others ...

He tries to teach others the same truth he has recognized, doing this, however, in the manner of a good teacher ...

In order to become a teacher and leader among his people he is always learning himself – he learns in schools, he learns from good and worthwhile books, journals, and he learns from the lives of other cultured and organized peoples ...

He comes out everywhere in favor of law and order as well as national-social discipline ...

In Family Life
He is to be an exemplary father (mother) or son (daughter). He must always remember that his family is a small monarchical nation and it is on the degree of order, love, fairness, and mutual respect which he demonstrates there that his test of social maturity as a member of the Hetman organization and the Ukrainian national patriotic community will depend.

If a Hetman member is a poor family member he will be even worse as a member of the Hetman organization ... The Ukrainian family is the beginning of the Ukrainian nation.

Sich, 1932

The New York branch of ODVU in 1935 during the visit of General Mykola Kapustiansky, a noted military leader during the Ukrainian struggle for independence in 1917–20.

The Nationalists

Nationalism was the last of the major ideological currents that swept through the Ukrainian communities of North America. Reeling from their setbacks in 1917–20, supporters of an independent Ukrainian nation-state were demoralized and disoriented throughout much of the 1920s. But in the next decade, Ukrainian nationalism adopted a radical, uncompromising form that propelled it once more to the forefront of Ukrainian organizational life in both Canada and the United States (henceforth adherents of the new, extremist variety of nationalism will be referred to as Nationalists, with a capital 'N').

Initially, the social base of the movement consisted of the several thousand war veterans who came to North America throughout the 1920s. In 1924, they formed the Ukrainska Striletska Hromada (Ukrainian Sharpshooters Association – USH), a veterans' association, in the United States, and four years later a similar organization arose in Canada. Meanwhile, in Vienna in 1929 Ukrainian émigrés, led by the charismatic Evhen Konovalets, created the clandestine Organization of Ukrainian Nationalists (OUN). Based on the new nationalism, it quickly developed a widespread, underground movement in Western Ukraine. Even

The Second Wave

The Fifth Convention of the Ukrainian National Federation, Toronto, 1938.

before OUN was established, Konovalets toured the United States and Canada in 1928 and again in 1929 to mobilize support. However, real work in establishing OUN affiliates in North America began in 1930 when a top OUN organizer, Omelian Senyk, came for a lengthy stay.

Using the veterans groups as a base, the Nationalists established the Organization for the Rebirth of Ukraine (ODVU) in 1929 in the United States and the Ukrainian National Federation (UNF) in 1932 in Canada. The new organizations grew quickly. As they expanded, they established their own affiliates. In the United States these included the Gold Cross, a women's organization, and Young Ukrainian Nationalists (MUN), a youth group. By the mid-1930s there were already 70 ODVU, 70 Gold Cross, and 41 MUN branches. Led by Alexander Granovsky, they included about 10,000 members. Moreover, ODVU members or sympathizers appeared in the leadership of other organizations. For example, in the UNA, the biggest Ukrainian-American fraternal organization, half of the executive committee consisted of ODVU members.

In Canada, the growth of the UNF was equally impressive: by 1939, it had 50 branches, its women's affiliates had 33, the youth affiliate had 38. There were, moreover, five student groups. In contrast to their counterparts in the United States, the Nationalists in Canada were able to attract members of the pioneer generation into their ranks. One of them, Alexander Gregorovich, became the president of the organization while other 'old' immigrants occupied important positions. None the less, the UNF consisted largely of members of the interwar immigration. By the late 1930s, the Nationalists were clearly on the rise, winning over great numbers of monarchists and effectively blocking the further spread of Communist influence in the Ukrainian communities.

A Nationalist Perspective

> This writer conceives of a Ukrainian Nationalist as one comparable to those 'rebels' in America who fought against oppression by a mother country. Our Nationalists rebel against oppression not of a mother country but of the traditional enemies of Ukraine. They do not wait for Hitler or Mussolini to guide them ...
>
> The Ukrainian Nationalist is intolerant of a quasi-intellectual, sentimental, pseudo-idealistic abhorrence of force when such is proven in fact to be the last resort, where all other means have been exhausted ... He is intolerant of those who would solve the problems of subjugated Ukraine by the radically different standards of life in free, rich and powerful America ... Above all, the Ukrainian Nationalist believes that to become free, Ukraine must be ready for freedom – her people must be bound with a common purpose and dedicated to a holy mission ... those furthering dissension at a time like the present are virtual traitors to the Ukrainian cause.
>
> Nationalist, *an ODWU periodical*, 1938

A patriotic Ukrainian play, Edmonton, 1933. The scene reflects the politicization and raised national consciousness that permeated Ukrainian communities in North America during the interwar period.

What did being a Ukrainian Nationalist in North America actually mean? And what did those who adhered to the ideology do? A major goal was consciousness-raising: both ODVU and UNF sought to create a new type of Ukrainian who was committed to the Ukrainian nation above all else. Reacting to the anarchy and chaos that characterized the struggle for independence of 1917–20 (and the situation within the immigrant communities as well), the Nationalists stressed discipline and commitment. As one activist put it: 'We realize that we cannot expect military discipline from Ukrainian immigrants ... but surely we can achieve more discipline than exists in other immigrant organizations.' But how were ODVU members to square their Ukrainian nationalism with their commitment to America? An oft-repeated response was that 'nationalism is love of country and a willingness to sacrifice for it ... A person brought up in Ukrainian nationalism will be a 100 per cent better American.'

ODVU and UNF branches put great emphasis on marking Ukrainian national holidays and commemorating national heroes, including Konovalets. These sombre occasions, called *akademii*, featured lengthy speeches, melodramatic, politically oriented plays, and fund-gathering for patriotic causes. Protests and demonstrations denouncing Polish and Soviet oppression were also frequently staged, sometimes giving rise to violent confrontations with pro-Communists. In larger centres, the Nationalists acquired

A pioneer celebration at Hryhoriw, Saskatchewan, 1937. The building in the background was typical of Ukrainian community centres throughout the prairies.

their own buildings and almost all branches supported heritage schools for children, choirs, and dance and theatrical groups. 'Nationalist Days' featuring picnics and dances were a favourite activity.

Like the monarchist UHO and for similar reasons, both ODVU and UNF stressed military drills and manoeuvres. Their members adopted the uniforms of the Sichovi Striltsi, a Ukrainian military unit in the war for independence. In the United States some ODVU branches formed units within the National Guard and the organization acquired a biplane to teach younger members the rudiments of flying. In Canada, UNF also sponsored an aviation school near Oshawa.

But while their ideology and aspirations were focused on their European homeland, the North American environment also exerted an impact on the Nationalists. They categorically rejected dictatorships and called for a republican form of government in Ukraine. Unlike the European-based OUN, both ODVU and UNF had a freely elected leadership and espoused the electoral principle in government. Meetings and congresses were held according to rules of parliamentary democracy. And every attempt was made to avoid involvement in religious conflicts, which, the Nationalists argued, only diverted them from their mission, the crusade to liberate Ukraine.

In 1938, it seemed that the event all non-Communist

Dual Loyalties

> Every American of Ukrainian descent has two equally fundamental duties to himself: 1) to support the democratic principles on which the United States was founded even to the point of sacrificing life itself; 2) to lend every support to the struggle of his 45,000,000 kinsmen in Europe for independence.
>
> Ukraine, a Ukrainian American periodical, 1939

Ukrainians had been hoping for had finally arrived. And it happened in the most unexpected of places. That year Nazi Germany began the dismemberment of Czechoslovakia. As a result, a Ukrainian government, closely linked to the OUN, emerged in Czechoslovakia's easternmost, Ukrainian-inhabited province of Transcarpathia, or, as it was now called, Carpatho-Ukraine. Although the position of the small state was extremely precarious, it seemed to Ukrainians that its appearance presaged independence for the entire land. In North America, all non-Communist Ukrainian organizations rushed to organize fund drives and other forms of support. But their euphoria turned to bitter despair when Germany allowed Hungary to crush the tiny Ukrainian state. Protesting the Hungarian action became the focus of Nationalist activity as the Second World War approached.

The oncoming conflict triggered another setback for the Nationalists. Their vociferous, anti-Soviet stance brought down the wrath of the Communists and their sympathizers upon them. Consequently, in the late 1930s, the Left launched a well-coordinated campaign to discredit the Nationalists. In the process, it also defamed much of the Ukrainian community. Indeed, the themes raised in the campaign had a historical significance for they became standard fare in anti-Ukrainian attacks in North America for the next fifty years.

A Nationalist View of the Ukrainian Left

For Ukrainians, wherever they may live, Communism is not only the enemy of their democratic way of life; it is also the destroyer of the Ukrainian nation-state. For more than 30 years, Moscow, the great proponent of Communism, has enslaved and maltreated the Ukrainian people. Under Soviet Communism, that people is now experiencing unprecedented political enslavement, social serfdom and unsurpassed economic exploitation. Therefore, for a Ukrainian the question – to be or not to be a Communist – is not merely a theoretical or academic consideration. A Ukrainian who, for whatever reason, joins the Communist cause is, from the Ukrainian point of view, not only an enemy of democracy but a traitor to the Ukrainian nation.

Novyi shliakh, a Nationalist newspaper, 1947

Participants in an anti-Soviet demonstration in New York City in the late 1930s. Efforts to bring Soviet policies in Ukraine to the attention of the American public preoccupied Ukrainian Americans for generations.

In Europe, from the time of its inception in 1929, the OUN did, in fact, maintain contacts with German military intelligence. Their cooperation was based on the fact that they shared common enemies, Poland and the USSR. As war with Germany approached, opponents of the Nationalists sounded two basic and predictable themes: in general, they equated Ukrainian nationalism with fascism and, more specifically, they accused OUN-affiliates in North America of serving the Nazis. Because of naïveté or left-wing sympathies, members of the media lent credence to these allegations. For example, *Time* proclaimed that Ukrainian separatism was 'a German imported article'; the *Chicago Daily News* ran the headline 'Nazi Groups Woo U.S. Ukrainians' (Kuropas, 293); a respected liberal author, Louis Adamic, in his book *Two Way Passage,* claimed that Nazi agents in the United States were seeking 'people of Ukrainian nationality who ... might serve as saboteurs in American industries' (ibid., 302). Another book, *Sabotage!* by Michael Sayers and Albert Kahn, announced that ODVU and UHO were 'two of the most dangerous espionage-sabotage organizations in the world' (ibid., 303). And the popular news commentator Walter Winchell repeatedly railed against 'Uka-rain-ian [sic] terrorists in our midst' (ibid., 312). Ukrainians in the United States never had so much publicity. Unfortunately, it was almost all bad.

They complained. And they tried to explain. But the American media paid no attention. 'Simply because we want our kinsmen in their native land to enjoy ... the freedom and democracy that we are so fortunate in having here as Americans, we have become the object of ruthless vilification,' declared Stephen Shumeyko, editor of the *Ukrainian Weekly*. Walter Dushnyk argued that the Ukrainian independence movement was not 'the invention of Hitler.' And one Nationalist organization after another declared its loyalty to the United States.

But things went from bad to worse. In 1940, the Dies committee on Un-American Activities in Congress launched a probe of ODVU. That same year, the FBI also began a three-year-long investigation. Stephen Kuropas, an ODVU activist, expressed the shock felt by many Ukrainians: 'We thought the whole thing was a misunderstanding ... We knew that the United States supported national self-determination and that most Americans hated the

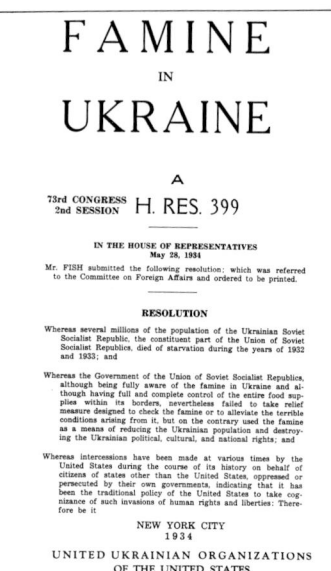

A copy of a House of Representatives resolution, sponsored by Rep. Hamilton Fish (R-NY) and disseminated by Ukrainian organizations, condemning the role of the Soviet government in the famine of 1933.

Defamation and the Results of an FBI Investigation

> With Myshuha as its head, *Svoboda* was converted into an organ of Axis propaganda and a medium for conveying instructions to ODWU spies. The *Svoboda* offices at 83 Grand Street, Jersey City, became a clearing house for espionage directives coming in from Berlin, Tokyo, and Rome. For many years, these directives have been regularly reaching the *Svoboda* offices by mail from Spanish and South American 'drops'; or through the special 'couriers' of the Axis spy systems. Liaison officers from Germany and Japan made their headquarters at 83 Grand Street when they visited the United States.
>
> Sayer and Kahn, Sabotage, 85

> In view of the fact that investigation has revealed the unreliable character of the original informants in this matter, and the fact that very extensive investigation in Ukrainian matters generally has failed to indicate any violation of the Registration Act and further since it appears that MYSHUHA is pro-democratic, pro-British, and pro-American, the outstanding leads in this case are being canceled, and this case is being considered closed.
>
> FBI report, 1943

Communists. We just couldn't bring ourselves to believe that the American people would be opposed to a free Ukraine once they knew the facts' (Kuropas, 295).

The FBI investigation found no evidence that Ukrainian organizations were engaged in subversion, sabotage, or espionage or that they maintained Nazi links. None the less, the investigation and the defamation campaign, launched in wartime when even the slightest hint of disloyalty among the foreign-born could have dire consequences, did irreparable harm to ODVU and its affiliates. Their membership dropped drastically. As noted above, other nationalistically inclined organizations such as UHO dissolved themselves. Even the non-political (but pro-nationalist) UNA came under fire.

The lead section of a 1933 protest march by Detroit Ukrainians against the man-made famine which occurred in Soviet Ukraine in that year.

In retrospect, it is perhaps understandable why ODVU's affiliation with OUN, which, in turn, had links with the Germans, made it vulnerable to attack. But there was a touch of irony in the situation. While Communist-inspired allegations sent congressional committees, the FBI, and the media on a wild-goose chase after spies among the Ukrainians, the Kremlin's agents were methodically establishing their networks elsewhere in America.

This traumatic episode also raised what became a long-standing concern of Ukrainian Americans: the ease with which the media could be manipulated into taking an anti-Ukrainian line. This issue was all the more disturbing when it was recalled how readily the American media turned a blind eye to news about the catastrophic Ukrainian famine of 1933. Especially painful to Ukrainians was the fact that Walter Duranty, the New York Times

Soviet correspondent, who systematically repressed and distorted information about the famine, received American journalism's highest award, the Pulitzer Prize, for the 'profundity, impartiality, sound judgement and exceptional clarity' of his dispatches from the USSR.

How vastly different, and stronger, was the position of the Ukrainians in Canada was evident in the experience of the UNF and other Nationalist organizations north of the border. As war drew closer, the pro-Communists also attacked their rivals on the right. In 1939, when their press called the UNF Aviation School in Oshawa a training ground for 'Ukrainian Nazis,' Canadian papers throughout the country picked up the story. There were also allegations that Nationalist aspirations, especially those involving the short-lived Carpatho-Ukrainian state, were part of a 'German intrigue.' But the Nationalists had influential friends. For example, Professor George Simpson of the University of Saskatchewan went on CBC radio to speak in defence of Ukrainian nationalist aspirations, comparing their links with Germany to those of American revolutionaries with absolutist France.

Apparently the European-based OUN also helped the UNF by practically severing their ties. According to informed sources, just before the war, a OUN leader declared that 'the UNF must carry on as an independent Ukrainian Canadian organization and in all respects conform its policies in accordance with the internal and foreign policies of Canada to whom UNF members owe their allegiance' (Prymak, 29). In any case, soon after England entered the war, the UNF sent a representative there to act as liaison and to assure the English of the support of the non-Communist Ukrainian Canadians. Moreover, the UNF worked energetically, if not successfully, for the creation of a Ukrainian-Canadian legion to fight on the Allied side. And in the person of Anthony Hlynka, a founding member of UNF and a member of Parliament, the Ukrainians had a forceful spokesman in the House of Commons. Thus, at least up to 1941, when the Soviets joined the Allies in the war against Hitler, the Ukrainian Nationalists in Canada faced few of the problems that bedevilled their colleagues in the United States.

St John the Baptist Ukrainian Catholic Church in Johnstown, Pennsylvania.

THE CHURCHES

After the First World War, the role of the churches, especially the Greek Catholic, in Ukrainian communities changed significantly. As other organizations proliferated, clergymen were no longer the only community leaders available. Increasingly, sometimes exclusively, the interest and activity of priests focused on church affairs. Moreover, a new spirit emerged among the predominantly Greek Catholic churchmen. It reflected much less of the patriotic social activism that characterized the American Circle of the pre-1914 era. Instead, a conservatism and discipline akin to that of the Roman Catholic clergy became more prevalent. When the Greek Catholic hierarchy had to choose between the dictates of Rome and the aspirations of Ukrainian nationalism, it almost invariably sided with the former.

To a great extent this new attitude facilitated the growing accommodation of the Greek Catholic church with the Roman Catholic hierarchy in North America. Whereas initially the very survival of the Byzantine-rite churches was highly questionable, by the 1930s they became an accepted part of North American Catholicism. However, accommodation came at a significant cost. Unhappy with the hierarchy's new approach, many Ukrainians, especially in Canada, joined the exodus to the more nationally oriented Ukrainian Orthodox church. Also the large, secular organizations often came into conflict with Greek Catholic bishops over their tendency to de-emphasize Ukrainianism. None the less, despite continuous tensions, the Catholic as well as Orthodox churches stabilized their positions and remained central – indeed, irreplaceable – pillars of Ukrainian communities.

The Catholics

After Bishop Ortynsky's death in 1916, Rome appointed two administrators for America's Byzantine-rite Catholics, Peter Poniatyshyn for those from Galicia and T. Maryniak for the Transcarpathians. The urbane, patriotic, and popular Poniatyshyn managed to dampen some of the conflicts that had embroiled his combative predecessor. And he was loath to discipline the clergy or to adjust to Roman Catholic models. This was not the case with his successor, Konstantyn Bohachevsky, who in 1924 was appointed bishop of what was now formally called the Ukrainian Catholic church. At the time it consisted of 144 churches, 102 priests, and about 237,000 faithful.

Bishop Bohachevsky's appointment ushered in a new era. As noted above, at the same time Bohachevsky was appointed, another bishop, Basil Takach, was assigned to the Transcarpathian Ruthenians. Thus, the division between two Byzantine-rite communities was institutionalized and each went its own way. For his part, Bohachevsky wasted little time in aligning his church with the Roman Catholic. From the outset, his epistles emphasized the primacy of the pope. Before long, he began to introduce Latin-rite practices: confessionals were installed in churches, the faithful were encouraged to use rosaries and to observe the stations of the cross, Latin feasts were celebrated, choirs rather than congregational singing were encouraged, altar boys replaced cantors (*diaky*), and, most infuriating for many traditionalists, the New (Gregorian) calendar came into use in some churches.

Among the older, foreign-born laity, protests mounted. Secular organizations, notably the UNA and its newpaper *Svoboda*, sharply criticized the prelate. An influential (and older) group of priests, the so-called New York Twenty Six, openly opposed their superior. But Bohachevsky had allies that his predecessor did not. A new and rising element in the clergy, the American-born (mostly products of the church's orphanages), not only accepted the changes but urged the younger generation of parishioners to do likewise. With such backing, Bohachevsky could confront his opponents with an ultimatum: either accept the changes or leave the church. Some did. Others, grudgingly, gave in. Consequently,

Konstantyn Bohachevsky, STD, became bishop of the Ukrainian Catholic church in 1924. He was elevated to Metropolitan-Archbishop of Philadelphia in 1958 and died in 1961.

Bishop Nykyta Budka surrounded by the faithful, 1926.

in 1929, when the Vatican issued the *Cum Data Fuerit* decree, which banned married priests in North America, declared that the bishop, not the lay trustees, owned the church property, and limited the influence of secular organizations in religious affairs, Ukrainian Catholics meekly accepted dictates that, a generation earlier, might have led to open rebellion.

In the meantime, Bohachevsky concentrated on strengthening his church. Unable to obtain enough priests from Ukraine, he invited the Basilian Order in Europe to aid him in staffing his parishes. From Canada he brought the Sisters Servants of Mary Immaculate to aid the Basilian nuns who taught in the dozen Ukrainian day schools. Secondary education also received much attention. In 1925 St Basil's, the first permanent day school, was established in Philadelphia; in the same city St Basil's Academy, a high school for girls, opened its doors in 1931. Four years later, a minor seminary and a high school for boys were founded in Stamford, Connecticut.

In Canada, events took a similar course: the stormy confrontations of the 1920s were followed by gradual stabilization and concentration on institution-building in the 1930s. When Bishop Budka also attempted to introduce Latinization, opposition developed among the nationalistic elements of the laity. But in Canada, unlike the United States, the latter were led by a new, Canadian-

The burial in national costume of Maria Khoma-Lypkova in Toronto, 1926.

educated intelligentsia that was even more militant than its compatriots in the United States. As noted above, in 1918 it formed the Ukrainian Orthodox church, which attracted many former Greek Catholics. The bitterness between the two churches was intense. For most of the 1920s, it led to harsh polemics, lawsuits, and even violent confrontations. Only in 1929, when a new bishop, Basil Ladyka, was appointed, did the Greek Catholic–Orthodox controversies subside, though they by no means disappeared.

The day-to-day church work was carried out, on the one hand, by the Basilian and Redemptorist orders and, on the other, by the nuns of the Basilian and Serving Sister orders. The Redemptorists were a noteworthy phenomenon: a Belgian Roman Catholic order, they created, under the leadership of Father Achilles Delaere, a Ukrainian Eastern-rite branch whose mission was to work among Ukrainians in Canada and Galicia. In addition to staffing most of the Ukrainian-Canadian parishes, both male orders established in the early 1920s, and greatly expanded in the 1930s, several high schools and seminaries. A major Basilian centre was located in Mundare, Alberta, while the Redemptorists were based in Yorkton, Saskatchewan, and Roblin, Manitoba. Meanwhile, the two orders of nuns maintained a growing network of elementary schools, an orphanage, and a hospital. To support the work of the church, in 1932 a lay organization, the

Brotherhood of Ukrainian Catholics (BUC), was founded. As of 1931, the Ukrainian Catholic church in Canada had about 100 priests, 350 parishes, and over 186,000 faithful.

The dedication of St Michael's Ukrainian Orthodox Church, Minneapolis, Minnesota, 1926. Officiating at the ceremony are Bishop Ioan Teodorovych (centre) with Reverends M. Zaparniuk and Iu. Zelechivsky.

The Orthodox

To comprehend the complicated history of the Ukrainian Orthodox church in North America, one should be cognizant of three basic points: (1) most of its members were discontented Greek Catholics (although the Bukovynians were Orthodox from the outset); (2) it had a strong Ukrainian national orientation; and (3) since there had been no Ukrainian Orthodox church for centuries, it faced huge problems in establishing its legitimacy and institutional structure.

The Second Wave

In Canada conditions for the development of the new church were more favourable than in the south: the influence of the pre-war Russian Orthodox church was weaker there than in the United States, many of the new intelligentsia joined its ranks, and it could count on attracting the Orthodox Bukovynians. None the less, when in 1918 the young activists of the Ukrainian Orthodox Brotherhood began expanding their church they were nearly overwhelmed by difficulties. Because the church had been founded without participation of a recognized bishop, it did not have canonical legitimacy. It seemed that this tenuous position was resolved in 1924 when Bishop Ioan Teodorovych, a patriotic hierarch of the newly founded Ukrainian Autocephalous church in Soviet Ukraine, arrived in America and accepted the leadership of Orthodox Ukrainians in North America. But keeping the church's diverse elements – former Catholics, Orthodox Bukovynians, and independents – together was a daunting task. Moreover, an extremely bitter polemical battle developed with the Ukrainian Catholics. And when in 1931 the mother-church in Ukraine was dissolved by the Soviets, legitimacy again became an issue.

Problems notwithstanding, the church made progress. Its image as a truly 'national' Ukrainian institution continued to attract those who rejected the Latinizing tendencies among the Greek Catholics. A highly supportive network of secular organizations, such as the Ukrainian Self-Reliance League (SUS), the Ukrainian Women's Association (SUK), and the Canadian Ukrainian Youth Association (SUMK), mobilized support on the grass-roots level. Thus, by 1941 the church had over 89,000 members and encompassed almost 30 per cent of the Ukrainian-Canadian community.

By comparison, the position of the Ukrainian Orthodox in the United States was weaker and even more complicated. Because they left their homeland earlier than their Canadian brethren and were therefore less influenced by its budding national movement, those Ukrainian immigrants in the United States who joined the Russian Orthodox church before 1914 generally remained loyal to it. Thus, when Bishop Teodorovych arrived, the fledgling Ukrainian Autocephalous Orthodox church (UAOC), which started out in Chicago, had only 8500 faithful and 14 priests. It received some reinforcement when a group of Greek Catholic priests who

Reverend Kiristiuk serving mass in Theodore, Saskatchewan, 1921.

Reverend Krupa and his parishioners, West Fort William, Ontario, c. 1922.

opposed Bohachevsky's reforms went over to Orthodoxy. But their defection was a mixed blessing. Bothered by the question of Teodorovych's canonical status, in 1928 the dissidents abandoned the UAOC, formed the Ukrainian Orthodox church (UOC), and placed it under patronage of the patriarch of Constantinople. Thus, in the United States two Ukrainian Orthodox churches emerged, the UAOC and the UOC. Both were relatively weak: in 1939 the former had only 24 parishes and 22 priests while the latter had 36 priests and 43 parishes.

The Second Wave

Protestants

The recurrent controversies, fissures, and lawsuits over property that rocked the two major denominations led some Ukrainians to consider a third option: Protestantism. Although it had no Ukrainian roots, it had the advantage of being a mainstream religion in North America. In the United States, Protestant inroads among Ukrainians were modest: in the late 1930s there were only five Presbyterian and four Baptist Ukrainian-language congregations. However, in Canada, where the Presbyterian and United churches mounted an energetic proselytizing effort among the immigrants, they attained considerable success. By the early 1940s, there were about 20,000 Ukrainian Protestants, half of whom belonged to the United church.

SECULAR ORGANIZATIONS

Women's associations

The urge to organize that swept through Ukrainian communities also encompassed women. Female activism was further encouraged by the budding feminist movement in North America and,

The Descent of the Holy Spirit parish of the Ukrainian Evangelical church celebrating its tenth anniversary, New York City, 1935.

even more, by the example of the strong and vibrant Ukrainian women's movement (Ukrainian Women's Union – Soiuz Ukrainok) that emerged in Galicia in the early 1920s.

Although women's groups, usually sisterhoods associated with parish churches, did emerge sporadically in the pre-1914 communities, they had no lasting impact. It was not until several years after the war that a more durable women's organization appeared. In 1925, several women's groups in the New York area combined to form the Soiuz Ukrainok Ameryky – Ukrainian National Women's League of America (UNWLA). A year later, in Saskatoon, a Canadian counterpart, Ukrainian Women's Association of Canada (SUK), appeared. Because the latter was linked with the Orthodox-controlled Mohyla Institute, its membership was drawn heavily from that denomination. In Canada, SUK enjoyed a promising start with twenty branches formed in the first year. Meanwhile, the American organization encompassed forty-two branches by 1932.

The organizations had similar objectives: they mounted campaigns to aid victims of natural disasters or political repression in the homeland, concentrated on raising the national consciousness of the youth, and sought to maintain cultural traditions. The last undertaking led the two groups to amass considerable collections of folk arts, which were eventually housed in museums that they founded. Leading activists in Canada were Savella Stechishin and Olha Woycenko and in the United States Helen Lotocky and Julia Jarema.

An appeal to Ukrainian women in North America to help political prisoners in their homeland, c. 1930.

162 UKRAINIANS IN NORTH AMERICA

The first congress of the Ukrainian National Women's League of America, New York City, 1932.

The various ideological organizations also developed women's affiliates. For example, in Canada female Nationalists belonged to the Olha Basarab Organization of Ukrainian Women while their counterparts in the United States formed the Gold Cross. Both pro-Communists and monarchists also had women's auxiliaries. Although it was established relatively late, the Ukrainian Catholic Women's League of Canada had two hundred branches by the early 1940s. In 1932, an event billed as the first congress of Ukrainian Women in America was held in New York. It adopted a constitution for the UNWLA and discussed a broad range of issues. Considerably later, in 1944, the major women's organizations in Canada formed their coordinating body, the Women's Council of the Ukrainian Canadian Committee.

For the most part these women's organizations focused much of their attention on traditional female concerns such as the care of the young, infirm, and needy and the maintenance of cultural traditions. They did not take an independent stand on the political and ideological controversies that shook their communities. But because they were able to establish ties with women's organizations beyond the Ukrainian community, their contacts tended to be more far-ranging and less insular than those of the male-dominated organizations.

A UNWLA Plan of Action

January – Christmas caroling to raise funds for various causes in Ukraine; ... commemoration of Ukrainian Independence Day.

February – Birthday of Lesia Ukrainka to be commemorated in an appropriate fashion along with the death of Olha Bassarab. Similar commemorative services should be planned for George Washington and Abraham Lincoln.

March – Commemoration of Taras Shevchenko. Branches should cooperate with other Ukrainian organizations in this observance or organize their own.

April – Classes should be organized for the teaching of Ukrainian Easter egg decoration to young Ukrainian girls ...

May – Every branch should organize a Mother's Day concert where the importance of Ukrainian motherhood is stressed along with the significance of raising children in the Ukrainian spirit ...

June – Children's month – During the month of June every mother should take her children to the doctor (to our doctor if there is one in the vicinity since he can communicate with you better) ...

July and August – While no formal suggestions are offered for the summer months, branches are urged to enlarge their treasuries through the sponsorship of picnics and other affairs.

September – School month – Every member is obligated to find ways to guarantee a higher education – college or university – for the more talented boys and girls in the community. Every member should also make sure that there is a local Ukrainian ethnic school (Ridna Shkola) in existence and that the teacher is qualified.

October – Book month – The significance of books and other reading material should be emphasized during October ...

November – This month should be devoted to the commemoration of the declaration of independence of the ZUNR (Listopadove Sviato) ...

December – During this month each branch is to take stock of its previous year's activity through the annual reports of branch officers ...

From a UNWLA publication, 1940

Ukrainian-American newspapers of the interwar period.

The press

During the interwar period, the community-oriented press came into its own. Like all ethnic media, it had the advantage of appearing in the readers' native language and providing Ukrainian-oriented news unavailable elsewhere. Moreover, illiteracy, so widespread among the immigrants of the pre-war period, declined considerably, adding to the potential readership. The ideological and political mobilization of the interwar period also made for a more sophisticated and interested readership. On the debit side, however, the impact of the Depression limited the growth of many newspapers and led to the demise of others.

Perhaps the most crucial feature of the Ukrainian press was that it was not independent. Almost every newspaper was associated with one type of organization or another, be it religious, fraternal, or ideological. This meant that publications, in reflecting interests of their organizations, tended to be highly biased, even confrontational. Adding to this tendency was the almost complete lack of professional training among the editors and journalists.

A cartoon, published in a Svoboda publication, depicting the growth in the Ukrainian national consciousness (and socio-economic status) of the once nationally confused immigrants.

For the most part, they were people with Old Country educations whose primary assets were dedication to a specific 'cause' and knowledge of the language. Their lack of familiarity with professional ethics was often reflected in the frequent personal smears and libellous accusations that were standard fare in the newspapers. None the less, the press as a whole was obviously of crucial importance to the community: it identified vital issues, presented various points of view, and informed its readers of important events. Moreover, many of the newspapers provided practical information about hygiene, agricultural techniques, labour conditions, immigration regulations, and the like. Finally, many an immigrant first learned to read by using a Ukrainian newspaper as his text.

In the United States, there were twenty-one Ukrainian newspapers and periodicals during the 1930s (the Transcarpathian community published an additional seven). As might be expected, the most influential and financially stable newspapers belonged to the fraternal associations. Under the able editorship of Luka Myshuha, the UNA's venerable daily *Svoboda*, which usually took a relatively moderate although distinctly pro-nationalist stance, was the most widely read. The other daily was *Ameryka* of the Catholic Providence Association. Rounding out the 'big three' was the left-leaning *Narodna Volya*, a weekly published by the UWA. A noteworthy development in the press of this period was the appearance of English-language papers geared to American-born children of immigrants. Of these, the most influential was the UNA's *Ukrainian Weekly*, founded in 1933 and initally edited by Stephen Shumeyko.

Since there were no major fraternal associations in Canada, the press depended on other bases of support. The earliest Ukrainian-Canadian newspaper, the weekly, *Kanadiisky farmer*, was founded in 1903 with the thinly veiled support of the Liberal party. Maintaining a moderate position on Ukrainian issues, it strove to expand Liberal party influence among Ukrainian-speaking voters. Later, the newspaper became a privately owned commercial enterprise. Religious denominations also sponsored newspapers. For example, the Presbyterian Synod provided funds for *Ranok* (1905), while the Catholic church sponsored *Kanadiisky Rusin* (1911), which was later renamed *Kanadiisky Ukrainets*. In the

Typical Contents of a Ukrainian Canadian Newspaper

Page one: column article denying report that 50,000 naturalised Ukrainians were going to exert their political power in 17 constituencies because of Non-Preferred restrictions.

Polish government oppresses Ukrainian peasants.

Polish emigrants leaving for Canada.

Memorial to Shevchenko in Detroit.

Lindbergh married!

Page two: Editorial as to whether it would be wise to have a Ukrainian political party in Canada; better in the interest of the Ukrainians and Canada to join the established parties.

Novel.

American delegates to Russia on their return report as they were told to report.

Page three: Canadian and American news from different districts.

Correspondence, etc.

Page five: Economic conditions in Canada.

Wheat Pool production.

Honey Pool in Ontario.

Tobacco industry in Canada, growth and development.

News from Dominion Parliament: new Canadian flag, etc.

Article on Ukrainians in Canada, their progress.

Page six: Correspondence, etc.

Letters from the old country re political prisoners in Lviv.

Article on higher education discussing coming series of lectures.

Article for farmers by Mr Prodan of Manitoba Department of Agriculture.

Pravda i Svoboda, 1929

Lonhyn Tsehelsky, standing, the administrator and editor of Ameryka, the daily newspaper of the Providence Association of Ukrainian Catholics, at work in Philadelphia, 1937.

interwar period, ideologically oriented newspapers came to the fore. Although founded in 1910, during the interwar period, the *Ukrainskyi holos*, edited by Myroslav Stechishin, became the organ of the Ukrainian Self-Reliance League (SUS). The Ukrainian Canadian Left also established a widely read paper, the *Ukrainski robitnychi visti*, edited by Danylo Lobay and Matthew Shatulsky. In 1930, *Novyi shliakh*, a militantly nationalist newspaper associated with the UNF, appeared. In addition, there were numerous, less widely read publications that catered to interests of various women's, youth, and religious groups. Another characteristic of the Canadian-based press was that almost all of it was concentrated in one city, Winnipeg.

Cultural activity

Having resolved, by and large, the basic problems of subsistence, the immigrants in the interwar period had more opportunities to turn to cultural pursuits. Compared to the pioneer era, there were now more people interested in and capable of working in this field. As might be expected, a favourite area of activity was folk-culture, which is unusually colourful and highly developed among the Ukrainians. Church choirs, amateur theatrical groups,

St Nicholas and company. Carollers in Calder, Saskatchewan, 1927.

and orchestras of various types appeared with the arrival of the earliest immigrants. However, the 1920s and 1930s brought notable changes. The choirs became larger, more sophisticated. In contrast to the earlier period, they frequently had no church connections and their repertoire included not only traditional folk melodies but also the patriotic songs that had emerged during the recent struggle for independence. Amateur theatricals also added plays of a political or historical content, often presented in exceedingly melodramatic form, to their traditional folkloric repertoire.

A new type of event, the national holiday, marked by sombre gatherings called *akademii*, made its appearance. By means of choral and orchestral performances, poetic recitations, and long, often stultifying, speeches, exuding patriotic pathos and rhetoric, these events commemorated national heroes such as Taras

The Ukrainian National Choir, led by Oleksander Koshyts, achieved renown during its highly successful tour of Europe and North America in 1920–4. It was dispatched abroad by the short-lived Ukrainian People's Republic to familiarize the West with the Ukrainian cause.

Oleksander Koshyts (1875–1944), the highly acclaimed composer and choral director.

Shevchenko, or important events such as the UNR's declaration of independence or the battle of Kruty in which three hundred young students perished.

But it was music and dance that attracted most participants, especially among the new, North American–born generation. And in this field there were impressive achievements. To a large extent they were linked with the arrival in North America of two exceptionally gifted émigrés, the dance master Vasyl Avramenko and the composer-conductor Oleksander Koshyts.

In 1920, the Ukrainian National Choir, consisting of some of the country's best singers and led by Koshyts, was sent abroad by the short-lived Ukrainian People's Republic to popularize the Ukrainian cause by means of song. After attaining spectacular successes thoughout Europe and North America, the choir chose to remain abroad. Settling in New York, Koshyts concentrated on composing and training new choral singers and directors. Soon a bevy of talented pupils duplicated his efforts by establishing prize-winning choirs in a number of major American cities. In 1941, the UNF brought the famed director to Winnipeg, where he continued to work with great success until his death in 1944. An example of his wide-ranging impact was the transformation of the Ukrainian melody 'Song of the Bells' into a North American Christmas classic.

A scene from Avramenko's film A Zaprozhian beyond the Danube. The sound-film, made in 1936–7, garnered little critical acclaim and even less financial profit.

What Koshyts did for singing, Avramenko did for dancing. Colourful, energetic, imaginative, and, quite often, exasperating, he was an impressario greatly reminiscent of the Music Man. Basing himself in New York in 1926, he travelled tirelessly through the United States and Canada, promoting the beauty and excitement of Ukrainian folk dancing. In close to a hundred communities he established dance groups, convinced parents to provide financial support, and awoke unprecedented enthusiasm among his young and numerous pupils. Avramenko was especially adept at bringing his efforts to an inspiring climax: huge extravaganzas, involving hundreds of his dancers and massed choirs led by Koshyts, were staged with great success and publicity, even in the English-language press, in the opera-houses of New York, Chicago, and Winnipeg. Even the White House invited him to give a performance.

Vasyl Avramenko (1895–1981), the famous choreographer and impressario.

Avramenko's Magic

Today we write with eagerness. We want to tell everybody about the unquestionably gorgeous and fascinating Ukrainian program under Vasile Avramenko on Saturday night in the old Metropolitan Opera House.

On this occasion it is hard to follow newspaper custom and put the last thing first. On the second day after we are still excited over the kaleidoscopic ardors of the dance, the richness of the chorus, the congeniality of the audience and the fairly inspiring naturalness of what really amounted to a brilliant Ukrainian folk festival. And we refuse to turn from this event to the other without first going on record for unrestricted immigration from the Ukraine. What this country needs is more Ukrainians! Through them Americans may learn to play.

(Henry Beckett, New York Evening Post, 1931)

Equally imaginative but less successful were Avramenko's attempts to create, in 1936, a 'Ukrainian Hollywood,' that is, to produce films. After producing several films, such as *Natalka Poltavka* and *A Zaporozhian beyond the Danube*, as well as several documentaries, he was forced to abandon these overly expensive undertakings. Ukrainians also had an outstanding representative in the world of high culture, Alexander Archipenko, another postwar émigré, whose modernistic sculptures gained widespread acclaim.

Enboldened by their cultural progress, Ukrainians were ready to display it to the North American public. An excellent opportunity came with the opening of the World's Fair in Chicago in 1933. Thanks to a massive and well-organized fund-raising campaign, a 'Ukrainian Pavilion' was built at the fair that included an impressive exhibition of Archipenko's sculptures. Ukrainians by the tens of thousands came to attend the opening ceremonies and most of the 1.8 million visitors to the fair also visited the pavilion. The success in Chicago was a high point for Ukrainians during the interwar period. A fitting follow-up came in 1939 at the New York World's Fair, where the Ukrainian exhibit featured a massive concert involving 1000 singers and dancers and a throng of Ukrainians numbering a reported 50,000.

The Ukraine Pavilion at the Chicago World's Fair in 1933. It was visited by 1.4 million persons during the course of the fair.

In Canada, song and dance extravaganzas were also staged but on a smaller scale. However, Ukrainian Canadians had cultural achievements that their brethren to the south did not. Most important of these was the vibrant Ukrainian-Canadian literature that emerged in the 1920s. Even before 1914 it had produced a literary phenomenon of note when the simplistic but catchy book of rhymes by Teodor Fedyk, *Pisni imigrantiv pro staryi i novyi krai* (Songs of Immigrants about the Old and New Country), which appeared in 1911, sold about 50,000 copies. During the 1920s and 1930s, poets and prose writers such as Ivan Danylchuk, Honore Ewach, and Mykyta Mandryka began to publish. In *The Sons of the Soil*, the novelist Illia Kiriak produced a work that depicted in epic form the Ukrainian settlement of the prairies. Meanwhile, in the pro-Communist camp, Myroslav Irchan emerged as a talented and prolific playwright. Writing mostly in Ukrainian, these authors frequently juxtaposed the confrontation of the old and new in the Ukrainian experience in Canada in skilful, often moving, fashion.

Education

Even though the bilingual schools were abolished in Canada in 1916, they had exerted a considerable impact. Thousands of Ukrainian schoolchildren in the approximately four hundred totally or largely Ukrainian school districts in the prairies had received primary education in the language of their parents. Moreover, many of the close to 250 teachers who had been trained to work in the bilingual system were employed in the all-English-language schools. Their familiarity with things Ukrainian balanced, at least in part, the strong, assimilationist attitudes of the Anglo-Saxon teachers.

The Szewczenko elementary school in Vita, Manitoba, c. 1930.

Mr Kupchenko, a teacher, with his best pupils, West Fort William, Ontario, 1924.

A school picnic, Myrnam, Alberta, late 1920s.

Another reflection of the strong commitment to the preservation of Ukrainian-language education was the numerous heritage schools that appeared. In many of the bloc settlements, public schools were utilized after hours, usually from 4 to 6 p.m., for courses in Ukrainian language, literature, history, and geography with public-school teachers of Ukrainian background often providing the instruction. In other cases, the ubiquitous *narodnyi dim* (community hall) doubled as a schoolhouse for heritage classes. Among the pro-Communists, these classes were especially well-organized and numerous. Thus, in the 1930s there were about 1500 children and 30 teachers among the non-Communists and over 2000 pupils in 50 schools among the pro-Communists attending supplementary courses.

Measures were also taken to ensure that the older, more

Preserving the Ancestral Language

> Our parents were such, you learn ten languages if you want but you must learn your own. It was a must in our home. There was never an English word spoken at meals. It was a rule. After supper, whether it was winter or summer, but not in harvest, we were all put behind the table like chickens and each one had to read and write. At that time I thought it was silly but now I thank them for it.
>
> *Recollections of a second-generation Ukrainian Canadian*

The Second Wave

The orchestra and drama club of the A. Kotsko Ukrainian Student Society, which was affiliated with the Michael Hrushevsky Ukrainian Institute in Edmonton, 1924.

advanced students retained and expanded their familiarity with Ukrainian subjects. As mentioned above, the *bursy* provided a well-organized and obligatory program in Ukrainian studies for the residents. Catholic high schools, such as the Sacred Heart Academy and St Joseph's College in Yorkton, also had heritage-related courses. For university students summer courses, which were organized at the University of Manitoba in 1924, gained in popularity in the late 1920s and 1930s as noted Ukrainian intellectuals such as the historian Dmytro Doroshenko were invited from Europe to lecture. Despite these efforts, only a small minority of Ukrainian youth were exposed to Ukrainian studies. The vast majority attended the public schools, which served as a primary means of transforming their pupils into 'good Canadians.'

If transmitting elements of a Ukrainian cultural heritage to the young was difficult in Canada, it was even more so in the United States. Few of the American-born ever attended a public school where the majority of students were of Ukrainian background, as

Ukrainian National Home in Windsor, Ontario, c. 1939. The building was typical of community centres in the cities of Canada and the United States.

frequently happened in the Canadian prairies. Teachers of Ukrainian background were rare. Since many of the children lived in urban ghettos, it was difficult enough to keep them in school, let alone attending supplementary Ukrainian classes. However, some progress, primarily regarding the heritage schools, was achieved.

After several failed attempts, in 1927 a blueprint for a network of coordinated heritage schools, under the name Ridna Shkola, was established. It sought to bring some coordination to the various community-run heritage schools by standardizing teaching materials, examinations, and the training of teachers. But it achieved little success. Communities were unwilling to give up control over the schools that they supported, and teachers remained, as before, mostly of the cantor-teacher type (diak-uchytel), with little training and even less ability to awaken the interest of their pupils. The fact that classes, usually held in damp, dark church halls, met from 4 to 6 p.m. five times a week made them even more unpopular with the youth. Basically, it was the strong commitment of parents and the pressure they were able to exert on their children that maintained the eighty-six heritage schools that existed in 1939.

Day schools were few and, as in Canada, associated with the Catholic church. In 1925, Bishop Bohachevsky established the first

The Second Wave

Clearly enamoured of Cossack traditions, these young Ukrainian Americans lead a parade in Detroit in the 1930s.

such school in Philadelphia and during the 1930s about a dozen more were established in major urban centres. In the opinion of one sophisticated observer, the function of Ukrainian subjects that were taught in these schools was not to produce patriotic Ukrainians but to engender just enough Ukrainian consciousness to ensure adherence to the Ukrainian Catholic church. In 1940, an ambitious campaign was launched to establish a Ukrainian college, but it failed to reach its objective.

A Ukrainian dance and drama troupe, Toronto, 1934.

Youth organizations

The need to form youth organizations was felt especially keenly in the United States. After the First World War, many Ukrainians who had originally planned to return to their homeland decided to stay. This decision forced them to consider the future of their ethnic community and, particularly, how to retain the youth's links with it. The prospects were sobering. Living in ethnically mixed neighbourhoods, exposed to the intense melting-pot ideology in the schools, and belonging to a hardly known nationality, young people were exceptionally prone to assimilation. There were, moreover, no organizations that catered to Ukrainian youth ever since the Sich gymnastics society adopted a monarchist stance and served an increasingly middle-aged membership. It was, therefore, with alarm that, in the early 1930s, community leaders realized not only that their organizations were failing to attract youth but that many young people actively rejected everything Ukrainian. Soon, in the press, at various congresses, at local meetings, in church sermons, wherever older, community activists gathered, one heard slogans proclaiming the need to 'Save Our Youth!'

The Second Wave

The Crisis of the Older Generation

> If we are honest with ourselves, we must realize that we are old and that the time to die is just around the corner. And let's ask ourselves if we really have anyone to whom we can leave that inheritance which we have developed in this new land. Will anyone be left to attend our churches, our schools, our national homes and the other institutions which now exist? ...
>
> Let us save our children, our blood, before it's too late. If we don't wish to save them from assimilation then we have no right to call ourselves their parents.
>
> Providence, a Ukrainian Catholic publication, 1931

An early attempt to confront the problem was the formation of the League of Ukrainian Clubs, an Orthodox-backed network of youth clubs, in 1931. It, however, dissolved a few years later. Much more lasting and broadly based was the undertaking that grew out of the Ukrainian participation in the Chicago World Fair in 1933. Capitalizing on the enthusiasm generated by the project and the involvement of numerous organizations, a group of young American-born activists, led by Stephen Shumeyko and backed by the UNA, formed the Ukrainian Youth League of North America (UYLNA). Committed to neutrality in politics and religion and emphasizing social functions and sports to attract the American-born, the new organization grew rapidly, forming fifty chapters by 1936. That year, a high point of its activity, the UYLNA hosted a Ukrainian Olympics in Philadelphia that attracted 150 athletes and 5000 spectators. Meanwhile, the UNA also used sports to attract the young, sponsoring, by 1940, about 30 baseball clubs, 21 basketball teams, and 33 bowling groups.

But the UYLNA stand on religion displeased the Catholics, who withdrew to form the Ukrainian Catholic Youth League (UCYL) in 1933. With the backing of the church, it formed 100 clubs in 35 communities. Political organizations also established youth-affiliates. The Nationalists formed the Young Ukrainian Nationalists (MUN) in 1932. It strove to attract members by emphasizing

Soldiers and nurses of Ukrainian background who served in the American armed forces participate in a flag-blessing ceremony in St George's Church in New York City, 1943.

sports, military drill teams, and flying. Meanwhile, the monarchists countered with Junior Siege (Sich), which sought to mix conservative ideology with boxing, track and field, and the 'aristocratic' sport of riding. As mentioned earlier, in 1933 the UNA began to publish the Ukrainian Weekly, an English-language weekly geared specifically to the young generation. The newspaper had a major impact and, as Myron Kuropas has noted, what the Ukrainian-language Svoboda did for raising the national consciousness of the first generation, the Ukrainian Weekly did in reminding the second generation of its ethnic origins.

Because most of them came to Canada with the intention of settling there permanently, Ukrainian Canadians were quicker to direct their attention to youth. This was evident in the establishment of the bursy during the First World War period. But, as in United States, the main thrust in establishing youth organizations

A Ukrainian baseball team sponsored by the UNF in Toronto in the 1930s.

came in the interwar period. In 1927, SUK provided the impetus for the formation of several youth clubs and soon afterwards SUS joined in. By 1931, these two Orthodox organizations sponsored the formation of SUMK. Thanks in large part to the organizing talents of H. Tyzuk, SUMK grew to encompass about two hundred branches. Like most youth groups, its activities consisted of social functions and sports. In 1938, the Catholics, unwilling to participate in the Orthodox-dominated SUMK, created the Ukrainian Catholic Youth (UCY). As in the United States, the Nationalists formed MUN. In contrast to their compatriots south of the border, however, the youth in Canada were much more active in forming student clubs. Especially noteworthy were the groups that existed at the universities of Manitoba, Saskatchewan, and Alberta.

Participants of a Ukrainian studies summer course at the Mohyla Institute, Saskatoon, 1947.

Fond Hopes

Our youth! Our youth! Surely they will not succumb to the bigotry and intolerance which have embedded themselves so deeply in the souls of their fathers? Surely they will not stop to don those old-fashioned and out-worn cloaks of their fathers' minds which have only served to disguise personal animosity and hatred? No! Our youth has been brought up in a new world, in a new environment, in a new age. And it is but logical that they should wish to garb their minds in raiment befitting this modern age ...

So lead on, Ukrainian youth! May your unprejudiced minds and wholesome attitudes conduct you on the journey of your life ... May the spirit of your good will toward fellow Ukrainians fuse your ranks into a harmonious and effective organization, thus supplying the means to attain your aim!

Zhinochyi svit, 1933

Umbrella organizations

As organizations multiplied, the need to coordinate their activities and to form an all-Ukrainian representative body grew. The Ukrainian Americans first addressed this need in 1922 when 130 delegates from 176 organizations met in Philadelphia to form the United Ukrainian Organizations of America (UUOA). During its eighteen years of existence this body achieved some notable results. It imposed a tax of $0.25 per month (albeit irregularly collected) on individual members that supported projects in the community and the homeland. Much effort went into staging demonstrations and rallies. For example, in 1930 the UUOA coordinated an impressive series of large, anti-Polish rallies thoughout the United States that involved 104,000 people, attending 160 rallies in 94 cities and towns. Other major efforts included drawing attention to the famine of 1933 and soliciting aid for Carpatho-Ukraine in 1938. However, difficulties associated with the defamation campaign of 1939 led to the dissolution of the UUOA and the formation of a new body.

As a result of an agreement among the leading fraternal associations, a congress was held in Washington in 1940. Attended by 805 delegates from 168 communities, it led to the creation of the Ukrainian Congress Committee of America (UCCA). As one of its first undertakings, the UCCA attempted, without notable success, to develop greater understanding in the American government of the aspirations of the Ukrainians in Europe.

The Ukrainian Canadians were much slower in forming an umbrella organization. And when they finally did so, it was largely because of the prodding of the Canadian government. Anxious to have a body that would mobilize Ukrainian-Canadian support for the looming war, in 1939 representatives of the federal government convinced the feuding ideological and religious organizations – the UHO, SUS, on the one hand, and UNF and the Catholic Brotherhood, on the other – to commence talks with the aim of forming the Ukrainian Canadian Committee (UCC). After much arm-twisting by the government and bargaining by the constituent groups, in 1940 the UCC came into being in Ottawa. Reverend Basil Kushnir was elected its first president.

The UCC mandate was to function as a coordinating and representative body for the Ukrainian-Canadian community. It did not, however, encompass the pro-Communists and their affiliated organizations and they remained adamantly opposed to it. Yet, as the Second World War began, the widespread organizational activity of the interwar period had clearly reached a watershed, in both Canada and the United States, and the stage was set for a new phase in the history of Ukrainians in North America.

THE THIRD WAVE

AFTER THE SECOND WORLD WAR

| Ukrainian DP's press forward to board the ship that will take them from Germany to the United States, c. 1949.

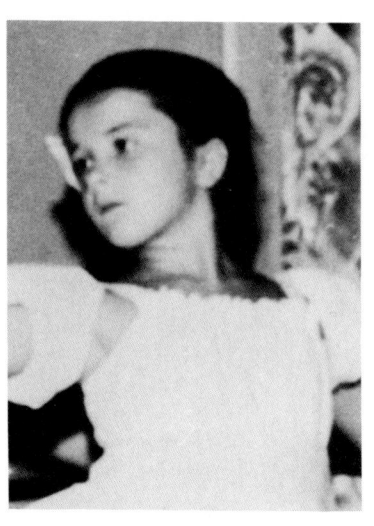

THE LATEST MAJOR WAVE of Ukrainians to come to North America consisted not so much of immigrants as refugees. The usual premeditated, basically economic, reasoning for coming to the New World was not uppermost in the minds of the newcomers. Forced to leave home by the turmoil of war, they would not return for fear of the Soviets. War-torn Europe had no place for them. Thus, the United States and Canada were perceived, first and foremost, as places of refuge and many hoped that their stay there would be only temporary, that they might return home when the opportunity arose.

Another striking aspect of this post–Second World War influx was its social composition. It contained a high percentage of the well-educated. Indeed, a large part of the West Ukrainian élite could be found in its ranks, since these people had most to fear from the Soviets. As might be expected, the highly nationalistic refugees were fervently anti-Communist. Much more varied than earlier immigrants in terms of the regions of Ukraine from which they came, the different political regimes under which they had lived, and the social strata that they represented, they did have a common, unifying experience: the postwar refugee camps of Germany and Austria.

THE GERMAN INTERLUDE

When the Second World War ended, Germany and Austria teemed with over 16 million foreign workers, prisoners-of-war, and refugees. Of these, about 2.2 million were Ukrainians. The overwhelming majority of them were the *Ostarbeiter*, mostly young boys and girls from Soviet Ukraine who had been forcibly torn from their homes and subjected to years of exhausting and demeaning labour in Germany. As soon as hostilities ceased, the Soviets sent in repatriation missions composed of officers and propagandists to convince Soviet citizens, by all means possible, to return home. Most of the *Ostarbeiter* returned, either voluntarily or involuntarily, to the USSR. But about 220,000 Ukrainians refused, under any circumstances, to do so. More than 2.5 million East Europeans also did not go back to their Soviet-dominated homelands. These people came to be called Displaced Persons (DP's).

To care for the masses of homeless refugees, the United Nations Relief and Rehabilitation Agency (UNRRA) was formed in 1945. Two years later, the International Relief Organization (IRO) took over this role. Basically, these organizations sought to provide the DP's with a modicum of food and shelter until they could be permanently resettled. Often grouped by nationality, the refugees were concentrated in 'camps,' that is, requisitioned schools, army barracks, and public buildings. Because they were allowed to elect their own leadership to look after administration as well as educational and cultural affairs, these camps, which were located in the U.S.-, British-, and French-occupied zones of Germany, were often referred to as 'DP republics.'

A group of Ukrainian DP's on the roof of the barracks that they constructed, c. 1946.

A memorial service for Ukrainian freedom fighters, Lindtorf DP camp, c. 1947.

About two-thirds of the Ukrainian refugees lived in the camps, eighty of which were all-Ukrainian. The remainder found private accommodation. Some of the major camps were located in U.S.-occupied Bavaria, most notably in Munich, Mittenwald, Regensburg, Berchtesgaden, and Augsburg. On the average, these large camps had a population of 2000 to 4000.

About 20 per cent of the Ukrainian DP's were political refugees par excellence. Consisting largely of members of the intelligentsia, they rejected the Soviet system and fled, often under harrowing circumstances, before the advancing Red Army. The vast majority were workers who had been forcefully brought to Germany during the war. By refusing the Soviets' insistent repatriation attempts, they too became refugees. About two-thirds of the DP's were from Galicia and belonged to the Ukrainian Catholic church, while the remaining third were from Soviet Ukraine and were Orthodox. Other important subgroups among the DP's were émigrés from the 1920s period, Ukrainian students in Germany, former German prisoners-of-war, and released inmates of the concentration camps. In Italy, there were about 10,000 members of the interned 'Galicia' division that had fought on the German side. And in 1947–8, several hundred soldiers of the anti-Soviet Ukrainian Insurgent Army (UPA), who had fought their way from the Carpathians through Czechoslovakia to Germany,

Students and faculty at the Ukrainian Free University in 1947. The university, which existed during the interwar period in Prague, was moved to Munich in 1946 to avoid the Soviet forces.

also joined the DP's. Thus, this largest of all Ukrainian political emigrations reflected Ukraine's various regions, religions, social classes, and cultural and political traditions.

Included in the large pool of well-educated people among the DP's were about 1000 teachers, 400 engineers, 350 lawyers, 300 physicians and an equal number of clergy, and close to 200 scholars. There were, moreover, over 2000 students on the university level. Judging by these numbers, it was clear that a large part of the West Ukrainian intelligentsia had chosen not to stay under Soviet rule.

For many of their inhabitants, the four to five years they spent in the camps was a unique and not altogether unpleasant experience. The 'DP republics' had a surfeit of young, energetic, and educated people. While simple food and shelter (although terribly crowded) were available, jobs in the shattered German economy were practically impossible to find. Therefore, partly in response to pressing needs, partly to express what had been long repressed, and partly to avoid boredom, the DP's generated an extraordinary amount of organizational, cultural, educational, and political activity.

Statistics underscore this point. Despite very limited material resources, the Ukrainian DP's maintained two university-level institutions, about forty gymnasia (secondary schools), and over a

The faculty of the Ukrainian Institute of Technology and Economics in 1947. This was another émigré institution that made the move to Bavaria to avoid the oncoming Soviets.

The Third Wave

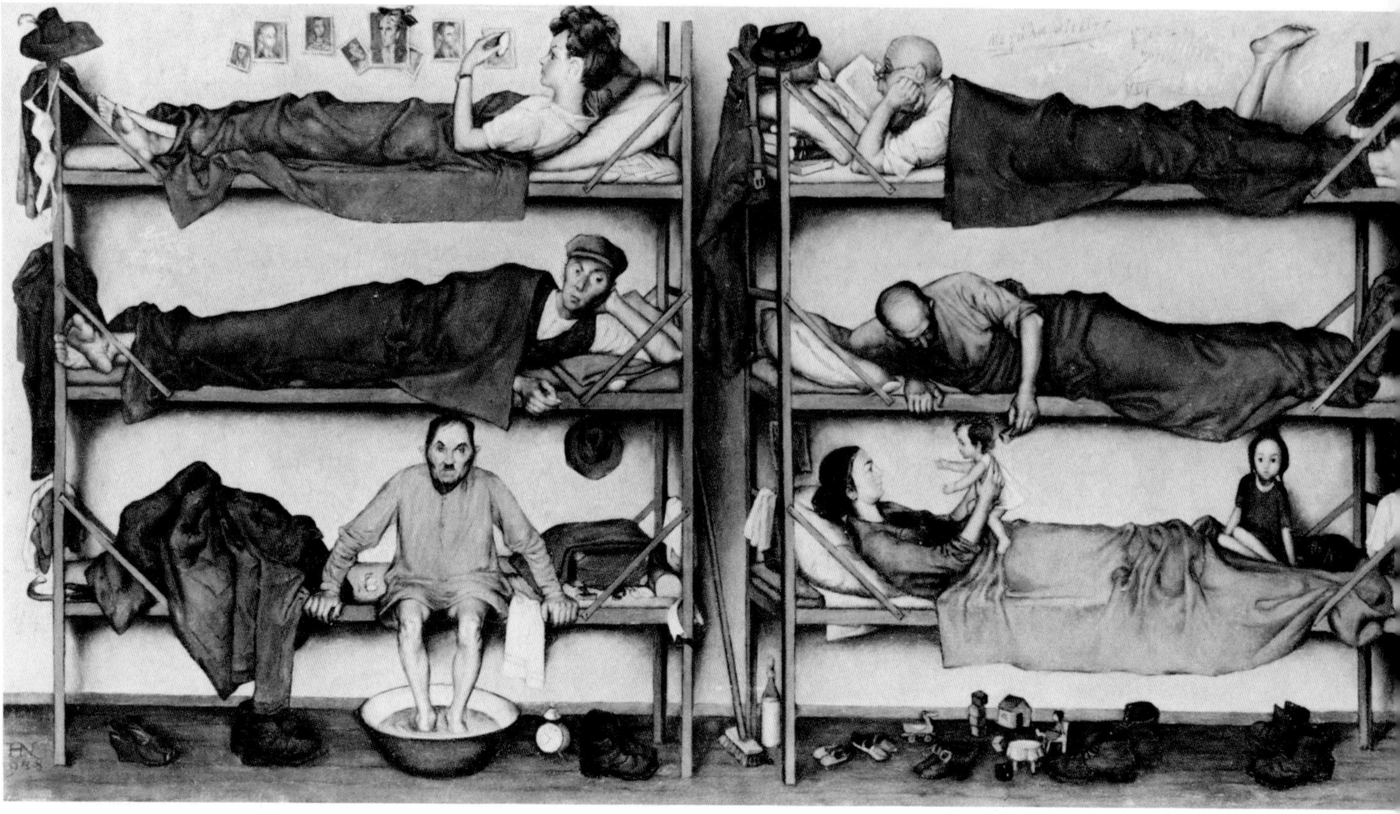

The Displaced Persons by
Jacques Hnizdovsky, 1948.

Jacques Hnizdovsky, painting
his Displaced Persons in 1948.

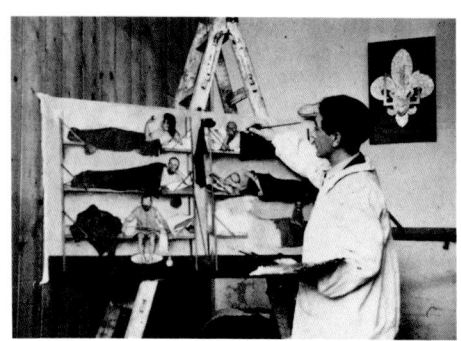

hundred elementary schools. They also established dozens of vocational courses and 85 parishes and rebuilt Plast, the scouting organization. Cultural activity was especially great. The camps had 35 libraries, 41 choruses, 13 orchestras, 33 theatrical groups, and 3 professional troupes. They staged over 1400 plays, 900 concerts, and 350 cultural-commemorative events (*akademii*). A vibrant if qualitatively uneven press produced about 230 periodicals and over 800 books. Young DP's also plunged into other activities. Forced to delay marriages and childbirth by the conditions of war, they established families at a rapid rate.

But the hothouse atmosphere of the camps also brought out negative features among the DP's. Forced to live in close proximity, West and East (Soviet) Ukrainians became painfully aware of the considerable social, cultural, and psychological differences between them. The Catholic-Orthodox split only exacerbated the problem. Most destructive were the feuds that broke out among the numerous political parties that emerged in the camps.

Between 1947 and 1951 the resettlement of the DP's to their permanent homes occurred. The approximate numbers of those

A group of Ukrainian Americans in Philadelphia, including Helen Stogryn, left, and Ray Karbiwnyk, centre, and Maria Omelian, prepare relief packages for their brethren in the DP camps.

who left Germany and Austria for various countries were as follows: United States, 80,000; Canada, 30,000; Australia, 20,000; Great Britain, 20,000; Belgium, 10,000; France, 10,000; Brazil, 7000; Argentina, 6000. Many of those who went to Britain, France, Belgium, and Latin America eventually settled in North America.

North America's Ukrainians and the DP's

As soon as they learned about the plight of the Ukrainian DP's, their compatriots in North America prepared to help. By late 1944, both umbrella organizations, the UCCA and the UCC, established aid committees. The American organization was called the United Ukrainian American Relief Committee (UUARC) while its Canadian counterpart was called the Ukrainian Canadian Relief Fund (UCRF). However, they had hardly started collecting funds and lobbying their respective governments to ease immigration, when the pro-Communists launched, especially in Canada, an energetic campaign to block all aid. They had good reason to fear the influx of the staunchly anti-Communist refugees, for they and their firsthand accounts of Soviet brutality were certain to undermine Communist influence in Ukrainian communities.

The Third Wave

A Leftist View of the DP's

The Ukrainian nationalist and pro-fascist press in Canada and the United States has again renewed its clamorous appeals for money for the so-called Ukrainian refugees in Europe ...

'Extend a helping hand to our brothers,' shouts the nationalist press.

For Ukrainians who remember the nationalists' 'silence of the grave' during Hitler's temporary occupation of Ukraine, their present 'moving' appeals appear boringly ludicrous.

Whence, may we ask, this sudden 'feeling'? Why did they not reveal it when the Hitlerite hordes were tearing Ukraine apart? Why did they not appeal for funds to aid the Ukrainian people in their heroic struggle against the German intruder? Why do they not appeal for funds now to help Ukraine rebuild itself?

Because for them 'Ukraine' and the 'Ukrainian nation' are the refugees, those who do not wish to return to Ukraine, those who are fleeing from the Ukrainian people, those who served the Germans in oppressing, plundering and pillaging Ukraine.

Everything is clear. The betrayers of the interests of their people in Canada wish to rescue the traitors of the Ukrainian people in Europe from just punishment for crimes against Ukraine. That is why they appeal so vociferously and so dishonestly for money for the so-called refugees who can no longer seek refuge under the wings of Hitler, Goebbels, Himmler or Rosenberg.

But he who donates money for this purpose will be helping war criminals to escape just punishment, will be opposing the vital interests of Ukraine and will be an accomplice in the further betrayal of his own people.

Ukrainske zhyttia, *a leftist publication,* 1945

Representatives of the Ukrainian Canadian Relief Fund visiting Ukrainian DP's in Augustdorf, Westphalia, in 1949.

The rationale of the pro-Communists was simplistic: essentially they argued that since the DP's fled from the Soviets or refused to return to their Soviet-occupied homeland, they must be Nazi henchmen. Following the general Soviet line regarding non-returnees, the pro-Communist press in Canada labelled the Ukrainian DP's as 'traitors,' 'enemies of the people,' and 'war criminals.' Several leading Canadian newspapers and influential parliamentarians accepted these allegations as fact, thereby greatly complicating the aid campaign.

In the United States the pro-Communists raised similar objections but with much less success. However, concerns about allowing DP's to immigrate to the United States were heard from other sources. Veterans groups, fearful of competion for jobs and housing, voiced their reservations. And a number of influential Jewish Americans accused Ukrainians and other East European DP's of collaboration with the Nazis. Typical of their statements was the one by Koppel Pinson of the American Jewish Joint Distribution Committee who wrote that 'a large group of Poles, Ukrainians, Russians and Balts' in the DP camps 'are some of the bloodiest henchmen of the SS and the Gestapo' (Kuropas, 398). Thus, in the controversies about DP's, the myth of Ukrainian 'war criminals,' which echoed Soviet-inspired propaganda, was born.

'Going to America.' The noted cartoonist Eko depicts the DP 'hurry-up-and-wait' process of emigrating to the United States.

The Third Wave

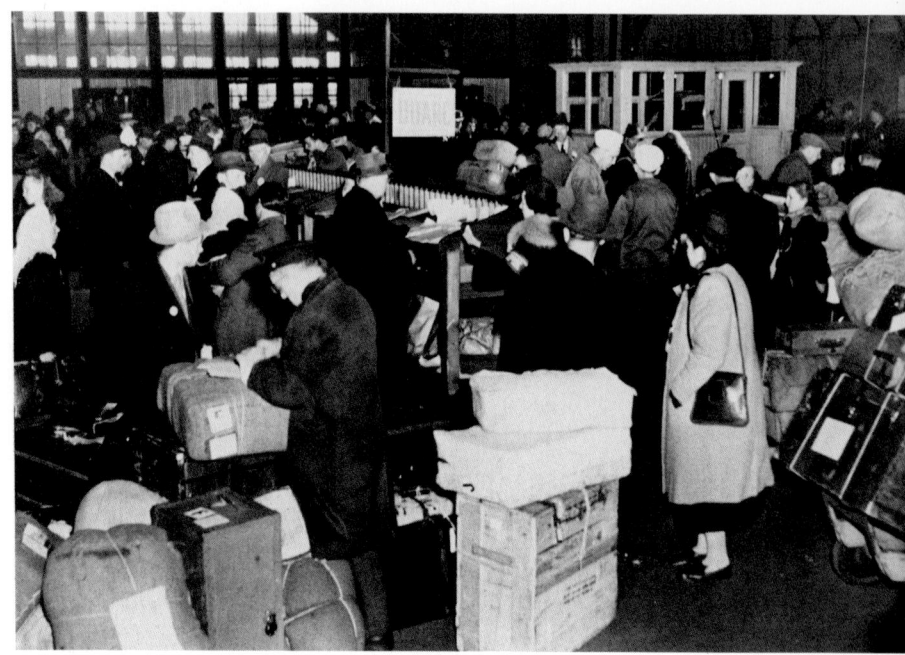

Upon arrival in New York City harbour, DP's gather their luggage and prepare for the formalities of entering the United States.

A Nationalist Defence of DP's

> Few people realize that our local Bolsheviks, especially those of Ukrainian background, defame the Ukrainian immigrants and unceasingly agitate against allowing them into Canada primarily because these people are fiercely anti-Bolshevik. In their homeland, they have experienced on their own skin the 'fruits' of the Bolshevik regime. Finding themselves abroad, they consider repatriation to their Soviet-rule homeland to be the greatest evil and misfortune. They can no longer be fooled by Communist propaganda. On the contrary, they can serve as the greatest contradiction of this propaganda ... They are needed not only by the Ukrainians in Canada, but by all Canadians.
>
> Novyi shliakh, *a Nationalist newspaper, 1947*

A DP family, bearing the identification buttons of the United Ukrainian American Relief Committee, arrives in New York City, c. 1949.

But there was also cooperation with Jewish groups on the DP issue. Desirous of bringing over a large number of Jewish DP's, the American Jewish Committee sponsored a campaign to create public sympathy for refugees in general. Other groups and charitable organizations, including the Ukrainians, joined in and the pro-DP lobby carried the day. By 1948, a bill was passed that allowed 205,000 DP's (later the number was raised to 395,000) to enter the United States. To ensure that undesirable elements were excluded, an elaborate screening process was applied. Meanwhile, in Canada, where the UCC and Anthony Hlynka, a member of Parliament whom some called 'the guardian angel of the Third Immigration,' energetically supported the immigration of DP's, things moved more quickly. In a decisive hearing in 1946, where both UCC and its pro-Communist rivals presented lengthy briefs, the Senate Committee decided in favour of the former. A year later, the first refugees began to arrive in Canada.

Troop-ships were the most prevalent mode of transportation, especially for those going to the United States. Although austere, they were certainly more comfortable than the steerage accommodations of the earliest immigrants. For the most part, the points of entry were New York and, in Canada, Halifax. The growing influx of the DP's reached its high point in 1948–9.

In 1948 a Boston newspaper featured a Ukrainian DP couple obviously grateful for their arrival in the United States.

The Third Wave

Resettlement

The resettlement of the DP's from the American and French zones of occupation was handled largely by UUARC, while the UCRF dealt with those in the British zone. Both were greatly aided by Ukrainians in the Canadian armed forces who, led by G.R.B. Panchuk and Stanley Frolick, transformed their club in London into a forepost of the North American relief organizations. The latter, and particularly the UUARC, found sponsors for the prospective immigrants, processed them in Europe, met and oriented them on arrival in North America, and sent them on to inland centres (usually community and church halls) where they were lodged until ready to strike out on their own. Ukrainian Catholic relief organizations were also actively involved in this effort. All in all, by the early 1950s, over 80,000 Ukrainians had come to the United States and about 34,000 to Canada.

The process of resettling the DP's was, in many ways, unique in Ukrainian immigration history. It was not, as earlier, a spontaneous movement of individuals or families who struck out on their own into the unknown. Already a cohesive group, the DP's arrived in North America with the aid of a well-organized effort on the part of their compatriots. Awaiting them were established communities and helpful countrymen. Despite this support, the initial period in the new land was fraught with difficulties that the new arrivals, like all immigrants, had to deal with on their own.

The DP's gravitated to large, urban centres, especially those that had large Ukrainian communities. In the United States this meant that New York received an especially large influx, making it the largest centre of Ukrainians in the country. Other favoured destinations were Philadelphia, Chicago, Detroit, Cleveland, Rochester, Buffalo, and Syracuse. Within these cities the DP's clustered in neighbourhoods where their compatriots from previous immigrations already lived and where Ukrainian churches existed. As in the interwar period, the small mining towns of Pennsylvania, the destination of the original immigrants, attracted relatively few of the newcomers.

A similar settlement pattern was evident in Canada. Toronto and the surrounding area received the vast bulk – close to 50 per

Checking for War Criminals

L. Scopes, British Foreign Office, to Canada House,
4 September 1950, Replying to Canadian Enquiry
with Respect to the 14th Galician Grenadier Division ...

CONFIDENTIAL

Sir,
With reference to your letter No. AR 408/7 of the 21st August regarding Ukrainian refugees now in the United Kingdom who formerly served in the German armed forces, I am directed by Mr Secretary Bevin to inform you that while in Italy these men were screened by Soviet and British missions and that neither then nor subsequently has any evidence been brought to light which would suggest that any of them fought against the Western Allies or engaged in crimes against humanity. Their behaviour since they came to this country has been good and they have never indicated in any way that they are infected with any trace of Nazi ideology ...

From the reports of the special mission set up by the War Office to screen these men, it seems clear that they volunteered to fight against the Red Army from nationalistic motives which were given greater impetus by the behaviour of the Soviet authorities during their earlier occupation of the Western Ukraine after the Nazi-Soviet Pact. Although Communist propaganda has constantly attempted to depict these, like so many other refugees, as 'quislings' and 'war criminals' it is interesting to note that no specific charges of war crimes have been made by the Soviet or any other Government against any member of this group ...

[sgd.] L. Scopes

* * *

MINUTES

29 August, [1950]

As will be seen from WR 2384 02685 (1947), these charges have been made against these Ukrainians before, but there is nothing to show that there is any truth in them. Let us inform Canada House of the facts at our disposal.

[sgd.] A.W.H. Wilkinson

cent – of the refugees. Winnipeg, Montreal, Sudbury, and Windsor absorbed much of the rest. Thus, the distribution of Ukrainians in Canada took on a decidedly eastward and urban shift. But unlike in the United States, many of the new arrivals had to delay settlement in urban centres by one or two years in order to pay off the costs of transportation by working in isolated lumber camps, on railways, and in mines. This requirement, plus more promising employment opportunities, attracted much of the intelligentsia to the United States.

Compared to the early immigrants, the Third Wave had a much easier time settling in. It was not the empty prairies or grim mines that they encountered but the far less demanding environment of the large, urban centres, with their various immigrant aid societies, social services, and established Ukrainian communities. With opportunities to obtain a higher education or to improve qualifications readily available, many commenced or continued their university studies soon after arrival. For the children there were, in the large cities, Ukrainian parochial schools (although most attended public and regular Catholic schools). And adults could count on the aid of sponsors, families, and friends in finding work. In most places where they settled there was the comforting presence of Ukrainian parishes and churches.

This is not to say that adaption came easily. Even the most educated had to start out by taking menial jobs. Frequently former lawyers, physicians, or professors found themselves washing dishes in restaurants or sweeping floors in office buildings. As the economy slowed down in the late 1940s, even these jobs were not easy to find. Moreover, the disorientation and depression that the highly educated suffered over their drop in social status was often painful and debilitating. While those with technical training, such as physicians or engineers, often obtained appropriate work, lawyers, teachers, and scholars found little demand for their skills. Indeed, the less educated manual workers, who had a ready market for their labour, often adapted to the new environment more successfully than did the intelligentsia. Unable to find appropriate employment, many of the latter gravitated to poorly paid positions in Ukrainian organizations and institutions.

After the initial wave of warm feeling, relations between 'old immigrants' and new arrivals often soured as a common ethnic

'The First Transport of Farmers to America.' Because those with a farming background were given preference by the U.S. immigration authorities, many dubious 'farmers' appeared among the DP's.

background failed to overcome the great social, political, and cultural differences between them. Usually of blue-collar and peasant background, 'old immigrants' were put off by what they perceived as the upper-class mannerisms of the newly arrived intelligentsia. Recalling the hardships of their own early days in the New World, they resented the newcomers' unwillingness to go through a similar experience and their aspirations to white-collar jobs and higher education. After having fought hard for decades to maintain their ethnic heritage, they were irritated by the condescending attitudes of the DP's to their poor command of Ukrainian and insufficient nationalistic fervour. For their part, the newcomers were impatient with the widespread assimilation and the ethnic inferiority complexes of their predecessors.

The attitudes of the old immigrants and the new arrivals towards American or Canadian society in general also differed markedly. Among the former, especially those who belonged to the First Wave, the lifestyle of the English-speakers was generally recognized to be more highly developed than their own. The DP's, especially those with a higher education, often did not share this view. Familiar with European culture, they were not impressed with the cultural standards of the usually lower-class or, at best, middle-class Americans and Canadians they came into contact with. And they were often astounded by their political naïveté, particularly regarding the Soviets. Consequently, educated DP's were much less likely to develop the feeling of cultural inferiority vis-à-vis the English-speakers that was widespread among the early Ukrainian immigrants to North America

THE ORGANIZATIONAL UPSURGE

The DP's were pre-organized when they arrived in North America, that is, they brought many of their organizations with them from Europe. Indeed, few newcomers to the New World were as cohesively and tightly knit as these post–Second World War refugees. Over 40 per cent of the youth, 60 per cent of the

Newly arrived DP's swelled the ranks of the more than 300 delegates at the fourth convention of the Ukrainian Congress Committee of America (UCCA) in Washington, DC, 1949.

adults, and about 70 per cent of the women belonged to one or more organizations. This predilection for organization can be explained, in part, by the fact that a large number of the community activists and leaders from Western Ukraine, and especially Galicia, which had a strong tradition of grass-roots organization, were included in this latest wave of newcomers.

Another important factor was that, during the hiatus of four to five years in the refugee camps of Germany and Austria, the DP's had ample opportunity to re-create, on a smaller scale, some of the associations and institutions that had existed at home. When the time came to go overseas, they systematically prepared to re-establish them in the new environment. Moreover, upon reaching Canada and the United States, the new arrivals did not have to expend their energies on building churches and schools since these were already in place thanks to the efforts of their predecessors. Another striking feature of the DP organizational network was that it was not limited to North America alone; it extended to Australia, Latin America, Great Britain, France, and Germany, wherever the refugees found a home.

The earliest of the DP institutions in America was Samopomich (Self-Reliance), a cooperative that was established in New York in 1947. Its goal was to provide the newly arrived with advice and information about housing and employment possibilities. Since

Prime Minister Louis St Laurent addressing the Fourth Ukrainian Canadian Congress, Winnipeg, 1953.

the cooperative placed special emphasis on developing a material base for aiding the community, this led to the creation of a network of credit unions that used part of their profits to support cultural and social activities. Thus, at the outset, the New York branch of Samopomich served as a core around which youth, women's, professional, and cultural groups formed and quickly developed into independent organizations.

The churches

The influx of DP's, with hundreds of priests among them, could not but exert a major impact on the Ukrainian churches in North America. There was, as might be expected, a rise in church membership, with that of the Ukrainian Catholics reaching close to 280,000 in the United States and about 190,000 in Canada. Another effect was that the churches became more avowedly Ukrainian. This was especially true of the Greek Catholic church, which had previously exhibited a strong tendency to adopt Roman Catholic ways. A galvanizing force in the movement to reassert the distinctiveness of the Ukrainian church was Archbishop and later Cardinal Josef Slipyj. Released from Siberian captivity in 1963, he took up residence in Rome. From there he

Ukrainian Catholic Bishop Basil Losten serves communion to young Plast members at their summer camp in East Chatham in the 1970s.

The Third Wave

Cardinal Josef Slipyj meets with President Gerald Ford in the White House, 1976.

Cardinal Josef Slipyj, the leader of the Ukrainian Catholic church who was released from Soviet imprisonment in Siberia in 1963, arrives to an enthusiastic welcome in Philadelphia, 1968.

worked energetically to unite the Ukrainian Catholics thoughout the West into an autonomous ecclesiastical body. By the late 1960s the Ukrainian church began to hold regular synods of its bishops. Supported enthusiastically by many of the newcomers, in the mid-1970s Slipyj adopted the title of patriarch and made a bid to establish a Ukrainian Eastern-rite patriarchate. Although the Vatican refused to sanction the creation of the patriarchate (and the American-born Ukrainian Catholic clergy was noticeably lukewarm in supporting it), the Holy See was, none the less, forced to pay greater heed to Ukrainian Catholic demands for special status. Meanwhile, in many parishes, newly arrived priests and laity sought to limit Latin-rite influences and to restore traditional Eastern-rite practices. This inevitably rekindled the old debates over married priests and the use of the Old versus the New Style calendar. In any case, these highly emotional controversies drove home the point to those who had hoped for the eventual amalgamation of the Ukrainian Catholics into the Latin-rite church that they would have to postpone their expectations indefinitely.

North America's Ukrainian Orthodox also benefited greatly from the new wave of immigrants. From the outset, they had had great difficulties finding suitable hierarchy and clergy. The latter could be found among the DP's not only in considerable quantity

With the bitter religious conflicts that wracked the Ukrainian communities in North America a thing of the past, Catholic Metropolitan Stephen Sulyk and the Orthodox Metropolitan Mstyslav Skrypnyk jointly officiate at a memorial service for the victims of the 1933 famine. South Bound Brook, New Jersey, 1983.

but also of impressive quality. This was because much of the leadership of the Ukrainian Autocephalous Orthodox church, which was renewed in Ukraine in 1942, was forced to flee from the Soviets. Thus, the eminent churchman and scholar Ilarion (Ivan Ohienko) became, in 1947, the metropolitan of the Ukrainian Greek Orthodox church in Canada. He and his associates contributed greatly to improving the intellectual level and training of his church's clergy. Meanwhile, in the United States, another recently arrived hierarch, Mstyslav (Stepan Skrypnyk), aided the ageing Bishop Teodorovych and, in 1971, took over the helm, with the title of metropolitan, of the Ukrainian Orthodox church in that country. Enlivened by the newcomers, the church, which in 1971 had over 90,000 members, greatly improved its organizational structure and expanded its new centre in South Bound Brook, New Jersey. The latter included the consistory, memorial church, a museum, a seminary affiliated with Rutgers University, and a cemetery where many prominent Ukrainians of all faiths would choose to be buried.

The Ukrainian Protestants, consisting of small, tightly knit, and highly religious Baptist communities, united in the Ukrainian Evangelical Alliance and, led by Pastor Oleksa Harbuziuk, also made noteworthy progress in the postwar period.

St Andrew's Memorial Church at the Ukrainian Orthodox centre in South Bound Brook, New Jersey. The church was built as a memorial to Ukrainian heroes and martyrs, and especially the victims of the Great Famine of 1933.

The Third Wave

Fiery political speeches were a standard feature on occasions such as this SUM conclave in Fox Chase, near Philadelphia, in 1952.

Politics

Since it was political convulsions rather than economic pressures that brought the Third Wave to North American shores, politics remained for many of its members an object of passionate concern and involvement. Having been exposed, often in traumatic fashion, to the Soviet and Nazi regimes and then having experienced North American democracy, the refugees were, by and large, highly sensitive to ideological issues.

There were, furthermore, among them many who had been active, even prominent, players in the dramatic political events that enveloped Ukraine during the first half of the twentieth century. They included ageing members of the short-lived Ukrainian governments of the 1917–20 period, who, after spending decades in exile in Czechoslovakia, Poland, France, and Germany, fled westward before the advancing Soviets; leaders of the large, legal, liberal interwar Galician parties such as UNDO, several of whom had served as parliamentarians and senators in the Polish parliament; prominent intellectuals from Soviet Ukraine who had managed to survive the murderous 1930s; members of the Carpatho-Ukrainian government that had briefly attained independence in 1939; and, most numerous and active, the members of the OUN underground who in the Second World War had fought the Poles,

Part of the festivities at the first World Congress of Free Ukrainians (WCFU) held in New York City in 1967.

Germans, and Soviets. Not suprisingly, many of them had politics in their blood.

Involvement in politics was, in general, narrowly circumscribed: it focused exclusively on issues relating to Ukraine and Ukrainians. Almost none of the DP's made a concerted effort to participate in the political processes of their host countries. For them, the key concerns were how to help their homeland obtain independence and, more immediately, how to establish themselves and their factions as the leaders in their communities of the liberation struggle. As might be expected, almost all the DP's were staunchly, sometimes virulently, anti-Soviet. But this point was one of the few the various political factions could agree on. For the most part, they tended to expend their considerable energies on blaming each other for political mistakes that were made in the homeland and for failure to consolidate their efforts abroad. In short, they succumbed, with great gusto, to the kind of internal squabbles that are characteristic of all political emigrations.

There were, to be sure, attempts to cooperate. At the initiative of Reverend Basil Kushnir and the Ukrainian Canadian Committee a serious effort to bring the fractious political groups together into a kind of parliament-in-exile was made already in Germany in 1947–8, before departure for North America. After lengthy negotiations, the Ukrainian National Council was formed to unite

The Third Wave

the liberals, socialists, and nationalists (only the monarchists refused to join) in a single body that would coordinate the political activities of Ukrainians in the West. But by 1950, the most powerful group in the council, the Bandera faction of the OUN, pulled out. Despite efforts of the Ukrainian Congress Committee of America (UCCA) in the early 1950s to reconstitute it, the Council and most of its constituent parties gradually receded into oblivion.

This failure highlighted an emerging pattern in the relationship among the political factions of the Third Wave. On the one hand, there were the various groups of liberals, socialists, monarchists, and moderate nationalists whose ideologies were generally considered to be, more or less, irrelevant in the current conditions and whose membership, while containing some prominent individuals, was very limited. Although frequently at odds with each other, they were often willing to cooperate or at least coordinate their activities and to accept democratic, pluralistic principles if only because each was too weak to stand on its own. On the other hand, there were the Nationalists of OUN, especially the Bandera faction, which frequently sought to establish its political and ideological hegemony over the entire emigration. Although they failed to gain a substantial following among the intelligentsia, the Banderites did exert a strong influence among the peasants and labourers who constituted the majority of the refugees, which made them a force to be reckoned with among the DP's.

Since the Bandera faction was much stronger than the other groups, it felt no need to compromise with them. Consequently, political and non-political undertakings often degenerated into manoeuvres in which non-Banderites sought to neutralize Banderite influence. Meanwhile, the latter usually attempted a take-over of a worthwhile project or institution. If they failed, the Banderites would often attempt to undermine it or set up their own.

Several factors accounted for Banderite influence. Because of their links with the Ukrainian Insurgent Army (UPA) underground that was still fighting against Soviet rule in the early 1950s, the Banderites laid claim to the leading role in the struggle for liberating the homeland. Their militancy appealed to many, particularly the youth. Moreover, the Banderites successfully established a widespread, tightly knit, and disciplined organizational network among the DP's.

The massed choirs and orchestras of the leftist Association of United Ukrainians of Canada at a festival in Toronto, 1951.

At its core was the semi-conspiratorial OUN-R (Revolutionary) party which controlled a series of affiliated organizations, foremost of which were the Organization for the Defense of Four Freedoms for Ukraine in the United States and the League for the Liberation of Ukraine in Canada. Established in 1947, the American organization had 29 branches and 2300 members by 1955; fifteen years later the number had risen to 48 branches and 8500 members. In Canada, the League for the Liberation of Ukraine was founded in 1948; by 1961 it had over 3000 members, most of whom were concentrated in Ontario. In addition, both American and Canadian organizations had youth, women's, and student affiliates. Rounding out the organizational network were credit unions and cooperatives in the larger centres, and a multifaceted press that included the Toronto-based *Homin Ukrainy*, a weekly that quickly grew to a readership of over 10,000. Regular collection of membership dues and frequent fund drives provided the

Banderites with financial resources that were much greater than those of their rivals.

The Banderites' quantitative assets were offset by qualitative deficiencies. Their authoritarian attitudes — all the more glaring in the context of North American society — not only alienated the community as a whole, but also led many talented activists to abandon their ranks. As a result, there was a dearth of politically skilled, well-educated talent in the leadership. Consequently, the Banderites' frequently heavy-handed efforts to establish predominance in the community were repeatedly rebuffed.

Implacably opposed to the Banderites were the Melnykites. As is often true between bitter enemies, they had much in common. Both were factions of a single organization, the OUN, which during the 1930s and the Second World War in Western Ukraine was the main proponent of militant nationalism. However, in 1939 OUN split, with older, more established members tending to follow Andrii Melnyk — hence the term *Melnykivtsi* — while the younger, more revolutionary members sided with Stepan Bandera and came to be called *Banderivtsi*. Throughout the war and during the DP period the two Nationalist factions continued to vie with each other, often in a most uncompromising and underhanded fashion. The resulting bitterness carried over to North America and became a central, recurrent feature in the internal politics of the new arrivals.

Unable to match their rivals in dynamism or numerical strength, the Melnykites liked to think that they were politically more sophisticated and, in terms of their links to the founders of OUN, more legitimate. In establishing themselves in North America, the Melnykites had, at the outset, certain advantages. Because the interwar Nationalist organizations in both the United States and Canada recognized Andrii Melnyk as the legitimate successor of Evhen Konovalets, the revered founder of OUN, they sided with the newly arrived Melnykites. In the United States, this meant that ODVU, the interwar Nationalist organization, which was revived in 1946, provided them with an organizational base. Moreover, other interwar organizations such as MUN and the Gold Cross also became part of the Melnykite camp.

The Melnykites, however, were unable to capitalize on this ready-made organizational base. On the one hand, the interwar

Nationalist organizations were only a shadow of their former selves, since most of the original, interwar membership had abandoned them because of advancing age, disinterest, or assimilation. On the other hand, the newly arrived Melnykites tended to have too many 'chiefs' who engaged in 'high politics' and too few 'Indians' who were willing to perform nitty-gritty organizational work on the grass-roots level.

In Canada, the situation was markedly different. There the old immigrants maintained, to a much greater degree than in the United States, their involvement in community life and, specifically, in such interwar Nationalist organizations as the UNF, which became the Melnykite stronghold. In the 1950s, UNF encompassed over 5000 members and maintained a wide range of activities such as summer camps, heritage schools, and dance groups. In Winnipeg, the organization supported the impressive Ukrainian Cultural and Educational Centre – Oseredok – and in Toronto it published the weekly *Novyi Shliakh*. Moreover, the newcomers helped to lay the foundations for a series of well-run and prospering credit unions. And a number of UNF-affiliated organizations, such as USH, OUK, and MUN, helped raise membership in the pro-Melnykite camp to an estimated 8000. Consequently, in Canada the two Nationalist factions were more evenly balanced. Furthermore, the still numerous activists from the pre–Second World War immigrations strove to prevent their constant feuding from exerting an overly deleterious effect on Ukrainian-Canadian community life as a whole.

An especially telling example of the impact that the different political constellations had within the postwar Ukrainian-American and Ukrainian-Canadian communities emerged in 1980s when the Banderites and their sympathizers gained control of the UCCA; a counter-organization, the Ukrainian American Coordinating Council (UUCC), was formed. Because of this split, Ukrainian Americans were deprived of a single, effective, generally recognized body that could legitimately claim to represent them all. Meanwhile, in Canada no single group was strong enough to dominate the internal politics of the Ukrainian community and this allowed UCC to function effectively as coordinating body within the community and its representative within Canadian society.

From a Report in a Leftist Newspaper

Marauding Nazi DP's on Loose

Timmins – The violence and terror of fascism was let loose in this city on Sunday, 11 December. As in Winnipeg eight weeks ago, more than 100 DP's launched an organized assault on the local hall of the Association of United Ukrainian Canadians. Similar assaults were attempted in Sudbury and South Porcupine.

Bricks, rocks and big chunks of ice were thrown through the windows of the Timmins hall into the midst of a meeting of Ukrainian Canadians – among them women and children.

The DP's used a sixteen-foot stair railing to smash down the doors of the hall. They seized Tom Kremyr, one of the leading members of the AUUC, threw him down the steps and put the boots to him. Kremyr is now in hospital with broken ribs and possible internal injuries. Seven others, including a bystander by the name of Mackenzie were injured. Mike Klapushchak required hospital treatment ...

In Sudbury on 7 December, twenty-five DP's began a similar organized attempt to disrupt an AUUC meeting, but a dozen police expelled them. In South Porcupine on Sunday afternoon a well-organized fascist DP gang tried three times, unsuccessfully, to break up an AUUC meeting. The DP's were finally dispersed by the police ...

Canadian Tribune, 1949

This is not to say that the existence of the two Nationalist factions was an unmitigated calamity that beset the post–Second World War Ukrainian communities. The Banderites and Melnykites had in their ranks many committed and patriotic Ukrainians. Especially impressive was the dedication of the factions' rank-and-file membership who, year after year, committed, without recompense or recognition, enormous effort, time, and money to the Ukrainian cause. Most of them sincerely believed that their group's tactics were not, as critics proclaimed, an attempt to gain hegemony within the Ukrainian communities but simply the most effective way of working for the liberation of Ukraine from abroad. Furthermore, the various affiliated organizations that the two Nationalist factions created added greatly to the infrastructure of the Ukrainian communities. Their dynamism forced rivals to match their efforts. And their undoubted commitment greatly strengthened the sense of mission that was a key characteristic of the Third Wave.

The rapid growth of the Nationalists in the post–Second World War era coincided with the steady and irreversible decline of the Ukrainian Left. In the United States it had practically disappeared by the 1960s, while in Canada, where the pro-Communists were much stronger, it managed to hold on for several decades longer. Initially, in the 1950s, when Canada's Ukrainian leftists were still willing to confront the Nationalists, clashes between the two camps were frequent and, at times, violent. But it was the latter who usually went on the offensive. And by the 1970s it was evident the ULFTA's old dynamism was quickly disappearing. Several factors accounted for this decline. As the Cold War set in, it became increasingly difficult, simply in terms of social pressure, to maintain pro-Communist views and positions. Moreover, Soviet behaviour such as the invasion of Czechoslovakia in 1968 and the systematic Russification of Ukraine greatly disillusioned many erstwhile sympathizers. Finally, because almost all the members of the Left belonged to the First and, even more so, Second Waves, their children were undergoing assimilation, political as well as cultural, into mainstream Canadian society. Consequently, the ULFTA lacked the fresh, young forces that the recently arrived Nationalists clearly had.

Young plastuny (scouts) at meal time at the Plast camp in East Chatham, New York, in 1954.

The raising of the American and Ukrainian flags at a Plast ceremony in East Chatham in the mid-1970s. The church in the background is modelled on those found in the Carpathian Mountains.

Youth groups

The DP's showed great concern for their youth since, in the view of many community leaders, its future role was to right the wrongs that the nation had suffered. This meant that assimilation was to be avoided at all costs. And one of the most effective means of doing so was to provide youth with an all-encompassing Ukrainian environment. Besides these patriotic reasons, there were pragmatic considerations. The involvement of their children in these organizations, especially in their summer camps, was a godsend to parents who usually had to work long hours to make ends meet. Moreover, as noted above, many of the newcomers had a low opinion of the behaviour and upbringing of North American youth and they hoped to isolate their children from the

Novaky, the youngest members of Plast, in a march past at East Chatham, NY, 1970s.

'demoralizing influence of the street.' Consequently, youth organizations, which were well established in the DP camps, were among the earliest to reappear in North America.

Plast, a scouting organization for boys and girls, had a venerable history. Founded in Galicia in 1911, it appealed especially to the children of the urban intelligentsia and many prominent individuals in Western Ukraine emerged from its ranks. Although it stressed patriotism, the organization was apolitical. None the less, it was banned by the Polish government during much of the interwar period. Re-created in the DP camps, it attracted about 10 per cent of the youth into its ranks. In 1948, as soon as large groups of DP's began to arrive, Plast groups sprang up in both the United States and Canada. By 1953 Plast had about 2300 members in the former country and close to 1000 in the latter,

Participants of the 1987 Plast jamboree on a camping trip in Algonquin Park, Ontario.

Outdoor mass in Algonquin Park during the 1987 Plast jamboree.

The ecstatic response of girls belonging to a Plast kurin (unit) from New Jersey upon learning that they won a scouting competition. East Chatham, New York, 1973.

and it was still growing rapidly. The organization was also quick to obtain about half a dozen summer camps in the United States and Canada, the largest of which was located in East Chatham in upstate New York. Each year about 1000 members spent a large part of their summer in these camps. In major centres such as New York, Philadelphia, Cleveland, Detroit, Chicago, Toronto, Montreal, and Winnipeg, buildings were purchased to provide places for year-round activities.

Since Plast tended to attract members from among the more educated of the new arrivals, it acquired an undertone of élitism within the Ukrainian community. Despite pressure to adopt a more nationalistic stance, Plast resisted, continuing to emphasize scouting and the development of self-reliant, self-motivated individuals who were patriotic Ukrainians as well.

A Sudbury, Ontario, SUM unit at a ceremony marking the blessing of its flag in the early 1950s.

The other major youth organization was the Ukrainian Youth Association (SUM), founded in 1946 in the Augsburg DP camp by members of the Bandera faction of the OUN. An avowedly ideological organization, SUM had as a goal the inculcation of youth with the principles, aspirations, and values of Ukrainian Nationalism. Taking 'God and Country' as its slogan, it stressed discipline and commitment to the cause among its members. To a great extent, SUM functioned in tandem with the Bandera OUN; while the latter attempted to establish its influence among the mass of adult refugees, most of whom were brought to Germany as forced labour, SUM concentrated on the 18–30 age group (later extended to 6–35).

Older members of SUM at attention, Acton, Ontario, 1950s. The impact of the Second World War and the commitment to the struggle for the liberation of Ukraine led to the stress on militarism in all DP youth organizations.

The presidium, including, on the extreme left, Iaroslav Stetsko, the leader of the Bandera faction of OUN, at the first major SUM rally in Canada, Toronto, 1952.

The Third Wave

With slogans proclaiming 'Freedom for nations' and 'Freedom for individuals' in the background, young members of SUM energetically perform the traditional Ukrainian hopak. The initials ABN stand for the Anti-Bolshevik Bloc of Nations, a militantly anti-Soviet organization of East European émigrés in which the Banderites played a leading role. Acton, Ontario, c. 1970.

The SUM Pledge

I, a son (daughter) of the great Ukrainian nation, solemnly swear before God and Ukraine, never to sully the honor of my nation and the blood of the millions of fallen fighters of the Association of Ukrainian Youth.

I swear to devote all my efforts and my knowledge for the struggle for an independent Ukrainian state. Therefore, when the proper moment shall arrive, I will proudly serve, with weapons in my hands, only under my national flag in the first cohorts of the Ukrainian Liberation Army and I will not lay down my weapons until I will drive out the last occupier from the sacred territory of my fatherland.

I commit myself to be a disciplined member of SUM and to fulfill uncompromisingly all the orders of my superiors.

From a SUM publication, 1954

Ukrainian-Canadian students at an anti-Soviet demonstration in Ottawa in the 1970s protesting against the repression of Ukrainian intellectuals.

By the time the exodus overseas began, SUM had almost twice as many members as Plast. The earliest North American branches were established in 1948 in Toronto and a year later in Philadelphia. By 1951, the rapidly growing organization had over 8000 members worldwide, of which 2500 were in the United States and 1400 in Canada. To add to its appeal, it borrowed some of Plast's scouting features but retained its militantly nationalist stance. It, too, acquired buildings and camp grounds, the best known of which is located in Ellenville, New York. Relations between these two major youth organizations were competitive and cool, but generally correct.

A third, much smaller organization was the Ukrainian National Democratic League (ODUM). Unlike Plast and SUM, which had a largely West Ukrainian membership, it consisted of East Ukrainians. Combining patriotism with emphasis on democratic values, its members also attended summer camps, although they placed less emphasis on discipline than did the other two organizations. After its establishment in New York in 1950 it spread to Canada, Germany, England, and Australia, and by the late 1950s it had a worldwide membership of about 2000.

Students were somewhat slower to organize since few had the linguistic skills or financial resources to enter universities immediately upon arrival. But by early 1950s, there were more than thirty student clubs and groups in American colleges and universities, and in 1953 they founded a coordinating body, the Federation of Ukrainian Student Organizations of America (SUSTA). Of its 500 members, only 60 were American-born. SUSTA also included student groups with ideological or religious affiliations such as the Ukrainian Student Association of Mikhnovsky (TUSM) and Zarevo, which were linked with, respectively, the Banderite and Melnykite factions of OUN, as well as Obnova, a Catholic group. Similarly, in Canada in 1953 representatives of about twenty student clubs met in Winnipeg to form the Ukrainian Canadian University Students Union (SUSK). Unlike its American counterpart, SUSK had a relatively high proportion of Canadian-born among its members. By the early 1960s, it encompassed about 800 of the 4000 Ukrainians studying in Canadian colleges and universities.

Professional groups

Given the relatively large number of professionals among the DP's and the fact that they had already formed professional organizations in the camps, it was not long before such groups were reconstituted in North America. Between 1948 and 1950 a series of professional associations did, in fact, emerge. Especially prominent were the Ukrainian Engineers Society (1948) and Ukrainian Medical Association of North America (1950), each of which eventually had a membership numbering over five hundred. Similar societies were formed by lawyers, university professors, librarians, teachers, and journalists. Businessmen's clubs appeared even before some of their members had established businesses. Initially, these associations concentrated on helping their members find employment, raise their qualifications, and obtain professional certification. In time they held conferences in their areas of interest and provided support for a wide range of community projects.

The impact the DP's had on the occupational profile of the Ukrainian-American community was reflected in the following statistics: in the 1930s there were only 25 physicians, 20 engineers, 40 lawyers, 200 schoolteachers, and less than 10 professors

Passing on the art of Ukrainian Easter egg decoration from generation to generation. Windsor, Ontario, 1970.

among the Ukrainian Americans. By the early 1960s, the number had risen to 1200 physicians, 700 engineers, 150 lawyers, 2000 teachers, and about 250 college and university professors. But while this was a vast improvement, Ukrainians in North America still lagged behind the Jews, Germans, Greeks, and Armenians in terms of the percentage of professionals among them.

Women's organizations

The post–Second World War influx greatly activated the women's organizations in the United States and Canada, although they were already heavily involved in resettling DP's. A major event in this area of activity was the creation in Philadelphia in 1948 of WCFU, a worldwide coordinating body of all Ukrainian women's organizations outside the Soviet bloc. Among the twelve founding organizations, the most influential and largest was the Ukrainian National Women's League (UNWL), which, as a result of the arrival of the new immigrants, expanded its ranks to about four thousand individual members. The UNWL also functioned in Canada, but it was not as widespread there as in the United States.

Members of the Ukrainian Canadian Servicemen's Association gather in 1945 in front of their London headquarters for the last time before returning home.

Veteran's and regional associations

An unusual variety of veterans groups emerged in the postwar period. Those Ukrainians who served in the armed forces of the United States formed veterans organizations. Canada's Ukrainian veterans were an especially tightly knit group. During the war about 5000 of them had belonged to the Ukrainian Canadian Veterans Club based in London, and in 1945 they quickly formed an association that allowed them to retain the ties they had forged in wartime. However, there was also an active and well-organized veterans group, the Brotherhood of the Former Soldiers of the First Ukrainian Division of the Ukrainian Army, which united those who had fought on the opposing side, in the 'Galicia' division of the German army. Finally, there was not one but two associations of veterans of the Ukrainian Insurgent Army (UPA), which had fought the Germans, Soviets, and Poles.

Yet another type of association that appeared frequently among the immigrants was the regional society which encompassed people from various towns and regions. The Lemkos, Transcarpathians or Carpatho-Ukrainians, Hutsuls, and Bukovynians all formed such associations. Since the Galicians were too numerous to unite in a single entity, they formed groups that united the former residents of cities and towns such as Lviv, Chortkiv, Berezhany, and Drohobych.

Heritage schools

Given the high level of national consciousness among the DP's, educating their youth in things Ukrainian was a priority. In doing so, they utilized the means that were already present in earlier immigrations but raised them to a higher organizational and intellectual level. Three types of schools were available to the immigrants: (1) the all-day parochial schools and high schools run by the Catholic church, (2) the Ukrainian heritage classes organized on Saturdays or Sundays by Catholic and Orthodox parishes, and (3) the non-denominational Saturday school of Ukrainian subjects commonly called Ridna Shkola. The Catholic schools, usually taught by North American–born nuns, invariably stressed religious education and downplayed Ukrainian subjects. Meanwhile, the resources of the parish-based courses were generally very limited. Consequently, DP's depended on the Ridna Shkola network to provide their children with a Ukrainian education, that is, instruction in language, literature, history, and geography. By the 1960s, there were over 50 such schools, with over 3500 students, in the United States. In Canada, where the tradition of the Ridna Shkola was stronger, it encompassed 8000 pupils in over 100 schools. Moreover, there were numerous higher-level Ukrainian studies courses, most notably in Toronto. SUM and UNF also organized heritage classes. While these courses were invariably on a higher level than those of the interwar period, they were, as might be expected, not on a par with regular schooling. And certainly the fact that students had to spend an extra day in school did not do much for the courses' popularity among them.

The Ukrainian Institute of America was founded by William Dzus, an industrialist, to promote Ukrainian culture. In 1955, Dzus donated this impressive mansion on New York City's Fifth Avenue to the institute.

A ballet school in New York City in the 1950s. While the DP's maintained a deep commitment to their folk art, they also sought to familiarize their young with classical culture.

Scholarship and culture

Prior to the arrival of the Third Wave, there were very few Ukrainian scholars and academics in North America. This changed dramatically when the DP's came, bringing along with them the scholarly societies they had established in Germany. First to be reconstituted was the Ukrainian Free Academy of Arts and Sciences (UVAN) in Winnipeg in 1949. It first president was the noted historian Dmytro Doroshenko. A year later, its American counterpart was established in New York under the leadership of Michael Vetukhiv and it soon attracted an impressive group of scholars in Ukrainian studies. While UVAN harkened back to the traditions of the All-Ukrainian Academy in Kiev, another scholarly association, the Shevchenko Scientific Society (NTSh), tried to carry on the work of its famous Galicia-based namesake. Although NTSh's main centre was moved from Germany to Paris in the mid-1950s where Volodymyr Kubiyovič directed its major project, the Ukrainian-language *Encyclopedia of Ukraine*, NTSh also established branches in New York and Winnipeg. Both scholarly institutions, but especially UVAN in New York, soon commenced an impressive publication program and provided a reputable forum for scholarly activity.

Valentina Pereyaslavec, formerly of the Kiev ballet, coaching Rudolf Nureyev in New York City, 1965.

The Dumka Choir of New York City in the 1950s.

The Third Wave

Led by Hryhory Kytasty and Volodymyr Bozhyk, the Ukrainian Bandurist ensemble, originally founded in Kiev and currently based in Detroit, has continued, since its arrival in North America in 1949, to delight audiences with its mastery of the bandura.

A performance by the Roma Pryma Bohachevsky ballet school at Soyuzivka, the UNA resort in the Catskills.

Among the new arrivals there were close to one hundred writers, poets, and literary critics. Moreover, there were dozens of painters and sculptors. Soon after arriving, they formed the Literary-Arts Club in New York, which provided a lively venue for demonstrating the fruits of their creativity. The great metropolitan centre, which quickly became the cultural capital of the new immigration, also became the home of the New York group of young poets. In addition, the Ukrainian Music Institute, several ballet schools, and Dumka, a first-rate chorus, were based in the city. Meanwhile, the Bandurist Capella, an ensemble that consisted of some of the best players of the *bandura* (a traditional Ukrainian instrument), made its home in Detroit, and frequently toured the major centres of the new immigration.

Sports

Given the many young people among them, sports was a popular activity with the DP's. Soon after their arrival, a series of clubs were formed that pursued such sports as soccer, volleyball, tennis, skiing, and track and field, as well as chess. Soccer was especially popular. Indeed, in this area Ukrainian teams achieved outstanding success, gaining dominance of the sport in North America in the late 1950s and early 1960s. Most impressive were the achievements of the Ukrainian Nationals, who represented the Trident Sports Club of Philadelphia. For four years (1960, 1961, 1963, and 1966) they won the soccer championship of the United States. New York's Ukrainian Sports Club did so in 1965, and Montreal's Ukraina Sports Club won the Canadian championship in 1957. Tennis and skiing were the specialties of the venerable Carpathian Ski Club, another of the associations originally founded in Western Ukraine and reconstituted in North America. The sports clubs eventually formed a coordinating body, the Association of Ukrainian Sports Clubs in North America (USCAK), which regularly organized tennis and swimming competitions at Soyuzivka, the UNA resort in the Catskills.

Members of the Ukrainian Nationals soccer team of Philadelphia shortly after winning the United States championship in 1960.

The Third Wave

Young participants in a Ukrainian festival in New York City, 1978.

A bilingual program class in Edmonton in 1987. The resources of the Canadian Institute of Ukrainian Studies at the University of Alberta helped to develop an innovative approach to bilingual Ukrainian-English teaching.

FROM ÉMIGRÉS TO ETHNICS

Compared to the organizational networks that the previous waves of immigrants had established, those of the Third Wave were clearly more multifaceted, comprehensive, and integrated. Almost from the outset, a multitude of organizations and associations emerged to address an unusually broad spectrum of the newcomers' interests, concerns, and needs. In the large centres like New York, Philadelphia, Chicago, Cleveland, Detroit, Toronto, Montreal, and Winnipeg one could attend church or engage in politics, borrow money or visit a doctor, send children to elementary schools and camps as well as ballet, music, or art classes, play tennis or ski, shop, or vacation – all in a Ukrainian context. Some institutions such as churches, schools, and fraternal associations were the products of earlier immigrations. But most of the organizations that created the backbone of the new, vibrant, and self-contained communities were the products of DP efforts and a reflection of their remarkable dynamism, an invigorating variety of social, religious, regional, and political components, and, most of all, commitment to the Cause.

An advertisement for income tax services in a Winnipeg shop window in the early 1980s.

The Third Wave

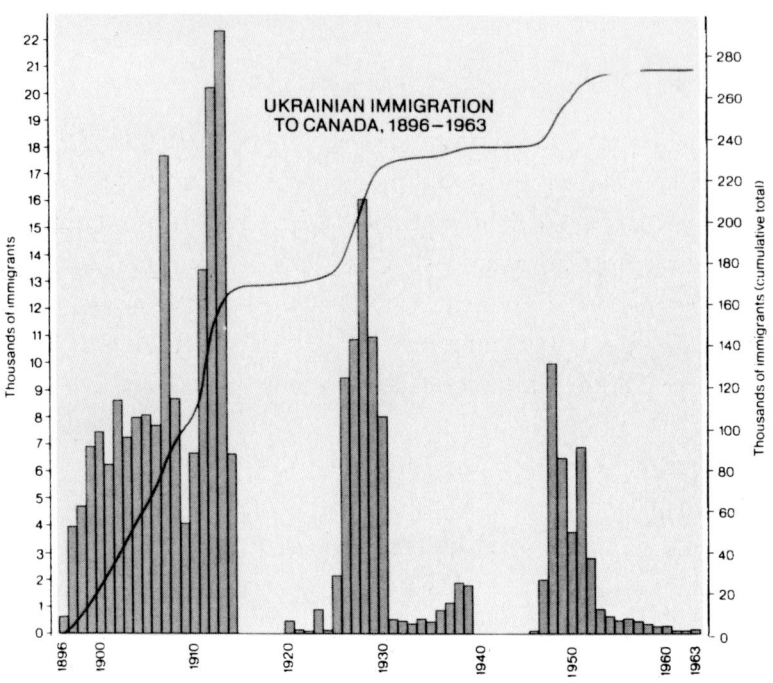

There was another noteworthy aspect of the DP organizational network: it was much more widespread than those of the earlier immigrations. The DP's were a tight-knit group. Many had close personal ties that reached back to their homeland or the refugee camps. Especially among the intelligentsia, which left en masse, there were numerous, clan-like family relationships. Others were friends from university days. Although dispersed to various cities upon arrival, they quickly re-established personal links. And since many of the DP's were activists, the organizations in which they were involved could spread quickly and widely by means of their personal contacts. Of course, the rapid growth of communications that occurred in the postwar era made the maintenance of far-flung ties that much easier. In any case, the DP organizations spread quickly not only from city to city or region to region, but also between Canada and the United States. For example, the largest youth organizations, Plast and SUM, were essentially parts of a whole. The same could be said for numerous other organizations. And the phenomenon of Ukrainians, both old and young, maintaining close and frequent contacts throughout the continent was not uncommon. Thus, the far-flung and well-integrated organizational network of the DP's helped to create a Ukrainian community that was, in many ways, North American in scope.

Yet, the pronounced in-group mentality, as well as the very different social, historical, and political contexts from which they had emerged, had another side to it: it prevented the DP's from attracting the largely assimilated Ukrainians of the First and Second waves into their ranks in appreciable numbers. Thus, the time and circumstances under which one arrived remained a crucial distinction among the Ukrainians of North America.

By 1990, those who arrived in the Third Wave had spent more than forty years in North America. It is an impressive time span, one that allows for drawing the outlines of the distinct, if not precisely delineated, phases through which this group passed. The initial phase encompassed, roughly, the period from arrival to the mid or late 1960s. As might be expected, getting established, both as individuals and as a community, was its hallmark. In socio-economic terms, this meant starting at the bottom of the socio-economic ladder, with even the highly educated taking on menial, poorly paid jobs. Women were frequently employed as cleaning ladies or in sweat shops. Housing usually consisted of a few rented rooms in the blue-collar neighbourhoods that the old immigrants had established around their churches. Whenever possible Ukrainian Catholic children were sent to parish schools. The Orthodox, however, preferred public schools from the outset. Many of the children belonged to youth organizations. For about the first two decades, the use of Ukrainian was widespread, especially in discourse between children and adults. Communities were self-contained, with limited social contacts and little intermarriage.

Fortunately for the new arrivals, they arrived at a propitious time. In the 1950s the universities entered into a period of rapid expansion, first in the United States and then in Canada. And many of the college-age newcomers were quick to take advantage of the relatively easy access to higher education. The initial phase also coincided with a period of unprecedented economic growth in both countries. This allowed the newcomers to move up the socio-economic ladder much more rapidly than had the previous waves. Consequently, the financial resources needed to support community institutions and activities were, if not abundant, at

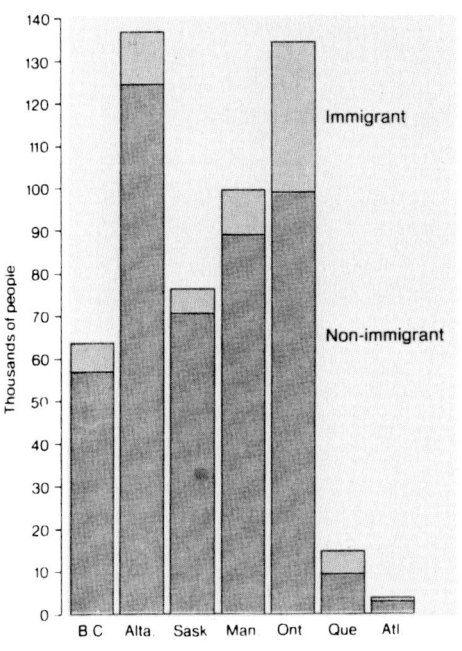

UKRAINIANS IN CANADA
UKRAINIAN POPULATION SHOWING IMMIGRANT/NON-IMMIGRANT STATUS

The Third Wave

A mounted policeman attempts to keep demonstrators in check during an anti-Soviet demonstration near the United Nations building in New York City, 1967.

least more readily available. There was, in comparison to their predecessors, yet another advantage that the DP's enjoyed. The prejudice and discrimination that the early waves of immigrants invariably encountered eased considerably in the 1960s and 1970s as the growing pluralism in North America made ethnic diversity much more acceptable in society as a whole.

In terms of organizational activity, this was the golden age. Relatively young, dynamic, and committed, the numerous activists of the Third Wave established almost all their organizations within the first decade of their arrival. Because a return to the homeland was a theoretical (although quickly fading) possibility, they viewed themselves not so much as immigrants but as 'Ukrainians living in an alien land' and tried to create 'a piece of Ukraine in North America,' that is, an environment that would allow them and especially their children to remain Ukrainian so as to make a return to, or at least links with, the homeland possible. In short, in the early days the goal was to maintain a kind of cultural-ideological holding pattern.

While all immigrants tend to be insular, at the outset members of the Third Wave were especially so. Sealed off from their homeland by the Iron Curtain and not yet ready to enter the North American mainstream, many focused their attention on the internal affairs of their communities. Émigré politics, especially the struggles between the Banderites and Melnykites, reached a high point. And the Cold War heightened the already virulent anti-Communism. The young, especially those in SUM, Plast, and ODUM, were inculcated with a sense of duty to their parents' homeland and an obligation to help it cast off Soviet oppression. Since this implied the need to struggle, summer camps and youth programs often had a militaristic aspect to them.

Several events marked both the culmination and conclusion of the initial period. In the summer of 1964 an estimated 100,000 Ukrainians, most from the United States and some from Canada, gathered in Washington, DC, to unveil, with the participation of former president Dwight Eisenhower, a statue of Taras Shevchenko. The event was viewed as an organizational tour de force, for it not only gathered a huge throng that included both new and old immigrants, but it also involved a large fund-raising campaign and, most impressive, demonstrated that the often fractious Ukrainian community could unite behind a single project. A similar event, on a smaller scale, had occurred in Winnipeg in 1961, when Prime Minister Diefenbaker participated in the unveiling ceremony (although, it should be noted, the Ukrainian Left in Canada was the first to erect a statue in North America to Taras Shevchenko when about 45,000 gathered in 1951 in Palermo, near Toronto, to mark the event). Topping off the organizational upsurge was the calling of the first World Congress of Free Ukrainians (SKVU-WCFU) in 1967 in New York. Over 1000 delegates, mostly from the United States and Canada but also from all Ukrainian communities outside the Soviet bloc, formed a body, the Secretariat of the WCFU, whose function was to coordinate efforts of all Ukrainians abroad to aid their homeland. Reverend Basil Kushnir of Canada served as the first president, and the Secretariat was initially based in Winnipeg.

An estimated 100,000 Ukrainians gathered in Washington, DC, in 1964 to witness Dwight D. Eisenhower unveil the Shevchenko Monument.

The Third Wave

Unveiling of the Taras Shevchenko monument in Winnipeg, 1961, with the participation of Prime Minister John G. Diefenbaker, coinciding with the seventieth anniversary of Ukrainian settlement in Canada.

Members of Plast, in foreground, and ODUM, in background, assembled at the 1961 festivities in Winnipeg.

The *second phase* in the history of the Third Wave encompassed the 1970s and much of the 1980s. By this time, the entrance of the DP's, and especially their grown children, into the Canadian and American mainstream was an accomplished fact. Along with this came the open acceptance of what had long been a foregone conclusion, namely, that they were in North America to stay. And, with signs of assimilation rapidly appearing, the central problem of the period was how to maintain what had been created in the preceding era. Much of the Third Wave was solidly ensconsed in the middle class by the 1970s. Despite the fact that many of the older generation earned only modest incomes, their general thriftiness allowed most to purchase their own homes. Meanwhile, their children began to reap the fruits of higher education. Many became professionals. Teaching and engineering were especially popular career choices. A considerable number also became well-paid physicians, lawyers, businessmen, and executives. In short, Ukrainian 'yuppies' made their appearance.

According to the 1980 census in the United States, only 5 per cent of the Ukrainians considered themselves to be poor, the third lowest percentage among fifty ethnic groups. And over 17 per cent described themselves as being wealthy, the twelfth highest percentage in the same sample. The census also revealed that

Debutantes at a ball in Chicago, 1988.

about 36 per cent of Ukrainian males were professionals or managers. Apparently the work ethic is still very strong among the Ukrainians.

But, as usual, moving up the socio-economic ladder meant moving away from the original, tight-knit ethnic community. In the United States this process was accelerated by the decay of the inner cities where most traditional Ukrainian neighbourhoods were located. Thus, the largest Ukrainian 'village' in North America, that of New York City, shrank dramatically as young families moved into the suburbs of New Jersey and elsewhere. A similar decline befell the Ukrainian neighbourhoods of Philadelphia, Detroit, Cleveland, Chicago, and other urban centres, leaving them as largely the preserve of the elderly. New centres did appear in some suburbs, but they were not as compact and concentrated as before. Yet, there was another aspect to dispersal. As young professionals followed career opportunities throughout the United States, they established new communities beyond the Northeast and Midwest, most notably in California, Colorado, Georgia, and Washington, DC. Meanwhile, the elderly from both countries congregated in Florida.

In Canada, the situation differed considerably. Although many of the young also moved into the suburbs, urban blight was less severe. In some cities, most notably Toronto, vibrant urban growth provided many Ukrainians with the incentive to remain in the inner city and in close proximity to their traditional neighbourhoods. Because many Ukrainians profited from Toronto's remarkable economic upsurge, its Ukrainian community became known as not only one of the largest but also the most active and wealthiest in North America. Indeed, by the 1980s it laid claim to being the informal capital of the Ukrainian diaspora. Meanwhile, rapidly growing Edmonton began to edge out Winnipeg as the leading Ukrainian centre in the West.

The initial social insularity of the DP's was long since a thing of the past. While the older generation still socialized primarily with 'their own,' the friends of their North American–educated children frequently came from outside their ethnic community. The use of Ukrainian declined steadily among the young, and only through the stubborn insistence of their grandparents on its

A day-care centre or sadochok in Toronto in 1988.

use was it still heard in the home. Intermarriage became a common although only grudgingly accepted phenomenon.

Compared to the socio-economic transformations, ideological and conceptual changes within this political emigration came slowly. Actually, the various ideologies that had existed among the DP's hardly changed; they simply became irrelevant. The militant nationalism of the initial period faded as it became evident that the immigrants' ability to affect the situation in their homeland was practically nil. Only a shrinking group of diehards showed interest in continuing the old feuds between the Banderites and Melnykites. Meanwhile, the pacifism of the post-Vietnam era along with the rise of the self-indulgent mentality of the 'me-generation' of the 1970s and 1980s greatly hastened the depoliticization of the erstwhile DP's and especially their children. Yet, many of the young still retained a strong sense of Ukrainian identity and sought new ways of expressing it.

An attempt to combine Ukrainian patriotism with the growing commitment to Canada or the United States was the 'two homelands' idea, which appeared with increasing frequency in the Ukrainian press. Its proponents argued that commitment to Ukraine, on the one hand, and Canada or the United States, on the other, was both possible and desirable, for by retaining one's

A sign of the Ukrainian presence in the Canadian West, Edmonton, 1978.

Ukrainian heritage an individual contributed to the cultural richness, diversity, and dynamism of his or her new homeland. In the United States in the 1970s, where renewed interest in and celebration of ethnic 'roots' was in vogue, this idea found ready acceptance among many young Ukrainians who were in the process of making the transition from émigrés to ethnics.

In Canada, Ukrainian 'ethnic pride' went much further. Citing the crucial role that Ukrainians played in the colonization of the prairies, Ukrainians – from all three waves of immigration – argued that they should be included, along with the French and British, among the 'founding peoples' of the country. They demanded that their cultural activity, and especially Ukrainian-language public education, receive government support analogous to that of the two dominant language groups. In fact, Ukrainians were in the forefront of the 'Third Element,' that is, the non-English or non-French ethnic communities in Canada, who pressed for not only government support in the preservation of their cultures but appropriate ethnic representation in government. While few of the specific Ukrainian desiderata were satisfied, multiculturalism was enshrined in the Canadian constitution in 1987, thereby improving the conditions for the retention of the Ukrainian cultural heritage in Canada.

Organizational activity, so dynamic and varied in the intial period, declined during the 1970s and 1980s. Contributing factors were the well-known litany of woes that befall many ethnic groups: the disintegration of traditional neighbourhoods; the ranks of activists thinned by death, ageing, or fatigue; the failure of an ageing European-bred leadership to adapt to modern ways; the increasing irrelevance of many, especially ideological, organizations; and, most crucial, the inability to attract young people. Indeed, many organizations became the preserve of the older generation, kept alive by little more than inertia. But the scene was not totally bleak. New types of associations – most notably the professional and business people's groups – appeared in several Canadian and, to a lesser extent, American cities. Largely non-political, although supportive of Ukrainian independence, they introduced a new sophistication to traditional cultural and social activity. Especially noteworthy in this regard was the Washington Group, based in the American capital.

Several events reflected the changing focus of interest, especially the shift from the political to the cultural aspects of Ukrainianism. Most notable was the Harvard Project, initiated in 1968 when a fund drive begun by students and headed by Stefan Chemych adopted the proposal of Omeljan Pritsak of Harvard University to establish chairs of Ukrainian history, literature, and language and a research institute at the prestigious American university. In what was the most successful fund drive in the history of Ukrainians in North America, about 10,000 of them donated over $6 million for the funding of the Harvard Ukrainian Research Institute (HURI). The selfless and enthusiastic efforts of numerous volunteers, as well as the publicity provided by the UNA's *Svoboda*, helped decisively in the successful completion of the project. Under the leadership of its director, Omeljan Pritsak, HURI contributed greatly to the academic legitimacy and scholarly quality of Ukrainian studies. It also provided a first-rate training ground for dozens of budding scholars.

In Canada, university-level courses in Ukrainian studies had existed at the universities of Manitoba, Alberta, and Toronto since early in the postwar era. None the less, the Harvard example was also an inspiration to Canadian Ukrainians. However,

Mama's Boy by Natalka Husar (1985).

Observations on Ukrainian Ethnic Culture

It's Ukrainian Day at the Vegreville Ukrainian Festival in June 1975. I wander among the booths set up in the recreation hall – it's a bazaar! – and realize that, these days, anybody can be a Ukrainian. (It's implied that someone will want to be.) Hot kobassa – the smell will always make me salivate – on a stick. Middle-aged women demonstrating how a pysanka is made. Teen-agers flogging T-shirts: Drink Molson's Ukrainian! Kiss me, I'm Ukrainian! Just outside the open doors, the crowd passes through the midway; kids in Ukrainian-style, machine-embroidered shirts ride on the ferris wheel eating popcorn. I look for Slavic features in their faces, a flaring cheekbone or a dusky complexion underneath the wild hair and Maybelline mascara. At a booth of old photographs, 'Taking Root in a New Land,' I peer at the picture of a woman and child standing stoically in front of their 'home,' a few slender logs propped upright under a mass of grasses and branches, and try to find my own face in her inscrutable expression.

The program begins. The opening remarks are in Ukrainian, followed by a much-abbreviated English version. 'Such days as today are very valuable for the patriotism of this country, etc.' We stand for the national anthems. First the Ukrainian nationalist one, 'The Ukraine Is Still Not Dead' (a rather negative way of putting it, I am thinking), and I am amazed yet again by the capacity of these people to be moved so artlessly and genuinely by the idea of the liberation of a country they have never seen.

A tourist I came, a tourist I leave. Like thousands and thousands of Ukrainian-Canadians of my generation and beyond, I only travel these ethnic sideroads when I need to find a breathing space awhile, away from the fumes of the cosmopolitan metropolis and all its works. But, metropolis is what I return to when it's time to go home. It is, after all, where Baba meant to have me live, when she mortgaged her life so mine would be deflected as much from the CPR quarter as from the kolkhoz, near Tulova, in Galicia ... [But] I have other skills now and assignments to fulfill that Baba never dreamed of. Not that she wouldn't be pleased.

Kostash, All of Baba's Children, 396, 399

Students at the Harvard Ukrainian Summer School, 1983.

they went about things differently. Because they constituted about 10 per cent of the province's population and since many of them held influential positions in provincial government and politics, Alberta's Ukrainians turned to the government for financial support. Led by Manoly Lupul and Peter Savaryn, they were successful in their efforts. And in 1975, the Canadian Institute of Ukrainian Studies (CIUS) began to operate at the University of Alberta. It, too, stressed high-quality scholarship and developed a prolific publications program.

Not to be outdone, the Ukrainian community of Toronto also established endowed positions in Ukrainian studies at the University of Toronto in 1979 and, in 1982, at York University. Toronto was also the base for several other projects. The Ukrainian Canadian Research and Documentation Centre (formerly the Famine Research Committee) produced a highly acclaimed and widely shown film, *Harvest of Despair*, which was most effective in informing North Americans about the famine of 1933. Another was the English-language *Encyclopedia of Ukraine* project based at the University of Toronto and funded by CIUS and the Ukrainian Studies Foundation.

Toronto also boasted several important patrons of Ukrainian scholarship. Especially noteworthy was Peter Jacyk, who provided, in addition to other major contributions, essential funding for the

Centre of Historical Research at CIUS; Lida and Erast Huculak, who endowed a chair of Ukrainian ethnography at the University of Alberta; and Yevhen Borys, who raised funds for the Ukrainian encyclopedia projects.

As the above-mentioned developments indicate, in recent years the focal point of community interests and undertakings has been on the non-political rather than political or ideological aspects of Ukrainianism. To a large extent, this reflects the growing realization in the diaspora that the fate of the homeland will be decided by those who live there, with little or no input from those who left. It also shows a marked preference in the communities for projects that unite rather than divide them into feuding factions. Preserving their cultural heritage is now the pressing priority among Ukrainians abroad. Only if this is achieved will they be able to survive as a community and retain their bonds with the ancestral homeland. In any case, being Ukrainian in North America no longer carries with it as many political and ideological associations as it did in the past.

THE NORTH AMERICAN DIASPORA

The descendants of the pioneers. Children of the Koziak family at the Dauphin, Manitoba, Ukrainian festival, 1980.

MORE THAN ONE HUNDRED years have passed since Ukrainians began to arrive in North America in large numbers. Today the immigrants and their descendants number close to 1.4 million, almost evenly divided between the United States and Canada. In terms of ethnic consciousness, they fall roughly into three categories. The largest consists of those whose forefathers left their homeland three, four, and even five generations ago. By and large, they no longer speak Ukrainian, have little or no contact with Ukrainian organizations, and are often only vaguely conscious of their ethnic roots. Another category, usually a generation or two removed from the homeland, is familiar with and even fond of Ukrainian culture but does little to preserve it. The third category is the small but committed minority that still manages to preserve its ethnic heritage. Composed largely of the post–Second World War émigrés and their children, but also including, especially in Canada, some members of earlier immigrations, it forms the core of the Ukrainian communities in North America.

THE UKRAINIAN AMERICANS

Ukrainians in the United States have been fortunate to live in a society that provides them with numerous opportunities and resources for developing their communal life. But for those who wished to maintain their ethnic heritage, there were also drawbacks. Economic constraints forced them to settle in urban centres where it was difficult to maintain the traditions of a peasant people. Until recently, the educational system was geared to assimilating immigrants into the American 'melting pot.' Although numerous compared to their compatriots elsewhere in the West, Ukrainians are relatively insignificant among the many ethnic groups in the United States. In terms of numbers, they rank twenty-first nationally and ninth in the Middle Atlantic states where they are concentrated. Moreover, their political influence is even less than might be expected. Even the large influx of DP's proved to be a mixed blessing. While they reinvigorated the Ukrainian community and greatly expanded its range of activities, their high degree of politicization, particularly the Melnykite-Banderite feud, has made the Ukrainian-American community the most politically fragmented in the West.

What socio-economic features distinguish the Ukrainian Americans from the average American? Traditionally, they have been marked by a relatively low level of education. This is not surprising in view of the fact that the early and most numerous immigrants came from one of the most backward regions in Europe and with an illiteracy rate of about 50 per cent. Consequently, even U.S.-born Ukrainians have long been overrepresented in blue-collar jobs and underrepresented in white-collar occupations. But recent studies indicate that the situation is changing. If current trends among younger Ukrainians continue, it is likely that they will surpass both the white population in the United States and some of the other East European ethnic groups in terms of educational level. The children of the post–Second World War refugees have been particularly successful in attaining managerial and professional status. Thus, it is safe to say that Ukrainians are now solidly ensconced in the American middle class.

Some of the 18,000 Ukrainians who gathered in Washington in October 1983 to commemorate the famine of 1933.

Another feature that sets off Ukrainians from the average American is their relative lack of mobility. Today, the vast majority of them are still concentrated in the Middle Atlantic region where they originally settled. On the whole, Ukrainian families are less 'modern' than the average American family: they have fewer single-parent families and more of them have their parents and other elderly relatives living with them. Moreover, they marry later, delay childbearing longer, and stay single more often. As befits their peasant origins, they tend to be conservative in their politics and mores.

Today the strongest Ukrainian institutions in the United States are those that the earliest immigrants established, that is, the churches and fraternal associations. The Ukrainian Catholic church encompasses about 200 parishes and 285,000 faithful, the various Ukrainian Orthodox churches have about 125,000 members, and the Baptists claim a membership of 50,000. Among the fraternals, the Ukrainian National Association (UNA), with 80,000 members, is by far the largest and richest. It publishes *Svoboda*, the oldest and most widely read Ukrainian daily in the West, and the lively, informative English-language *Ukrainian Weekly*. The Ukrainian Fraternal Association (previously called the Ukrainian Workingmen's Association) has about 25,000 members and publishes *Narodnia volya* and the well-edited *Forum* magazine. Meanwhile the Providence Association of Ukrainian Catholics has 19,000 members. Its press organ is the daily *Ameryka*. The list of other periodicals is too lengthy to enumerate.

Continuing in the Galician tradition, the post–Second World War immigrants to the United States have established a growing network of savings-and-loan associations and credit unions. Together with similar institutions in Canada and elsewhere in the world, they have a membership of 122,000 and combined assets of close to $1 billion. Another carry-over from the Old Country is a well-organized women's association, the Ukrainian National Women's League (3700 members and 83 branches). Of the numerous youth organizations, the strongest are the scouting association Plast, and the more nationalistic Association of Ukrainian Youth (SUM). Both have a membership of about 4000. Numerous professional societies unite Ukrainian engineers, physicians, professors, teachers, writers, journalists, and businessmen. Young people are often drawn to the dance ensembles and choruses that are usually found in Ukrainian communties.

Clearly the past looms large in the consciousness of American Ukrainians. Some might argue that this is because their future as a community is not promising. Prior to the 1980s, new emigration had practically ceased. Links with their Soviet-controlled homeland have been, until recently, tenuous and fraught with mutual suspicions. Many organizations are obviously on their last legs. And assimilation is moving apace. In 1980, of about 730,000 people of Ukrainian descent in the United States only 123,000 declared Ukrainian to be their primary language. But there are also hopeful signs. Unlike its predecessors, the post–Second World War immigration, thanks to its many youth-oriented organizations, has had notable success in raising a new generation of community activists. Most of them are professionals by occupation who know the American environment well. Meanwhile, a new tolerance for ethnic diversity has emerged in the United States. Finally, many American-born Ukrainians are beginning to discover the psychological and social advantages of belonging to an ethnic 'in-group.' It is, therefore, possible that the century-old Ukrainian-American community has more life in it than many pessimists contend.

THE UKRAINIAN CANADIANS

Of all the Ukrainian communities in the West, the Ukrainian Canadians are in the most advantageous position. Numbering over 600,000, they are not far behind their compatriots in the United States in terms of numbers. But their profile and influence in their country are much greater. Because the population of Canada is only one-tenth that of the United States, the Ukrainian Canadians are, in effect, a bigger fish in a smaller pond. While Ukrainians in the United States hold the twenty-first position in terms of ethnic group size, in Canada they rank fifth. Moreover, as the people who settled much of the Canadian prairies they lay claim to pioneer status. Some Ukrainians even argue that they are one of the 'founding nations' of the country. Because they settled in solid blocs, the early immigrants to Canada have withstood assimilation much better than their counterparts to the south. This is reflected in the relatively large number of third-, fourth-, and even fifth-generation Ukrainians who still speak the language of their forefathers and participate in Ukrainian community affairs.

Yet, foreboding developments also confront Ukrainian Canadians. As has so often happened with Ukrainians, modernization is threatening their sense of community. The global trend towards urbanization is breaking up the rural bloc settlements in the prairies, the bastions of Ukrainian life in Canada. In 1931, over 80 per cent of Ukrainian Canadians lived in a rural setting; today over 75 per cent are city-dwellers. Edmonton, Winnipeg, and especially Toronto, where many DP's settled, are now the centres of Ukrainian life in Canada. Although each city has a large and active community of about 70,000 to 80,000 Ukrainians and part-Ukrainians, urban life in Canada is clearly not conducive to the retention of Ukrainian ethnic identity. A variety of statistics bear this out. In 1921, over 90 per cent of Ukrainian Canadians declared that their mother tongue was Ukrainian; in 1971 only 49 per cent did so, and the percentage has been dropping rapidly since then. In 1931, over 80 per cent intermarried within their own group; today less than 50 per cent do so. Even the churches face an uncertain future. While in 1931 the Ukrainian Catholic and Orthodox denominations encompassed 82 per cent of Ukrainians, today the figure is only 52 per cent.

But if Ukrainian Canadians have problems that are similar to those of their compatriots south of the border, they are better equipped to deal with them. In general, they are more effectively organized than the latter. For example, Ukrainian Canadians have managed to preserve a single, generally recognized umbrella organization – the Ukrainian Canadian Committee (UCC). Many of the organizations that the DP's established in the United States can also be found in Canada. And the ties between them are close. However, while in the United States many of the 'old immigrant' organizations – except for the churches and the fraternal associations – have faded, in Canada a considerable number, notably SUS and UNF, continue to exist. Moreover, Canada has a strong network of Ukrainian professional and businessmen's clubs that have been able to attract a young, upwardly mobile, professional membership. Especially popular with the grandchildren and great-grandchildren of the early immigrants are the numerous dance ensembles. In Western Canada alone there are over 150 such groups, with about 10,000 members. But the organizational strength of the Ukrainians in Canada should not be exaggerated. Only an estimated 10 to 15 per cent belong to the community organizations. In order to attract new members, some groups are de-emphasizing political and nationalist features and concentrating on cultural and social activities.

Unlike their southern compatriots, Ukrainian Canadians have developed a cultural tradition of their own. Writers such as Iliia Kiriak skilfully depicted, in both Ukrainian and English, the experiences of the pioneer generation. The nationally famous painter

Visitors to Canora, Saskatchewan, learn quickly that many of the town's inhabitants are of Ukrainian background.

The inauguration of Ramon Hnatyshyn as governor-general of Canada in Ottawa in 1990.

A section of the coat-of-arms of the new governor-general, containing a Ukrainian trident symbol.

William Kurelek frequently utilized Ukrainian motifs. The architect Radoslav Zuk has intertwined traditional and modern elements in the architecture of Ukrainian churches. On the debit side, however, Ukrainians in Canada, particularly those in the West, tend to be more provincial and folklore-oriented in their approach to Ukrainian culture than those in the United States. This may be due, in part, to the fact that a smaller portion of the Ukrainian intelligentsia emigrated to Canada than to the United States.

A striking feature of the Ukrainian-Canadian community is the relatively large number of its members who have achieved high political office. Ukrainians are or have been mayors of such large cities as Edmonton and Winnipeg. Close to a hundred Ukrainian Canadians have been elected to provincial legislatures, primarily in the prairie provinces. About thirty have been members of the federal parliament. Moreover, there have been five Ukrainian senators and dozens of federal and provincial cabinet ministers. Recently John Sopinka was appointed to the country's Supreme Court and Ramon Hnatyshyn became Canada's governor general. Although far from being a major political force in Canada, the Ukrainian Canadians wield more political influence than any other Ukrainian community in the West.

THE HOMELAND AND THE DIASPORA

Although initially many Ukrainians arrived with the thought that they might, sooner or later, return home, it has long since become clear to them and especially to their children that they are in North America to stay. None the less, many, especially the members of the Third Wave, have been loath to sever all their links with the homeland. Consequently, those who live abroad permanently but still identify with their homeland have come to refer to themselves as the Ukrainian diaspora.

Throughout the more than one hundred years that Ukrainian communities have existed in North America, they have shown remarkable longevity and dynamism. In part this is because their immigration was fortuitously spaced, with each of the three waves coming roughly twenty years apart. The earliest arrivals established the organizational backbone of the community – the churches and fraternal organizations – that were expanded during the interwar period by another wave of immigrants. The post–Second World War immigrants arrived just in time to replace the 'old' immigrants. With many institutions and organizations already in place, they were able to concentrate on forming new ones. Thus the Ukrainians in North America have been able to maintain a sense of continuity and growth. However, today, as the half-century mark since arrival of the Third Wave approaches, it is clear that reinforcements from the homeland are long overdue if the pattern sketched above is to be maintained.

As mentioned above, the fact that most of the immigrants came from Galicia, where the tradition of grass-roots community organizations was strong, is another reason for the community's

Celebrating the feast of Jordan at Hawkstone, Ontario, in 1977.

impressive record of activism. Finally, and perhaps most important, almost from the outset many Ukrainians in North America have had a sense of mission in regard to their homeland. As they benefited from the political freedom and economic bounty of the United States and Canada, many felt duty bound to aid their less fortunate brethren in the homeland. And the desire to help was heightened by the numbing litany of misfortunes that befell Ukraine throughout the twentieth century: the poverty of the peasants, the chaos of the civil war in 1918–20, Polish repression, Stalinist terror and the horrible famine of 1933, the devastation and horror of the Second World War, Russification, the brutal suppression of dissent in the 1970s, and, finally, the Chernobyl disaster in 1986. Thus, for many being a Ukrainian in North America implied a commitment to The Cause, that is, the welfare and freedom of a beloved and unfortunate homeland. And this has served as a compelling motivating force for activism.

The North American diaspora in the era of glasnost and perestroika

The epochal changes that have occurred in the USSR under Mikhail Gorbachev could not but exert a great impact on the Ukrainians of North America. As the generation-old barriers that separated the diaspora from the land of their parents and grandparents crumbled in the late 1980s, the two-way flow of visitors between the Ukrainian communities of North America and Ukraine increased dramatically. And a probing, expanding, and often bitter-sweet process of reacquaintance for some and discovery for others began.

Initially, it was family ties that expanded as the Soviet Union eased restrictions on individual travel, thereby allowing thousands of Ukrainians, mostly of the Third Wave, to visit Ukraine or to invite their relatives to visit them. As changes in the USSR progressed, formal contacts between diaspora organizations and institutions and the government of Soviet Ukraine developed. At first these ties were non-political, usually charitable and cultural in nature. Then they progressed to exchanges of professionals and specialists. Finally, by 1990, they reached the most sensitive levels, those of religion and politics. Although all contacts have been fraught with problems, complications, and setbacks, it became increasingly evident that Ukrainians in both the diaspora and the homeland are eager and ready to set aside their long, fruitless separation and to establish a mutually beneficial, harmonious relationship.

One of the results of the increased familiarity between Ukrainians abroad and in the homeland was the collapse, or at least, radical modification of the stereotypes they have had about each other for generations. Those in the West realized that their view, tinted by nationalist ideology, of Soviet Ukrainian society as a mass of oppressed, suffering patriots thirsting for independence and repressed by brutal imperialists in the Kremlin with the aid of their Russified lackeys in Kiev was too simplistic and one-dimensional. Meanwhile, the traditional Soviet propaganda image of Ukrainians in North America as consisting of progressive workers, on the one hand, and malicious bourgeois nationalists, on the other, was also far off the mark. Encouragingly, both sides

Many Ukrainians in North America greeted the onset of glasnost and perestroika with scepticism. The Kremlin's handling of the nuclear disaster at Chernobyl in 1986 confirmed the suspicions of these demonstrators in Ontario.

now seem ready to modify their views. Especially in Ukraine, where information about compatriots in the West has been grossly distorted or suppressed, the topic has evoked great interest and received unprecedented coverage in the media. Indeed, there has been a tendency to go to the other extreme and to present the achievements of North America's Ukrainians in near-mythical terms.

Given their stereotypical views of each other, it is not surprising that, at the outset of their rapprochement, unrealistic expectations abounded on both sides. In the communities of North America, the turbulent events of 1989–90 gave rise to euphoric, and naïve, expectations that the extensive Russification of their homeland could be reversed quickly and that independence would soon be achieved. For their part, Soviet Ukrainians greatly overestimated the capacity of the North American diaspora to help them. And all too often they waited, passively, for aid from abroad to resolve their myriad problems.

At least part of the problem of the new relationship that is evolving between the diaspora and Ukraine is that it is essentially asymmetrical in nature. Brought up with a sense of obligation to their unfortunate land of origin, those Ukrainians in North America who sought to aid their homeland generally did so for altruistic motives. For them it was a chance to turn the age-old

Responding to Perestroika

Suddenly it's chic to be Ukrainian. Over the past few months, as a direct result, we believe, of the great national renaissance in Ukraine, we have heard many persons here in North America speak proudly of their Ukrainian heritage. Concurrently, we have witnessed a great reawakening of interest among Americans and Canadians of Ukrainian descent in their Ukrainian roots, an intensive thirst for information about current events and past history to provide the background needed to understand today's news. Even among non-Ukrainians we've seen evidence of a vastly increased interest in Ukraine – all thanks to the remarkable events unfolding on a daily, or even hourly, basis in Ukraine. (How many of us have had friends or acquaintances approach us to say, for example, 'How about Ukraine's sovereignty proclamation? What do you think?')

During these heady times, as we scan the newspapers and newsmagazines, listen to the all-news radio stations, and perpetually switch channels on our TV sets in hopes of catching just one more report about unprecedented events in Ukraine, we should pause to think about our relation to those events.

Is it enough to sit back and take all this in? Or do we have a role to play in all of this?

Many Ukrainian Americans and Ukrainian Canadians, apparently, have decided that now is the time to help, to become involved, to donate their efforts or their money. Many have come to believe that yes, indeed, Ukrainians worldwide are one nation; that we need each other to survive, to flourish.

Ukrainian Weekly, 1990

hopes and dreams of their parents and grandparents into a reality. Few expected any concrete rewards for their efforts. But often their good intentions were greater than the actual help they delivered. Their compatriots in Ukraine, however, had, of necessity, a more pragmatic approach to this relationship: finding themselves in exceedingly straitened circumstances, they had little patience for pious sentiment and great eagerness for concrete aid and benefit. Moreover, both sides soon realized that in the course of their lengthy separation very considerable differences of attitude and mentality, reflective of those between the North American and Soviet societies, had developed between them. Consequently, today they often approach each other both as brethren and as strangers.

Yet this was to be expected and could not overshadow the great satisfaction, even euphoria – reminiscent of the reaction to the Ukrainian revolution in 1917 and the proclamation of Carpatho-Ukraine in 1938 – that swept the North American communities in connection with the changes in the USSR. And both sides have been clearly inclined to emphasize the positive. The ever-increasing numbers of Soviet Ukrainian visitors to North America have been surprised and favourably impressed by the size and organization of the diaspora communities, by their well-established position in Canadian and American societies, and, most of all, by their preservation of the Ukrainian cultural heritage, much of which was suppressed in their homeland. Indeed, one often encountered cases where second-generation Ukrainians in the diaspora had better command of their parent's language than their counterparts in the more Russified areas of Ukraine. For their part, North American communities welcomed the sudden emergence in Ukraine of national sentiment, all the more unexpected after the Soviet regime's long and brutal campaign to obliterate it. And they were pleased by the intelligent and enlightened policies of Ukraine's democratic reformers. Consequently, both sides realized that they still had much in common, most notably the desire to aid Ukraine.

Ukrainians in the United States dispatch aid to victims of Chernobyl in Newark, 1989.

New and growing links

Ironically, the disaster that occurred on 26 April 1986 at the nuclear reactor in Chernobyl, near Kiev, helped bring about a dramatic improvement in relations between the diaspora and Ukraine. When it became evident, after the initial few years, that the Soviet government could not adequately deal with the massive impact of the nuclear catastrophe, the North American communities began to mobilize aid for their homeland, and especially for the children suffering from the effects of radiation. Organized by Taras Hunczak, Nadia and Zenon Matkiwsky, and Irene Labensky of New Jersey, the Children of Chernobyl Relief Fund dispatched in early 1990 several plane-loads of medical supplies for the victims of the disaster. The aid received wide publicity in the Soviet Ukrainian media and supported the emergence of a new, much more favourable image of Ukrainians in the West: no longer viewed as implacable ideological enemies, they were now welcomed as long-lost brethren who were coming to the aid of their compatriots in their time of need.

Aid shipment to Ukraine aboard a Soviet cargo plane.

The North American Diaspora

The changes in the USSR also allowed for the development of closer contacts between professional, charitable, and cultural organizations in North America and Ukraine. Thus, from 5 to 16 August 1990 the North America–based World Federation of Ukrainian Medical Associations (WFUMA), led by Achilles Chreptowsky, held its world congress in Kiev. This unprecedented and very successful event occurred with the aid and participation of the republic's Ministry of Health and numerous Soviet Ukrainian colleagues. And it facilitated the transfer of Western medical aid and expertise to the republic. It also led to the establishment of a diaspora-supported hospital in Lviv.

Soon afterward, from 27 August to 3 September, the newly formed International Association of Ukrainian Studies, an organization of Western, East European, and Soviet scholars, also held its first congress in Kiev and elected George Grabowicz of Harvard University as its president. The congress, which symbolized the willingness of scholars in the East and West to cooperate, also allowed Soviet Ukrainians to familiarize themselves, in many cases for the first time, with the impressive achievements of their North American colleagues. It also raised the possibility that the standards of international scholarship might be applied to Ukrainian studies, a field that was long and purposely neglected and degraded by the Soviet regime.

Meanwhile, numerous delegations of Ukrainian businessmen visited the homeland of their parents to explore possibilities for joint ventures. Especially notable was the visit of a high-level delegation of Ukrainian Canadians and Canadian government economists that met with their counterparts in 1989. With the aid of Canadian-educated and Geneva-based Bohdan Hawrylyshyn, an affiliate of the International Management Institute was established in Kiev to teach, in Ukrainian, Western business techniques. And a number of Ukrainian entrepreneurs from North America also initiated several projects in the USSR. However, the difficulties of doing business in the chaotic Soviet economy cooled some of their early enthusiasm.

Besides the concrete benefits that these burgeoning contacts provided, they also had a broader, politico-cultural significance: by exposing Soviet Ukrainians to modern Western technology, expertise, and methods by means of their native language and

The Ukrainian Youth Ensemble of Toronto in Lviv during its tour of Ukraine in the summer of 1990.

through the intermediary of other Ukrainians — that is, by encouraging the view that modernization was attainable without recourse to the Russian language and without Moscow acting as its conduit — North America's Ukrainians may have contributed to slowing the Russification of Ukraine. And, in the long run, this could prove to be their greatest contribution.

Cultural exchanges also proliferated in the late 1980s. While the novelty of numerous choirs, singers, musicians, painters, and poets from Ukraine freely performing before their countrymen in North America was striking, even more astounding was the sight of North American ensembles appearing before enthusiastic audiences in Ukraine. An especially noteworthy example of cultural cooperation was the Chervona Ruta Festival of popular Ukrainian music, which included hard-rock renditions of Shevchenko's poetry. It was organized by Toronto-based businessman

The Canadian Friends of RUKH, a support group for the democratic movement for reform in Ukraine, at their inaugural rally in Toronto in 1989.

Mykola Moros, in Chernivtsi in 1989. The success of these ventures, and especially the promise of international exposure they engendered, raised hopes that the heretofore stagnant – in both East and West – Ukrainian cultural scene would receive a much-needed stimulus.

On the organizational level there was also considerable progress. Plast, the scouting organization, put down new roots in Ukraine, especially in Lviv. By 1990, the North American leadership observed with satisfaction as newly formed troops, encompassing hundreds of new members, appeared throughout Ukraine and launched their first camping trips into the Carpathian Mountains. New branches of another diaspora organization, the women's association Soiuz Ukrainok (UNWL), were also formed in Kiev and Lviv.

But organizational expansion extended in the opposite direction as well. Enthused by the formation, in September 1989, of RUKH, Ukraine's democratic movement for reform, Ukrainians in North America quickly formed support groups in about three dozen cities. The Canadian Friends of RUKH, especially the large Toronto branch, was especially active. In both the United States and Canada these support groups collected funds that were used to provide the reform movement with the technology necessary to maintain communications and to get its message out to the populace. Aid was also dispatched to the victims of Chernobyl. Other forms of support included arranging meetings for leading members of RUKH with influential politicians in Ottawa and Washington and familiarizing the North American media with the reform movement and its goals. In the course of their work, the support groups experienced something new: the North American media – for the first time – evinced an interest in Ukraine, especially when the dramatic changes of 1989–90 brought the nationalities issue in the USSR to the fore.

An indication of Ukraine's improving international presence was the announcement in 1990 by the governments of Canada and the United States that they planned to open their respective consulates in Kiev. This was a goal the communities of North America had long sought to attain. It also raised hopes that this was only the beginning of Ukraine's long-delayed recognition by the international community.

Yet, perhaps the most significant of the links that were forged or restored between the diaspora and the homeland in the era of perestroika were those involving the churches. For several generations the Catholic and Orthodox churches in the West had existed in near isolation, cut off from their roots in Ukraine. Their fate depended, basically, on the longevity of the communities in North America. And, prior to the reforms, their prospects were not encouraging. Meanwhile, in the homeland, the Ukrainian Catholic church had been forcibly dissolved in 1946, although it continued to exist clandestinely, and the Ukrainian Orthodox church, which was briefly renewed during the Second World War, was also liquidated. Therefore, the religious revival that occurred in 1989–90 in Ukraine was truly awe-inspring, indeed wellnigh miraculous. Initially, the Ukrainian Catholic church emerged 'from the catacombs' and, despite Communist (and Orthodox) opposition, began to reclaim, with notable success, the position it had held prior to 1946. Aid from North America, spearheaded by Bishop Basil Losten, helped considerably. A high point in this ecclesiastical rebirth came on Palm Sunday of 1991 when the church's leading hierarch, Cardinal Myroslav Lubachivsky, returned to his see in Lviv, thereby symbolically reuniting the Ukrainian Catholics in the West with their brethren in the homeland.

Cardinal and Patriarch Myroslav Lubachivsky during his return to his see of Lviv in 1991.

Patriarch Mstyslav, centre, leader of the UAOC in the West, during his enthronement as Patriarch of Ukraine in the Cathedral of St Sophia in Kiev, 1990.

Equally dramatic events occurred among the Orthodox. The loosening of Moscow's control in Ukraine meant that the dominant Russian Orthodox church also lost influence in the republic. Consequently, on 5–6 June 1990, at a synod held in Kiev and attended by 7 bishops and about 540 priests who had defected from the Russian Orthodox fold, the Ukrainian Autocephalous Orthodox church (UAOC) was resurrected. Declaring that 'we are the independent church of an independent nation,' the synod broke all ties with the Moscow-based church and proclaimed the creation of its own patriachate. Its choice for the new patriarch was Mstyslav, the leader of the UAOC in the West. And, on 20 October, the 92-year-old heirarch travelled to the homeland he had not seen for 46 years, where he was greeted by vast throngs and, in a moving ceremony held in St Sophia Cathedral, was proclaimed Patriarch of Kiev and all Ukraine. Because the new patriarch retained his residence in South Bound Brook, New Jersey, Metropolitan Ioann was appointed as his representative in Kiev.

The restoration of bonds between the churches of the diaspora and the homeland was certainly a development of major historical significance, especially for the communities in the West. It indicated that their long, hard struggle to retain Ukrainian churches abroad was justified, for it contributed to the renewal of religious life in the homeland. And this realization was a morale-booster that the faithful in the West greatly needed and appreciated.

Recent events have clearly been a watershed not only in the history of Ukraine but in that of the Ukrainian communities abroad as well. Long isolated from each other, the homeland and the disapora now have an unprecedented opportunity to interact freely. From the point of view of the former, the communities abroad have already fulfilled and can still fulfil several important functions. They have preserved the political and cultural values of non-Soviet Ukraine. And they have spoken up for Ukrainian interests, when compatriots in the homeland were forced to remain silent. Now they can serve as Ukraine's sorely needed window to the West. But the diaspora, most notably the communities of North America, has also benefited from the changes in the homeland. The growing contacts with Ukraine have clearly revitalized the communities, broken their sense of isolation, and reassured them that their efforts on behalf of their compatriots were not for naught. Therefore, as Ukraine emerges to claim its rightful place among the countries of the world, the Ukrainians of North America can take justifiable pride in having done their share for the Cause.

ABBREVIATIONS

CIUS	Canadian Institute of Ukrainian Studies
DP	Displaced Person
FBI	Federal Bureau of Investigation
HURI	Harvard Ukrainian Research Institute
IRO	International Relief Organization
IWO	International Workers Organization
MUN	Molodi Ukrainski Nationalisty – Young Ukrainian Nationalists
NTSh	Naukove Tovarystvo im. Shevchenka – Shevchenko Scientific Society
ODUM	Obednannia Demokratychnoi Ukrainskoi Molodi – Ukrainian National Democratic League
ODVU	Orhanizatsiia Derzhavnoho Vidrodzhennia Ukrainy – Organization for the Rebirth of Ukraine
OUN	Orhanizatsiia Ukrainskykh Natsionalistiv – Organization of Ukrainian Nationalists
SKVU	Svitovyi Kongres Vilnykh Ukrainstiv – World Congress of Free Ukrainians
SUK	Soiuz Ukrainok Kanady – Ukrainian Women's Association of Canada
SUM	Spilka Ukrainskoi Molodi – Ukrainian Youth Association
SUMK	Soiuz Ukrainskoi Molodi Kanady – Canadian Ukrainian Youth Association
SURO	Soiuz Ukrainskykh Robitnychykh Orhanizatsii – Association of Ukrainian Toilers
SUS	Soiuz Ukrainskykh Samostiinykiv – Ukrainian Self-Reliance League
SUSK	Soiuz Ukrainskykh Studentiv Kanady – Ukrainian Canadian University Students Union
SUSTA	Soiuz Ukrainskykh Studentskykh Tovarystv Ameryky – Federation of Ukrainian Student Organizations of America
TUSM	Tovarystvo Ukrainskoi Studiiuiuchoi Molodi im. M. Mikhnovskoho – M. Mikhnovsky Ukrainian Student Association

UACC	Ukrainian American Coordinating Council
UAOC	Ukrainian Autocephalous Orthodox Church
UCC	Ukrainian Canadian Committee
UCCA	Ukrainian Congress Committee of America
UCRF	Ukrainian Canadian Relief Fund
UFSPA	Ukrainian Federation of Socialist Parties of America
UHO	United Hetman Organizations
ULFTA	Ukrainian Labour and Farmers Temple Association
UNA	Ukrainian National Association
UNDO	Ukrainske Natsionalne-Demokratychne Obednannia – Ukrainian National Democratic Union
UNF	Ukrainian National Federation
UNR	Ukrainska Narodna Respublyka – Ukrainian People's Republic
UNRRA	United Nations Relief and Rehabilitation Administration
UNWLA	Ukrainian National Women's League of America
UOC	Ukrainian Orthodox Church
UPA	Ukrainska Povstanska Armiia – Ukrainian Insurgent Army
USCAK	Ukrainska Sportova Tsentrala Ameryky i Kanady – Ukrainian Sports Association of America and Canada
USH	Ukrainska Striletska Hromada – Ukrainian Sharpshooters Association
UUARC	United Ukrainian American Relief Committee
UUOA	United Ukrainian Organizations of America
UVAN	Ukrainska Vilna Akademiia Nauk – Ukrainian Free Academy of Arts and Sciences
UWA	Ukrainian Workingmen's Association
UYLNA	Ukrainian Youth League of North America
WBA	Workers Benevolent Association
WFUMA	World Federation of Ukrainian Medical Associations

SELECTED READINGS

BIBLIOGRAPHIES

Boshyk, Y., and B. Balan. *Political Refugees and Displaced Persons, 1945–54*. Edmonton 1982

Momryk, M. *A Guide to the Sources for the Study of Ukrainian Canadians*. Ottawa 1984

Sokolyshyn, A., and V. Wertsman. *Ukrainians in Canada and the United States: A Guide to Information Sources*. Detroit 1981

CANADA – STUDIES AND SOURCES

Czumer, W. *Recollections about the Life of the First Ukrainian Settlers in Canada*. Edmonton 1981

Darcovich, W. *Ukrainians in Canada: The Struggle to Retain Their Identity*. Ottawa 1967

Ewanchuk, M. *Pioneer Profiles: Ukrainian Settlers in Manitoba*. Winnipeg 1981

Goa, D., ed. *The Ukrainian Religious Experience: Tradition and the Canadian Cultural Context*. Edmonton 1989

Gregorovich, A. *Chronology of Ukrainian Canadian History*. Toronto 1974

Hryniuk, S., and L. Luciuk, eds. *Canada's Ukrainians: The Changing Perspectives, 1891–1991*. Toronto 1991

Isajiw, W., ed. *Ukrainians in the Canadian City*. Special issue of *Canadian Ethnic Studies* 12 (1980)

Kaye, V. *Early Ukrainian Settlers in Canada 1895–1900: Dr. J. Oleskiw's Role in the Settlement of the Canadian Northwest*. Toronto 1964

Klymasz, R. *The Ukrainians in Canada 1891–1991*. Special issue of *Material History Bulletin*. Toronto 1991

Kolasky, J. *The Shattered Illusion: The History of Ukrainian Pro-Communist Organizations in Canada*. Toronto 1979

Kolasky, J., ed. *Prophets and Proletarians: Documents on the History of the Rise and Decline of Ukrainian Communism in Canada.* Edmonton 1988

Kordan, B., and L. Luciuk, eds. *A Delicate and Difficult Question: Documents in the History of Ukrainians in Canada 1899–1962.* Kingston 1986

Kostash, M. *All of Baba's Children.* Edmonton 1977

Luciuk, L., ed. *Heroes of Their Day: The Reminiscences of Bohdan Panchuk.* Toronto 1989

Luciuk, L., and B. Kordan. *Creating a Landscape: A Geography of Ukrainians in Canada.* Toronto 1983

Lupul, M., ed. *Ukrainian Canadians, Multiculturalism and Separatism: An Assessment.* Edmonton 1978

– *A Heritage in Transition: Essays in the History of Ukrainians in Canada.* Toronto 1982

– *Visible Symbols: Cultural Expression among Canada's Ukrainians.* Edmonton 1984

– *Continuity and Change: The Cultural Life of Alberta's First Ukrainians.* Edmonton 1988

Martynowych, O. *Ukrainians in Canada: The Formative Years, 1891–1924.* Edmonton 1991

Marunchak, M. *The Ukrainian Canadians: A History.* Winnipeg 1970

Piniuta, H., ed. and trans. *Land of Pain, Land of Promise: First Person Accounts by Ukrainian Pioneers, 1989–1914.* Saskatoon 1978

Petryshyn, J. *Peasants in a Promised Land: Canada and the Ukrainians, 1891–1914.* Toronto 1985

Petryshyn, W. *Changing Realities: Social Trends among Ukrainian Canadians.* Edmonton 1980

Prymak, T. *Maple Leaf and Trident: The Ukrainian Canadians during the Second World War.* Toronto 1988

Rozumnyj, J., ed. *New Soil – Old Roots: The Ukrainian Experience in Canada.* Winnipeg 1983

Skwarok, J. *The Ukrainian Settlers in Canada and Their Schools, 1891–1921.* Toronto 1929

Swyripa, F. *Ukrainian Canadians: A Survey of Their Portrayal in English-language Works.* Edmonton 1978

Swyripa, F., and J. Thompson. *Loyalties in Conflict: Ukrainians in Canada during the Great War.* Edmonton 1983

Woycenko, O. *The Annals of Ukrainian Life in Canada,* 4 vols. Winnipeg 1961–9

Young, C. *The Ukrainian-Canadians: A Study of Assimilation.* Toronto 1931

Yuzyk, P. *The Ukrainians in Manitoba.* Toronto 1953

UNITED STATES – STUDIES

Basarab, S., et al. *The Ukrainians of Maryland*. Baltimore 1977
Chyz, Y. *The Ukrainian Immigrants in the United States*. Scranton 1932
Dragan, A. *The Ukrainian National Association: Its Past and Present 1894–1964*. Jersey City 1964
Ewanchuk, M. *Hawaiian Ordeal: Ukrainian Contract Workers, 1897–1910*. Winnipeg 1986
Halich, W. *Ukrainians in the United States*. Chicago 1937
Isajiw, W., ed. *Ukrainians in American and Canadian Society*. Jersey City 1976
Kuropas, M. *The Ukrainians in America*. Minneapolis 1972
– *Ukrainian Americans: Roots and Aspirations 1884–1954*. Toronto 1991
Lushnycky, A., ed. *Ukrainians in Pennsylvania*. Philadelphia 1976
Magocsi, P. *Our People: Carpatho-Rusyns and Their Descendants in North America*. Toronto 1980
Magocsi, P., ed. *The Ukrainian Experience in the United States: A Symposium*. Cambridge, MA, 1979
Markus, D. *Ukrainians in Chicago*. Chicago 1991
Markus, V. '[Ukrainians] in the United States.' In V. Kubijovyč, ed., *Ukraine: A Concise Encyclopedia*, vol. II, 1100–51. Toronto 1971
Pekar, A. 'The Historical Background of the Carpatho-Ruthenians in America.' *Ukrainskyi Istoryk* 13 (1976):87–103 and 14 (1977):68–84
Procko, B. 'Pennsylvania: Focal Point of Ukrainian Immigration.' In J. Bodnar, ed., *The Ethnic Experience in Pennsylvania*. Lewisburg 1973
– *Ukrainian Catholics in America: A History*. Washington 1982
Stefaniuk, M., and F. Dohrs. *Ukrainians in Detroit*. Detroit 1979
Wolowyna, O., ed. *Ethnicity and National Identity: Demographic and Socioeconomic Characteristics of Persons with Ukrainian Mother Tongue in the United States*. Cambridge, MA, 1986

INDEX

Acton, 220, 222
Adamic, Louis, 148
akademiia, 144, 194
Akron, 17
Alaska, 12
Alaska Herald, 12
Alberta, 36, 37, 42, 43, 44, 56, 58, 60, 83, 84, 85, 87, 89, 91, 177, 184
Alberta, University of, 233
alcoholism, 7, 34
Algonquin Park, 218
All-Ukrainian Academy, 228
Ambridge, 73
American Circle, 64, 65; role of, 75, 76; socialist inclinations of, 131
American Jewish Committee, 199
American Jewish Joint Distribution Committee, 197
American Plan, 65
Ameryka, 62
Ameryka (Catholic newspaper), 78, 166, 168, 253
Anglo-Saxons, 45, 58, 59, 60, 87, 92, 175
Anti-Bolshevik Bloc of Nations (ABN), 222
Anti-Defamation League (Jewish), 139
Archipenko, Alexander, 174
Ardan, Ivan, 64, 65, 132
Argentina, 195
Armenians, 225
assimilation, 34, 35, 40, 46; in Canada, 58–60, 82, 111, 112; in Second Wave, 181, 251

Association of Ukrainian Sports Clubs of North America (USCAK), 231
Association of United Ukrainians of Canada, 211, 214
Association to Aid the Liberation Movement in Western Ukraine, 124
Athabasca, 44
Augsburg, 192
Australia, 204, 223
Austria, 4, 7, 96, 97, 191, 195
Austro-Hungarian empire, 3, 4, 13, 35, 94, 99
Avramenko, Vasyl, 171–3

babske pravo, 34
Bachynsky, Iuliian, 30, 94, 119
Balan, Dmytro (Balan, Danytra), 42
Bandera, Stepan, 210, 212
Banderites (*Banderivtsi*), 210–13, 215, 220, 221, 237, 241, 251
Bandurist Cappella, 231
Baptists, 140, 207, 253
Basilian order, 81, 155
Bavaria, 192
Belgium, 156, 195
Berchtesgaden, 192
Berezhany, 226
Besida Choir, 79
biculturalism, 113
bilingual schools, 85, 175; controversy over, 87
Binghamton, 17
bloc settlements, 45, 46, 58–9
boarding-house, 19, 22, 24, 29–30

Bodrug, Ivan, 82, 89
Bohachevsky, Konstantyn (bishop), appointment of, 154, 179
Bohemia, 4, 35
'Bohunks,' 35
Bolsheviks and Bolshevism, 59, 96, 122, 132, 198
Bonchevsky, Antin, 64, 65
Borshchiv, 84
Borys, Yevhen, 247
Bossy, Volodymyr, 136, 137
Boston, 199
Boychuk, John, 123
Bozhyk, Volodymyr, 230
bratstva. See fraternal benefit societies *and* brotherhoods
Brazil, 38, 78, 195
Britain and British, 59, 242
British Canadians, 37
British Columbia, 88
Bronx, 79
Brotherhood of the Former Soldiers of the First Ukrainian Division of the Ukrainian Army, 226. *See also* 'Galician Division'
Brotherhood of St Nicholas, 74
Brotherhood of Ukrainian Catholics (BUC), 156
Budka, Nykyta (bishop), 82–4; declaration by, 99, 136, 155
Buffalo, 17, 200
Bukovyna and Bukovynians, 4, 15, 36, 45, 50, 52, 55, 73, 81, 85, 118, 157, 226
business and businessmen, 15, 22, 27, 108
Byington, Margaret, 24

Byzantine rite, 62, 65, 70. *See also* Greek *and* Ukrainian Catholic
Byzantine Ruthenian Catholic Church, 67, 71
Byzantine style, 69

Calder, 169
Calgary, 40
California, 12, 13, 240
Canada, western, 37, 38
Canadian Broadcasting Corporation, 151
Canadian Communist Party. *See* Communist Party of Canada
Canadian Friends of RUKH, 266, 267
Canadian Institute of Ukrainian Studies (CIUS), 233; founding of, 246
Canadian Pacific Railway, 38, 41, 52
Canadian Tribune, 214
Canadian Ukrainian Youth Association (SUMK), 158, 184
'Canadianization.' *See* assimilation
Canora, 255
Canora district, 57
Carnegie Steel Company, 24
Carpathian Ski Club, 231
Carpatho-Ukraine, 146, 151, 186, 208, 226, 262
Catholicism and Catholics, 83, 194
Chekhovtsev, Arsenii, 81
Chemych, Stefan, 243
Chernivtsi, 15
Chernobyl disaster, 258, 260, 263, 267
Chervona Ruta festival, 265
Chicago, 17, 69, 114, 136, 158, 172, 200, 219, 233, 239, 240
Chicago Daily News, 148
Chicago World's Fair, 174, 182
Chortkiv, 226
church-building fever, 68–9
churches, 61–2; architecture of, 69; building of, 68–9; in Canada, 80–4

chytalni (reading-rooms), 76, 78, 83, 85
Chyz, Yaroslav, 132
clergy, 63–8, 72, 81
Cleveland, 17, 200, 219, 240
Cold War, 237
Colorado, 62, 240
Communism and Communists, 108, 123, 131, 134, 138, 143, 146, 150, 177, 190, 195, 197, 198
Communist Party of America, 132
Communist Party of Canada: Ukrainian role in, 122, 128
conservatism, 108
crime rate, 34, 56
Cum Data Fuerit, 154
Czechoslovakia, 97, 104, 119, 146, 192, 208, 215
Czechs, 8

Danylchuk, Ivan, 174
Dauphin Ukrainian festival, 249
Delaere, Achilles, 156
Demydchuk, Semen, 95
Depression, 102, 108, 121, 127, 165
Detroit, 17, 114, 167, 180, 200, 219, 230, 231, 233, 240
diaky (cantors), 154
Diefenbaker, John, 237, 238
Dies, Martin, 139, 148
discrimination, 127; in United States, 34–5; in Canada, 58–9
Displaced Persons (DP's), 191–203 and passim
Dmytriw, Nestor, 63, 64, 65, 78; in Canada, 80, 91
Dmytryshyn, A., 132
Doroshenko, Dmytro, 178, 228
Drahomanov, Mykhailo, 89
Drohobych, 226
Dumka choir, 229, 231
Duranty, Walter, 150
Dushnyk, Walter, 148
Dzus, William, 227

East Chatham, 205, 216, 218, 219
East Europeans, 17, 22, 25, 35, 69, 104, 134
Eastern Christianity, 82
Eastern Rite, 156
Edmonton, 37, 40, 42, 46, 49, 53, 88, 89, 178, 233, 240, 247, 254, 256
Edmonton Bulletin, 87
Edna-Star, 36; settlement in, 37
Eisenhower, Dwight, 237
Eko, 197
Eleniak, Vasyl, 37
Ellenville, 223
Ellis Island, 16, 17
Elmira, 17
Encyclopedia of Ukraine, 228
Encyclopedia of Ukraine (Entsyklopedia Ukrainoznavstva), 246
English (language) and the English, 8, 31, 34, 35, 37, 93, 111, 151, 233
Ewach, Honore, 174

Famine of 1933, 128, 133, 207, 252, 258
Famine Research Committee. *See* Ukrainian Canadian Research and Documentation Centre
farming, 20, 50–2
Federal Bureau of Investigation (FBI), 139, 149
Federation of Ukrainian Student Organizations of America (SUSTA), 224
Federation of Ukrainians, 96
Fedorky, Julia, 85
Fedyk, Teodor, 174
Ferley, Taras, 89, 91
First World War, 19, 29, 48, 52, 53, 56, 60, 86, 91, 92, 96, 97, 108, 134, 181
Florida, 240
Ford, Gerald, 206
Forum, 35

foundries, 22, 26, 93
France, 104, 151, 195, 204, 208
Franko, Ivan, 89
fraternal benefit societies, 77, 124; role of, 74
French Canadians, 81
Frolick, Stanley, 200
Fund for Liberation, 96

Galicia and Galicians, 17, 21, 32, 37, 40, 42, 47, 50, 52, 55, 64, 65, 66, 69, 70, 73, 74, 85, 86, 92, 94, 97, 118, 122, 161, 192, 217, 226, 257; priests from, 63
Galicia, Eastern, 4, 6, 8, 37
'Galician Division,' 192, 201, 226
Galician Radical Party, 64, 67
Galician-Transcarpathian schism, 65–8, 72
Genik, Cyril, 82, 89
Georgia, 21, 240
Germany and Germans, 13, 17, 34, 37, 93, 134, 138, 148, 150, 191, 204, 208, 223, 226
Gold Cross, 142, 163, 212
Gorbachev, Mikhail, 259
Grabowicz, George, 264
Granovsky, Alexander, 142
Great Britain, 195
Greek Catholic church, 66, 70, 75; appointment of bishop for, 72; in Canada, 80–4, 95
Greek Catholic rite, 68, 69
Greek Catholic Union, 66, 75
Greek Catholicism, 32
Greek Catholics, 63, 69, 71, 78
Gregorian calendar, 154
Gregorovich, Alexander, 143
Gregory (Svarich), Annie, 85

Habsburgs, 6, 113
Haidamaky, 107, 131
Halifax, 38, 199
Hamilton, 90
Harbuziak, Oleksa, 207

Harvard Project, 243
Harvard Ukrainian Research Institute (HURI), 243
Harvard Ukrainian Summer School, 246
Harvard University, 243, 264
Harvest of Despair, 246
Hawaii, 13, 21, 78
Hawaiian senate, 13
Hawrylyshyn, Bohdan, 264
Hayward, 13, 89
Hazelton, 17
Hetmanites, 109
Hitler, Adolf, 148, 151
Hlynka, Anthony, 199
Hnatyshyn, Ramon, 256, 257
Hnizdovsky, Jacques, 194
Holy See, 206
Holy Synod, 81
Homestead, 17, 24
Homin Ukrainy, 211
Honcharenko, Ahapii, 12, 13
Horlytsko, 15
Hrushevsky (Michael) Ukrainian Institute, 178
Hrushka, Hryhorii, 75, 76, 77
Hrynevetsky, Stepan, 134
Huculak, Erast, 247
Huculak, Lida, 247
Hudson's Bay Company, 37
Hunczak, Taras, 263
Hungarians, 13, 35, 63, 75, 146
'Hunkies,' 35
Husar, Natalka, 244
Hutsuls, 226

ideologies, 79, 108
Ilarion (Ivan Ohienko) (metropolitan), 207
Illinois, 114
immigration policies, 102
Independent Greek church, 82
intelligentsia, Ukrainian, 6; and church, 82; in Canada, 85, 87, 93, 102, 157, 192, 193, 202, 217, 234, 256

International Association of Ukrainian Studies (MAU), 264
International Management Institute, 264
International Relief Organization (IRO), 191
Ioan (metropolitan), 268
Irchan, Myroslav, 174
Irish, 17, 34, 35, 37
Iron Curtain, 237

Jacyk, Peter, 246
Jacyk Centre of Historical Research, 247
Jamestown, 12
Jarema, Julia, 161
Jersey City, 32, 75, 77
Jewish Americans, 197, 199
Jews, 7, 19, 29, 37, 38, 60, 97, 225
Johnstown, 17

Kahn, Albert, 146
Kanadiisky farmer, 89, 166
Kanadiisky Rusin (Ukrainets), 166
Karbiwnyk, Ray, 195
Kharkiv, 127
Khyliak, Pavel, 15
Khyliak, Semen, 15
Kiev, 12, 13, 83, 228, 229, 230, 263, 264, 266, 267
Kiriak, Illia, 255
Klapatniuk, George (Klapcyuk, Giorgi), 42
Klapushchak, Mike, 214
Konovalets, Evhen, 141, 144, 212
Konstankevych, Ivan, 64, 65, 75
Koshyts, Oleksander, 170–1, 173
Kostash, Myrna, 54, 55, 56, 59, 109, 245
Kotsko Ukrainian Student Society, 178
Koziak family, 249
Krat, Pavlo, 59
Kremlin, 150, 259, 260
Kremyr, Tom, 214

Kruty, battle of, 171
Kubiyovč, Volodymyr, 228
Kurelek, William, 41, 256
Kuropas, Myron, 149, 183, 197
Kuropas, Stephen, 148
Kushnir, Basil, 209, 237; election of, 186
Kuzmych, Basil, 74
Kytasty, Hryhory, 230

Labensky, Irene, 263
Ladyka, Basil (bishop), 136, 156
Latin rite, 154
Latinization, 155
League for the Liberation of Ukraine, 211
League of Ukrainian Clubs, 182
Lehigh Valley, 17
Lemko region (Lemkivshchyna) and Lemkos, 13, 15, 17, 70, 226
Liberals, 85, 89, 90, 91, 166
Literary-Arts Club, 231
Lobay, Danylo, 128, 168
London, 226
Losten, Basil (bishop), 205, 267
Lotocky, Helen, 161
Lubachivsky, Myroslav (cardinal), 267
Luhy, 15
Lupul, Manoly, 246
Lviv, 37, 62, 65, 72, 94, 95, 226, 264, 265, 266
Lypynsky, Viacheslav, 108

Magyarones, 65, 66, 97; characteristics of, 64
Magyarophiles, 77
Makar, Stefan, 64, 65
Mandryka, Mykyta, 174
Manhattan, 27
Manitoba, 37, 45, 47, 50, 51, 53, 57, 86, 91, 167, 175, 184, 249
Manitoba, University of, 178
Marunchak, Michael, 96
Marx, Karl, 89

Marxism and Marxists, 107, 128
Maryniak, T., 154
Masaryk, Tomaš, 97
Matkiwsky, Nadia, 263
Matkiwsky, Zenon, 263
McAdoo, 78
McKees Rocks, 17
Mckeesport, 17
Melnyk, Andrii, 212
Melnyk, Giorgi, 42
Melnykites (Melnykivtsi), 212–13, 215, 237, 241
Mennonites, 37
Michigan, 32
militarism, 137, 138
Millville, 31
mining, 22
Minneapolis, 70
Misery of Galicia, 8
Mittenwald, 192
Mohyla Institute, 83–4
Montana, 21
Montreal, 114, 136, 202, 219, 233
Moros, Mykola, 266
Moscow, 127, 128
Mstyslav (Stepan Skrypnyk) (patriarch), 207, 268
Mt Carmel, 17
Mukachiv, eparchy of, 64, 65, 66
MUN. See Young Ukrainian Nationalists
Mundare, 83, 156
Munich, 192
Muscophiles, 73. See also Russophilism
Myrnam, 177
Myshuha, Luke, 166

Narodna Volya, 78, 166, 253
Natalka Poltavka, 174
National Festival, 128
National Guard (U.S.), 138, 144
'Nationalist Days,' 144
Navis, John, 124
Nazaruk, Osyp, 136
Nazis, 139, 148, 151, 197, 208

Nebyliw, 37
Nebyliw Group, 37
Negrych, Ivan, 82, 89
New Castle, 17
New Jersey, 21, 32, 114, 240, 263
New York City, 17, 18, 96, 107, 131, 163, 171, 172, 183, 198, 199, 200, 204, 209, 223, 227, 228, 229, 231, 233, 236, 240
New York Evening Post, 173, 232
New York harbour, 15, 16, 17
New York State, 17, 21, 76
New York Times, 150
New York Twenty Six, 154
New York World's Fair, 174
Newark, 263
North Dakota, 20, 21
Novyi shliakh, 168, 198, 213
Nureyev, Rudolf, 229

Obnova, 224
ODUM. *See* Ukrainian National Democratic League
Ohio, 114
Oklahoma, 21
Oleskiw, Josef, 37, 38
Olha Basarab Organization of Ukrainian Women, 163
Olyphant, 17
Omelian, Maria, 195
Ontario, 90, 167, 176, 179, 260
Organization for the Defense of the Four Freedoms of Ukraine, 211
Organization for the Rebirth of Ukraine (ODVU), 142, 144, 149
Organization of Ukrainian Nationalists (OUN), 141, 146, 208, 210, 211, 212, 220, 224
Orthodoxy and Orthodox, 32, 49, 136, 192, 194, 206; growth of in United States, 70–1; in Canada, 81–4
Ortynsky, Soter (bishop): 69, 78, 154; appointment of, 65; funeral of, 70; activity of, 72

Oshawa, 114, 136, 151; aviation school in, 144
Ostarbeiter, 191
Ottawa, 187, 223, 256, 267

Palermo, 237
Panchuk, G.R.B., 200
Paris, 99
Passaic, 33
patriarchate, 206
peasants and peasantry, 6, 7, 62, 65, 109
Pennsylvania, 13, 17, 19, 21, 24, 26, 29, 33, 35, 62, 65, 67, 72, 73, 74, 80, 91, 97, 114
perestroika, 259, 261
Pereyaslavec, Valentina, 229
Petliura, Symon, 97
Philadelphia, 17, 67, 70, 72, 78, 95, 97, 114, 168, 180, 182, 186, 200, 208, 219, 223, 225, 231, 233, 240
Pidhoretsky, Mykola, 64, 65
Pinson, Koppel, 197
Pittsburgh, 17, 67
Plast, 194, 205, 216, 234, 237, 238, 253; growth of, 217–19; re-emergence in Ukraine, 266
Plum Ridge school, 86
Poles and Polish, 13, 17, 19, 33, 34, 38, 66, 94, 97, 102, 124, 144, 148, 197, 208, 226
Polissia, 119
Poniatyshyn, Petro, 79, 154
Popowich, Matthew, 123
Potocki, Andrżej, 94
Pravda i svoboda, 167
prejudice. See discrimination
Presbyterian church, 82, 84, 160
Presbyterian synod, 166
Prešov, eparchy of, 64
Pritsak, Omeljan, 243
Procko, Bohdan, 63
Prosvita, 51, 76, 83, 85
Protestantism, 82, 89
Providence Association of Ukrainian Catholics, 78, 253
Pryma Bohachevsky, Roma, 230
Prymak, Thomas, 151
Pulitzer Prize, 151
Pylypiw, Ivan, 37

Quebec, 36
Quebec City, 38

Radical party, 122
Ranok, 166
Red Army, 192
Red Cross, 137
'Red Scare,' 123
Redemptorist Order, 156
Regensburg, 192
Ridna Shkola, 95, 164, 179; activity of, 227
Roblin, 156
Rochester, 17, 200
Roman Catholic church, 70, 82
Roman Catholic hierarchy, 63; attitude toward Greek Catholics, 69; in Canada, 81, 92
Romania, 118
Rome, 70, 83, 154
Ruryk (Melnyk), Nancy, 85
Russia and Russians, 1, 3, 12, 71, 81, 92, 96, 97, 167
Russian empire, 2, 3, 37, 81, 96, 97, 118
Russian Orthodox church, 70, 71, 73, 92, 268; in Canada, 81
Russian Orthodox Mission, 70
Russian Revolution, 131
Russification, 215, 260, 265
Russkyi narodnyi soiuz (Ruthenian National Association), 75. See also Ukrainian National Association (UNA)
Russophilism, 71, 81, 91
Rusyn, 3, 65, 66, 71. See also Ruthenians, Transcarpathia
Ruthenian National Union, 74. See also Ukrainian Workingmen's Association (UWA)
Ruthenian Training School, 85, 87, 89, 91
Ruthenians, 3, 42, 60, 66, 71, 73, 77, 154; abandonment of term, 94

Sabotage, 148
Sacred Heart Academy, 178
St Andrew's Memorial Church, 207
St Basil's Academy, 155
St Basil's school, 155
St George's Church, 183
St John the Baptist, church of, 73
St Joseph College, 178
St Laurent, Louis, 205
St Michael, church of: in Gardenton, 57, 63, 67; in Shenandoah, 62
St Nicholas, brotherhood of, 62
St Raphael's Ukrainian Immigrants Welfare Association, 119
St Sophia's Cathedral, 268
St Volodymyr, church of, 73
Saints Cyril and Methodius Society, 72
Sts Peter and Paul, church of, 73
Samopomich (Self-Reliance), 204, 205
Sandul, Maria, 50
Sandul, Sanda, 50
Saskatchewan, 57, 58, 83, 87, 169, 184, 255
Saskatchewan, University of, 151
Saskatoon, 83, 161
Savaryn, Peter, 246
Sayers, Michael, 148
Scots and Scottish, 17, 35, 37
Scranton, 17, 78
Second World War, 146, 187, 190, 202, 212, 220, 251, 253, 257, 258
Sembratovych, Sylvester (bishop), 62
Senyk, Omelian, 142
Seraphim (bishop), 80, 82
Shakespeare, 113

Shamokin, 17, 72
Shandro, Andrew, 91
Shatulsky, Matthew, 124, 168
Sheho, 58
Shenandoah, 17, 62, 63, 67
Sheptytsky, Andrii (metropolitan), 72, 95; in United States, 94
Shevchenko, Taras, 12, 42, 167, 171
Shevchenko Scientific Society (NTSh), 228
Shumeyko, Stephen, 166, 182
Siberia, 206
Sich (Junior Siege), 183
Sich movement, 137, 181
Sichinsky, Myroslav, 94, 132
Sichovi Striltsi (Sich Sharpshooters), 145
Sifton, Clifford, 38, 58
Simenovych, Volodymyr, 63
Simpson, George, 151
Sisters Servant of Mary Immaculate, 81, 155
Skoropadsky, Danylo: visit in the U.S. and Canada, 138
Skoropadsky, Pavlo, 134, 138
Slav Invasion, 35
Slavs and Slavic, 17, 22, 24, 34, 35
Slipyj, Josef (cardinal), 205, 206
Slovak, 13, 17, 19, 33
Smoky Lake, 89
Social Democrats, 90
socialism and socialists, 104, 107, 108, 131
Socialist Party of Canada, Ukrainian branch, 89
sokol, 77
Sons of the Soil, 174
Sopinka, John, 257
Soroka, S., 132
South Bound Brook, 207, 268
South Dakota, 20
Soviet Ukraine, 128, 259
Soviet Union and Soviets, 2, 128, 144, 146, 151, 190, 192, 208
Soyuzivka, 230, 231

Stalin and Stalinism, 113, 128
Stamford, 155
Statue of Liberty, 16
Stechishin, Myroslaw, 89, 168
Stechishin, Savella, 161
Stefanovych, Mykola, 64, 65
Stetsko, Iaroslav, 221
Stogryn, Helen, 195
Storozuk, Ivan, 91
Stuartburn, 47, 50, 51, 91
Stundists (Evangelicals), 20, 21
Sudbury, 202, 214, 220
Sudzilovsky-Russel, Nicholas, 13
Sulyk, Stephen (metropolitan), 207
SUM. See Ukrainian Youth Organization
Surma Book and Music Store, 27
Surmach family, 27
SURO – Souiz ukrainskykh robitnychykh orhanizatsii (Association of Ukrainian Toilers), 132
SUS. See Ukrainian Self-Reliance League
Svarich (Porayko), Stella, 85
Svoboda, 32, 66; founding of, 76, 78, 91, 93, 166, 243, 253; support for, 77
Swystun, Wasyl, 84
Syracuse, 17, 76, 200
Szalapaj, Sawa, 44
Szczepanowski, Stanisław, 9
Szewczenko school, 175

Takach, Basil (bishop), 154
Teodorovych, Ivan (bishop), 158, 207
Texas, 21
'Third Element,' 242
Time, 148
Tkach, George, 132
Tkachuk, H., 132
Topolnitsky, Nykola (Tapylnitzki, Nycola), 42
Toronto, 114, 136, 200, 211, 219, 221, 223, 233, 240, 242, 243, 246, 251, 265, 266
Toronto, University of, 246
Toronto Globe, 59
Toth, Alexis (bishop): role of, 70–1
Transcarpathia and Transcarpathians, 4, 13, 17, 64, 66, 68, 69, 70, 71, 73, 75, 92, 97, 146, 154, 166, 226; priests from, 63
Transcarpathian-Galician feud, 68. See also Galician-Transcarpathian schism
Trident (Tryzub) Sports Club, 231
Tsehelsky, Lonhyn, 168
Tsehlynsky, Mykola, 132
Two Way Passage, 148
Tymkevych, Pavlo, 64, 65
Tyzak, H., 184

Ukraina (North Dakota), 20
Ukraina Sports Club, 231
'Ukrainchiks,' 66
Ukraine, Eastern, 20, 21
Ukraine, Western, 38, 95, 97, 141, 217
Ukraine Pavilion, 174
'Ukrainian': introduction of term, 94
Ukrainian Alliance of America, 96
Ukrainian American Coordinating Council (UUCC), 213
Ukrainian Autocephalous Church, 158
Ukrainian Autocephalous Orthodox Church (UAOC), 158, 207; re-emergence in Ukraine, 268
Ukrainian Brotherhood, 89
Ukrainian Canadian Citizens Committee, 99
Ukrainian Canadian Committee (UCC), 186, 195, 205, 209, 255
Ukrainian Canadian Committee, Women's Council, 163
Ukrainian Canadian Relief Fund (UCRF), 195, 197, 200
Ukrainian Canadian Research and Documentation Centre, 246

Ukrainian Canadian Servicemen's Association, 226
Ukrainian Canadian University Students Union (SUSK), 224
Ukrainian Canadian Veterans Club, 226
Ukrainian Catholic church, 63, 68, 69, 83, 96, 136, 180, 192, 205, 235, 252; re-emergence in Ukraine, 267
Ukrainian Catholic Providence Association, 166, 168
Ukrainian Catholic Women's League of Canada, 163
Ukrainian Catholic Youth (UCY), 184
Ukrainian Catholic Youth League (UCYL), 182
Ukrainian Congress Committee of America (UCCA), 195, 204, 210
Ukrainian Cultural and Educational Centre (Oseredok), 213
'Ukrainian Day,' 96
Ukrainian Diet, 96
Ukrainian Emigrants Aid Society, 119
Ukrainian Engineers Society, 224
Ukrainian Evangelical Alliance, 207
Ukrainian Federation of Socialist Parties in America (UFSPA), 131
Ukrainian Fraternal Association, 253. See also Ukrainian Workingmen's Association
Ukrainian Free Academy of Arts and Sciences (UVAN), 228
Ukrainian Free University, 193
Ukrainian Greek Orthodox Brotherhood, 84
Ukrainian Greek Orthodox church, 83, 84
Ukrainian Institute of America, 227
Ukrainian Institute of Technology and Economics, 193
Ukrainian Insurgent Army (UPA), 192, 210, 226

Ukrainian Labour Farmer Temple Association (ULFTA), 123, 124–9, 132; decline of, 215
Ukrainian Labour Temple Association, 123
Ukrainian Medical Association of North America, 224
Ukrainian Music Institute, 231
Ukrainian National Association (UNA), 73, 78, 91, 93, 96, 167, 182, 230, 231, 243, 253; founding of, 75; activity of, 76
Ukrainian National Choir, 170–1
Ukrainian National Council, 96, 209
Ukrainian National Democratic League (ODUM), 223
Ukrainian National Democratic Union (UNDO), 208
Ukrainian National Federation (UNF), 143, 144, 151, 168, 171, 186, 213, 227, 255
Ukrainian National Federation Aviation School, 151
Ukrainian National Women's League of America (UNWLA), 161, 163, 164, 225, 253, 266
Ukrainian Nationals, 231
Ukrainian Olympics, 182
Ukrainian Orthodox Brotherhood, 158
Ukrainian Orthodox Church (UOC), 73, 153, 159, 235, 252, 267
Ukrainian People's Republic (UNR), 96, 97, 99, 170, 171
Ukrainian Red Cross, 99
Ukrainian Self-Reliance League (SUS), 158, 168, 255
Ukrainian Student Association of Mikhnovsky (TUSM), 224
'Ukrainian Threat,' 68
Ukrainian Weekly, 158, 183, 253, 261
Ukrainian Women's Association of Canada (SUK), 161, 184

Ukrainian Women's Union (Soiuz Ukrainok), 161
Ukrainian Workingmen's Association (UWA), 74, 78, 132, 166
Ukrainian Youth Ensemble, 265
Ukrainian Youth League of North America (UYLNA), 182
Ukrainian Youth Organization (SUM), 227, 234, 237; formation of, 220–3
Ukrainianism, 76
Ukrainianization, 108, 128
Ukrainians, East, 2
Ukrainians, West, 2, 8, 104, 190, 223
Ukrainka, Lesia, 164
Ukrainska Striletska Hromada (USH), 141, 213
Ukrainske zhyttia, 196
Ukrainski robitnychi visti, 168
Ukrainskyi holos, 168
Un-American Activities Committee, 148
United Hetman Organization (UHO), 138, 148, 149
United Nations, 236
United Nations Relief and Rehabilitation Agency (UNRRA), 191
United Ukrainian American Relief Committee (UUARC), 200
United Ukrainian Organizations of America (UUOA), 186
USSR, 191

Vatican, 66, 155
Vegreville, 85
Vegreville Ukrainian festival, 245
Vestnik (Viestnik), 66, 68, 77
Vetukhiv, Michael, 228
Vienna, 4
Virginia, 12, 20, 21
Vita, 175
Volhynia, 118
Voliansky, Ivan, 74; activity of, 62–3

Washington, DC, 96, 181, 204, 237, 252, 267
Washington Group, 243
Waskewicz, Stefan, 43
Welsh, 34, 35
West Fort William, 176
West Ukrainian Peoples Republic (ZUNR), 96
Wilkes-Barre, 17
Wilson, Woodrow, 96
Wilton, 20
Winchell, Walter, 148
Windsor, 179, 202, 225,
Winnipeg, 38, 39, 41, 46, 48, 49, 51, 52, 54, 55, 59, 80, 81, 82, 85, 87, 89, 90, 99, 101, 114, 119, 124, 127, 171, 172, 202, 205, 213, 214, 219, 228, 233, 237, 238, 240, 254, 256
Winnipeg Free Press, 60
Winnipeg Telegram, 58
Woodsworth, J.S., 60
Worker's Benevolent Association (WBA), 124
Worker's Party of Canada, 123. See also Communist Party of Canada
World Congress of Free Ukrainians (WCFU–SKVU), 209, 225, 237
World Federation of Ukrainian Medical Associations (WFUMA), 264
Woycenko, Olha, 161
Wyoming Valley, 17

York University, 246
Yorkton, 156, 178
Young, Charles, 57
Young Ukrainian Nationalists (MUN), 142, 182, 184
Youngstown, 17
Yuzyk, Paul, 105

Zahara, Wasyl, 50
Zahara, Wasylyna, 50
'Zaporozhian beyond the Danube,' 172, 174
Zaporozhian Sich, 76
Zarevo, 224
Zhdynia, 15
Zhinochyi svit, 185
Zuk, Radoslav, 256

PHOTO CREDITS

INSTITUTIONS

National Archives of Canada (Ottawa): Pages 10 (C68842), 35 (C137280), 36 (PA 10402), 38 top (PA 27942), bottom (C6196), 40 (C84298), 41 top (PA 127145), 43 (PA 178587/178595), 44 (C24876), 47 top (C6608), 48 (C88572), 49 top (PA 127150), bottom (PA 21244), 50 (C8805), 51 (C6607), 53 (PA 122554), 54 (PA 88504), 56 (PA 178586/PA 113842), 57 (PA 123571), 59 (C37274), 60 (C5131), 82 (PA 139320), 83 (PA 88616), 84 (PA 139306), 85 (PA 178598), 87 (PA 178583), 89 bottom (PA 19879), 98 (C14104), 106 (C26782), 110 (C28439), 118 (PA 178592), 119 (C30325), 123 (C35491), 142 (PA 138727), 144 (PA 178591), 145 (PA 88435), 175 (PA 178591), 178 (PA 88424), 181 (PA 178584), 185 (PA 88619), 197 (PA 124487), 205 (PA 124489)

The Ukrainian Museum (New York): Pages 2, 27, 29, 33, 62, 67, 69, 70, 72, 75, 76, 78, 79, 93, 104, 108, 115, 131, 134, 141, 147, 152, 160, 162, 170, 172, 180, 183, 188, 190, 194 bottom, 195, 198, 199 bottom, 204, 206, 207, 227, 228, 229, 230, 237, 252

Ukrainian Cultural and Educational Centre (Winnipeg): Pages 42, 51, 52, 54 bottom, 86 bottom, 105, 109, 112, 113, 114, 116, 124, 155, 159, 169, 176, 177, 179, 238

Ukrainian Diocesan Museum and Library (Stamford, Conn.): Pages 63, 64, 74, 95, 97, 107, 154, 168

Manitoba Archives (Winnipeg): Pages 45, 48 bottom, 55, 80, 101, 120, 121

Ontario Archives (Toronto): Pages 90, 126, 136, 221 bottom, 222, 223, 258

University of Maryland Baltimore County Library (Baltimore): Pages 14, 18, 22, 23, 24–5, 25, 26

International Museum of Photography – George Eastman House. Lewis Hine collection (Rochester): Pages 16, 17, 28, 31

Immigration History Research Center, University of Minnesota (St Paul, Minn.): Pages 139, 157, 199 top

Harvard Ukrainian Research Institute (Cambridge, Mass.): Page 246

PUBLICATIONS

Jerome Davis, *The Russians and Ruthenians in America* (New York 1922): Page 30. Antin Dragan, *Ukrainski Narodny Soiuz u mynulomu i suchasnomu (1894–1964)* (Jersey City 1964): Page 77. Walter Halich, *Ukrainians in the United States* (Chicago 1937): Page 165. Vladimir Kaye, *Early Ukrainian Settlements in Canada, 1897–1900* (Toronto 1964): Pages 40 bottom, 53 top, 58 top. Peter Krawchuk, ed., *Our Stage: The Amateur Performing Arts of the Ukrainian Settlers in Canada* (Toronto 1984): Pages 52 bottom, 125, 127, 130. Volodymyr Kubiovyč, *Ukraine. A Concise Encyclopedia* (Toronto 1971), vol 2: Page 20. Lubomyr Luciuk and Bohdan Kordan, *Creating a Landscape: A Geography of Ukrainians in Canada* (Toronto 1989): Pages 46, 234, 235. Wasyl Luciw, *Ahapius Honcharenko, 'Alaska Man'* (Toronto 1963): Page 13. Alexander Lushnycky, ed., *Ukrainians in Pennsylvania* (Philadelphia 1976): Page 74 top. Michael Marunchak, *The Ukrainian Canadians: A History* (Winnipeg 1982): Page 91. Volodymyr Maruniak, *Ukrainska emigratsia v Nimechchyni i Avstrii po druhi svitovii viini* (Munich 1985): Pages 191, 192, 193. Luka Myshuha, *Propamiatna knyha* (Jersey City 1936): Pages 150, 166. *Spilka Ukrainskoi Molodi na chuzhyni* (London 1954): Pages 208, 220, 221. *Svoboda*: Pages 238 bottom, 239. *Tryzub. Desiat rokiv futbolnoi druzhyny* (Philadelphia 1967): Page 231. *Ukrainian Weekly*: Pages 232, 242, 248, 263; pages 205 bottom, 216 bottom, 217, 219 (Roma Hadzewycz); page 267 (Marta Kolomayets); page 268 (Yaroslav Kulynych)

INDIVIDUALS

Menno Fieguth: Pages 233, 241, 255. Stanley Frolick: Page 226. Dmytro Gutiw: Page 111. Stephanie Hnizdovsky: Page 194. Natalka Husar: Pages 156, 184, 244. Isaacs/Inuit Gallery: Pages 41, 47. Peter Krawchuk: Pages 88, 129, 211. Vladimira Luczkiw: Pages 89, 103, 171, 173. Meva Photo Studio: Page 206. Slavko Novytski: Page 236. Agnes Palanuk: Pages 21, 61. Lev Piaseckyj: Page 218. Orest Subtelny: Page 216. Lou Taskey: Pages 225, 250, 260, 266. Bertrand Thibeault: Page 256

Photo Credits

This book is set in a digital version of Eric Gill's Joanna. Designed in 1930, the face is named after his daughter, Joan, and was created for use by Hague and Gill, the private press run by Gill and René Hague, Joan's husband. In 1939 Monotype adapted it for the exclusive use of J.M. Dent. It was not issued for general use until 1958. Though it is not widely used, many consider it to be the most successful and individual of Gill's type designs, which also include Gill Sans and Perpetua. Born in Brighton, England, in 1882, Gill was a highly noted craftsman and artist of his day, active also as a wood- and stone-engraver and sculptor. In his views of art, craft, religion, and living he was both idiosyncratic and vocally opinionated.